"A *classic* example of the American regional community cookbook, reflecting the bounty and hospitality of one of the nation's most singular cities."
—*The Pilot*, Pilot Mountain, NC

"No matter what style of entertaining readers may enjoy, this book provides some *delicious* offerings."
—*Publishers Weekly*

"Filled with recipes you've always yearned for when sampling your way through a holiday buffet."
—*This Week*, Portland, OR

"A very good collection, and *a real boon* to anyone who entertains more than once a year."
—*The Herald*, Rock Hill, SC

"A cookbook with *true Southern flavor.*"
—*News & Reporter*, Chester, SC

"In the endless flood of new cookbooks, this one is the *keeper.*"
—*Richmond Times-Dispatch*, Richmond, VA

"People who can't find something in this book to titillate their taste buds are in sad shape."
—*Beaumont Enterprise*, Beaumont, TX

"*Secrets* for fine cooking and entertaining."
—*The Knoxville News Sentinel*, Knoxville, TN

"Like raiding your mother's recipe box."
—*Madera Tribune*, Madera, CA

"Two hundred pages on *nonstop yumminess,* recipes good not just for fancy entertaining, but for picnics, cookouts, and your own family occasions."
—*The Brunswick Beacon,* Shallotte, NC

# PARTY RECEIPTS

FROM THE

## CHARLESTON JUNIOR LEAGUE

# PARTY RECEIPTS

FROM THE

## CHARLESTON JUNIOR LEAGUE

**HORS D'OEUVRES • SAVORIES • SWEETS**

Collected by
The Junior League of Charleston, Inc.

Edited by Linda Glick Conway

ALGONQUIN BOOKS OF CHAPEL HILL
1993

Published by Algonquin Books of Chapel Hill
Post Office Box 2225
Chapel Hill, North Carolina 27515-2225

a division of
Workman Publishing Company, Inc.
708 Broadway
New York, New York 10003

20 19 18 17 16 15 14

Library of Congress Cataloging-in-Publication Data

Party receipts from the Charleston Junior League:
hors d'oeuvres, savories, sweets/
edited by Linda Glick Conway.
p. cm.
ISBN-13: 978-0-945575-84-9
ISBN-10: 0-945575-84-X
1. Appetizers.  I. Conway, Linda Glick.
TX740.P335   1993
641.812—dc20                          93-11669
                                       CIP

Front cover and chapter opening illustrations,
    and interior food illustrations: Diana LeMasters
Cover inset photograph: Paul Barton
Cover and book design: Diana LeMasters

# CONTENTS

*I*n Charleston, South Carolina, any holiday, occasion, or season of the year can be the excuse to entertain friends and family — the Christmas Parade of Boats, the Spoleto Festival U.S.A., the Moja Arts Festival celebrating the city's rich heritage of African and Caribbean cultures, an oyster roast on the beach at Sullivan's Island.

As Robert Rosen says in his *Short History of Charleston*, "Like their ancestors, Charlestonians still prefer a party to any other activity." At any rate, entertaining is so ingrained in the life of the city that the pressures of the two-career family and other hard facts of contemporary life have not put an end to socializing but have just inspired a somewhat different approach. Because time with the family becomes more precious the less there is of it, many parties involve the whole family and are centered on outdoor activities — picnics at the beach, boating parties, and hunting expeditions where fathers are accompanied not only by sons but by daughters. The subtropical climate of the Lowcountry (the narrow coastal plain in which Charleston is situated), the ocean, the creeks, the Sea Islands with miles of white sand beaches all combine to make outdoor life a key attraction. Other entertainments for the whole family are Christmas Eve drop-ins; Easter Egg hunts; Bar Mitzvah and Hannukah parties.

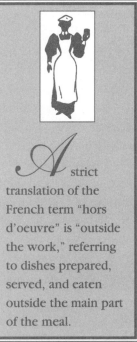

*A* strict translation of the French term "hors d'oeuvre" is "outside the work," referring to dishes prepared, served, and eaten outside the main part of the meal.

"*C*ooking was always a fine art in Charlestown, and a lady was expected to keep her own recipe books, know how to supervise servants, and entertain lavishly."

**A Short History of Charleston,**
*Robert Rosen*

The "savories and sweets" included in this book reflect a nationwide trend away from complicated sit-down dinner parties. Occasions for serving party food can range from hors d'oeuvres and drinks before dinner for a few friends, to tea parties, to a cocktail buffet that takes the place of dinner. In Charleston, as in most cities, such gatherings may be at home, in a

public place before or after a charity or cultural event, or connected with a business meeting. Just as many people prefer to choose a restaurant meal from among the appetizer selections, so is an hors d'oeuvre buffet a popular way to dine.

In deciding what recipes to include in this book we have used the guideline that the food must be able to be eaten standing up, in one or two bites, possibly with a fork but never needing a knife. The "savories" include spreads, dips, pâtés, mousses, biscuits and other baked morsels — many using ingredients so abundant in the Lowcountry: shrimp, crab, game, fruits and vegetables benefiting from an extensive growing season, benne seeds, pecans. The sweets are not sit-down desserts but items that can be passed on a tray — cookies, cakes, small tarts, candies — not only for tea parties but because even the most fitness-conscious like to top off a party with a goodie. And we have also included a section of soups and appetizers. The soups can be served in the living room or outdoors, in mugs or even paper cups. Most of the appetizers can be served to standing guests but some might best be used as first courses for a proper meal. In short, we have defined "party food" in the broadest possible way.

The key to a successful party is planning and preparing ahead so that you can have as much fun as your guests. Think about having a balanced "menu," not only in terms of ingredients but in technique, texture, and color. (Pretend you are preparing a balanced meal, with tinier portions.) Serving several baked items will cause logistical problems as well as repetitious flavors; too many fresh vegetables will leave your guests hungry. Plan on five or six helpings per person for a cocktail party before dinner; ten to twelve if the hors d'oeuvres *are* the dinner. Be sure to have plenty of napkins on hand (three per person) and place them in various locations. Think about presentation. The

*"The word RECEIPT's been handed down*

*For generations. Its renown*

*Is well established. RECIPE*

*From scholarship to pedantry*

*Has now evolved. However, we*

*Can use them interchangeably."*

**Louise Frierson Kerr,** *from* **Two Hundred Years of Charleston Cooking**

"*We* had arrived here without knowing a soul, and if Charleston's inner life was closed to outsiders that was quite understandable. It had the reputation of being snobbish, but to us it just seemed contented. And we were contented too."

**Charleston:**
**A Golden Memory,**
*Charles R. Anderson*

food should look appetizing and beautiful and be arranged in a spacious fashion; if you are serving canapés, place them in one layer, with plenty of room between pieces, allowing guests to pick them up easily. Garnish the individual items and/or the serving platter, remembering that the garnish must be appropriate to the food (if no garnish is called for in a recipe, be creative). In general it is more pleasing to put only one kind of hors d'oeuvre on a tray, both for aesthetic reasons and because you don't want the guest to have to interrupt a conversation to carefully peruse the selection. If you are having a buffet table, use a variety of containers (keeping in mind the tone of the occasion — informal or elegant). For variety, use serving pieces of different shapes and heights; pedestal cake plates, for example, work nicely for biscuits or canapés as well as cakes and cookies. When it comes to beverages, be sure to include a selection of nonalcoholic juices and sparkling waters at cocktail hour and herbal and decaffeinated teas at teatime.

With the recipes in this book you can create a menu for almost any occasion. A menu that best fits your life-style, available time, and guest list. Whether you have a busy young family with both parents working, or are retired and cutting back on the rigors of entertaining, the fun can start with reading *Party Receipts from the Charleston Junior League* — for recipes, tips on entertaining, and a glimpse of the special place that is Charleston.

The Junior League of Charleston has long been associated with fine food and gracious hospitality. Many of the fund-raising activities it has undertaken since its founding in 1923 have involved food and entertaining. In the early days the group ran a tearoom open to the public, a lunchroom at the bagging factory, and the Junior League Milk Station. In 1950, the League embarked upon its most significant fund-raising project and published *Charleston Receipts*, a collection of traditional southern recipes passed down through the generations. With more than 700,000 copies in print, it is the oldest Junior League cookbook still in print. A second cookbook followed in 1986, *Charleston Receipts Repeats*, featuring contemporary Lowcountry cuisine. *Party Receipts* continues the tradition of sharing Charleston secrets for fine cooking and entertaining with a collection of recipes for lighter fare, from soups to sweets, as they meet the needs of today's host and hostess.

## MEETING STREET CRAB MEAT

The Junior League of Charleston Cookbook Committee caters one or two events a year to publicize their cookbooks. Meeting Street Crab is always on the menu.

*1 pound white crab meat*
*4 tablespoons butter*
*4 tablespoons flour*
*½ pint cream*
*4 tablespoons sherry*
*¾ cup grated sharp cheese*
*Salt and pepper to taste*

Make a cream sauce with the butter, flour and cream. Add salt, pepper and sherry. Remove from fire and add crab meat. Pour the mixture into buttered casserole or individual baking dishes. Sprinkle with grated cheese and cook in a hot oven until cheese melts. Do not overcook. Serves 4 (or more if served with crackers as an hors d'oeuvre). (1½ pounds of shrimp may be substituted for the crab.)

*Mrs. Thomas A. Huguenin (Mary Vereen),*
*from* **Charleston Receipts**

# THE JUNIOR LEAGUE OF CHARLESTON

*T*he Junior League of Charleston, Inc., is an organization of women committed to promoting voluntarism and to improving the community through the effective action and leadership of trained volunteers. Its purpose is exclusively educational and charitable. The Junior League of Charleston reaches out to women of all races, religions and national origins who demonstrate an interest in and a commitment to voluntarism.

The organization has been responsible for the establishment of such major projects as The Charleston Speech and Hearing Center, Horizon House (a refuge for troubled young people), and the Lowcountry Children's Center, a facility for the assessment, treatment, and intervention of abused and neglected children.

A few of the many other community projects supported by the Charleston Junior League's volunteer efforts include the Charleston Museum "Discover Me" room, the Child Guidance Bureau, "Kids on the Block," "I'm Special," Teen Outreach, "Woman to Woman," and the Voluntary Action Center. Funding for these projects has been largely supported by the sale of cookbooks published by the Junior League of Charleston, *Charleston Receipts* and *Charleston Receipts Repeats*. The publication of *Party Receipts from the Charleston Junior League* will continue that tradition.

*A*n important feature of Charleston Receipts, the first cookbook published by the Junior League of Charleston, is the quotations from the Gullah language scattered throughout the text. The only creole language spoken on the mainland of the United States, it is known by many descendants of slaves living in Charleston and on the nearby Sea Islands.

# PARTY RECEIPTS

# RECEIPTS

FROM THE

## CHARLESTON JUNIOR LEAGUE

# ACCOUTREMENTS:
# NUTS·NIBBLES
## AND
# BEVERAGES

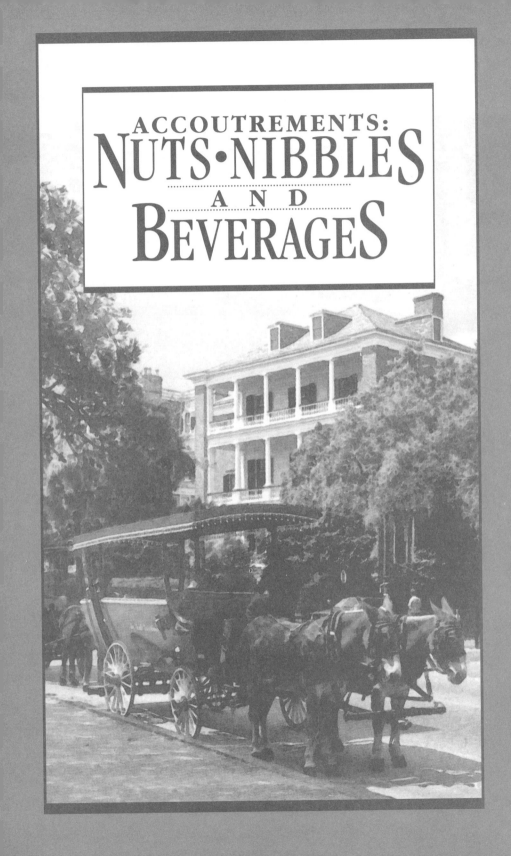

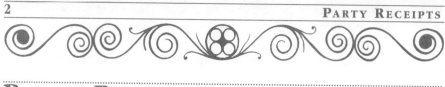

# BOILED PEANUTS

This is my husband's recipe for boiling peanuts, a traditional favorite at sailing events and all outdoor parties. They freeze well sealed in airtight containers.
— *Heidi Speissegger Whaley* (Mrs. John Seabrook Whaley, Jr.)

*Yield: 6 quarts*

6 quarts green peanuts in the shell
2 cups salt

**1.** Place the peanuts and salt in a 12-quart pot and add enough water to cover the peanuts.
**2.** Bring the water to a boil and boil the peanuts, uncovered, until they are tender, 1½ to 2 hours. Stir occasionally and add water as needed.
**3.** When the peanuts are tender, turn off the heat and let the nuts stand in the liquid until they reach the desired saltiness, approximately 1 to 2 hours.
**4.** Drain the nuts and serve at room temperature.

# PEANUTS CALIENTE

Warn your guests—these are hot!
— *Kara Anderson Berly* (Mrs. J. Anderson Berly III)

*Yield: 1 pound*

4 tablespoons butter
1 pound raw peanuts
4 teaspoons chili powder
¾ teaspoon paprika
1 teaspoon salt
½ teaspoon ground cumin
½ teaspoon cayenne pepper

**1.** Preheat the oven to 300°F. Melt the butter in a jelly-roll pan.
**2.** Shell the peanuts, add to the butter, and toss to coat. Bake for 30 minutes, stirring occasionally.
**3.** Combine the chili powder, paprika, salt, cumin, and cayenne in a small bowl. Sprinkle the mixture over the nuts and toss to coat. Return the pan to the oven and bake for an additional 30 minutes.
**4.** Transfer the peanuts to paper toweling and let cool.

"Mr. Redcliff, much diminished by the common touch, was serving chicken fricassee from a great silver platter. Vinny accepted her heaped plate with reservations. A suspicion stirred that Etta hadn't taken the trouble to have party food for them. Macaroni and sweet potatoes and guinea-squash — anybody could have those."

**Three O'Clock Dinner,**
*Josephine Pinckney*

# WALNUTS PARMESAN

There's no way to stop at just a few of these!

— *Suzanne Williams Chesnut (Mrs. Robert C. Chesnut)*

*Yield: 2 cups*

*1½ to 2 cups walnut halves*
*1 tablespoon butter, melted*
*¼ teaspoon liquid smoke or seasoned*
  *salt*
*¼ teaspoon salt*
*¼ cup shredded Parmesan cheese*

**1.** Preheat the oven to 350°F.
**2.** Spread the walnuts in one layer in a 9 x 13-inch baking pan and bake for 10 minutes.
**3.** Combine the butter, seasoned salt, and salt in a small bowl. Pour over the walnuts and toss to coat. Sprinkle the cheese over the walnuts and toss again.

**4.** Spread the nuts into a single layer and bake until the cheese is melted, 3 to 4 minutes. Immediately remove from the baking pan and cool on wax paper. Store in an airtight container; do not refrigerate.

# CHINESE FRIED WALNUTS

These lightly sugared nuts keep for up to two weeks in a tightly covered container. The recipe was given to me by Susan Proefke Brock.

— *Charlotte Nancie Quick*

*Yield: 4 cups*

*6 cups water*
*4 cups walnut halves*
*½ cup sugar*
*Vegetable oil*
*Salt, to taste*

**1.** Bring the water to a boil in a large saucepan. Add the walnuts and cook for 1 minute. Drain the nuts under hot running water and transfer to a large bowl. Wash the saucepan and dry it well.
**2.** Add the sugar to the hot walnuts

and stir until the sugar is dissolved (it may be necessary to let the mixture stand for a few minutes to let the sugar dissolve completely).
**3.** In the clean saucepan, heat 1 inch of oil to 350°F. With a slotted spoon, add half the walnuts to the oil and fry until golden brown, about 5 minutes. Remove the walnuts to a colander and sprinkle with salt. Toss lightly and cool on paper toweling.
**4.** Repeat the process with the remaining walnuts. When completely cool, store the nuts in an airtight container.

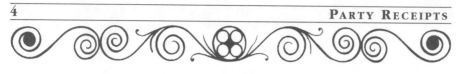

# TERIYAKI TOASTED NUTS

A tasty, light hors d'oeuvre.

*—Judy Nuss Werrell (Mrs. William Gresham Werrell)*

---
*Yield: 2 cups*
---

2 cups shelled pecan halves
2 tablespoons margarine, melted
2 teaspoons teriyaki sauce
2 teaspoons fresh lemon juice
2 cloves garlic, crushed and chopped
2 teaspoons finely chopped fresh ginger
½ teaspoon kosher salt

**1.** Preheat the oven to 350°F.
**2.** Spread the nuts on a jelly-roll pan in a single layer. Bake for 8 minutes, stirring once.
**3.** Combine the margarine, teriyaki sauce, lemon juice, garlic, ginger, and salt in a small bowl and mix well. Spoon or brush the mixture over the nuts.
**4.** Return the nuts to the oven and toast them until they are crisp and lightly browned, about 7 minutes, stirring twice.

# SPICY NUTS

Here is an easy way to dress up plain nuts.

*—Allison Ralston Leggett (Mrs. Leon D. Leggett, Jr.)*

---
*Yield: 2 cups*
---

⅓ cup margarine, melted
1 tablespoon Worcestershire sauce
½ teaspoon Tabasco sauce
¼ teaspoon freshly ground pepper
1 teaspoon salt
1 pound pecans or peanuts

**1.** Preheat the oven to 300°F.
**2.** Combine the margarine, Worcestershire, Tabasco, pepper, and salt in a small bowl.
**3.** Place the nuts in a jelly-roll pan, pour over the butter mixture, and toss to coat. Spread the nuts into a single layer and bake for 20 minutes, stirring frequently. Drain on paper toweling.

# GOLDEN NUT CRUNCH

The sweetness of the graham cereal makes this snack mix particularly irresistible.
— *Barbara D. Hall*

*Yield: 5 cups*

1 can (12 ounces) mixed nuts
¼ cup melted butter
¼ cup grated Parmesan cheese
¼ teaspoon garlic powder
¼ teaspoon ground oregano
¼ teaspoon celery salt
4 cups Golden Grahams cereal

**1.** Preheat the oven to 300°F.
**2.** Combine the mixed nuts and melted butter in a large bowl and add the Parmesan cheese, garlic powder, oregano, and celery salt. Toss well.
**3.** Spread the mixture in an ungreased roasting pan and bake for 15 minutes, stirring occasionally. Stir in the cereal and let cool.

# SNACK MIX

Here's an hors d'oeuvre the whole family can enjoy.
— *Julie Anne Dingle Swanson (Mrs. Arthur Pringle Swanson)*

*Yield: 3 quarts*

3 cups popped popcorn
2 cups Pepperidge Farm Goldfish
2 cups Cheerios cereal
2 cups thin pretzel sticks
2 cups Oysterette crackers
1 cup salted cashew nuts
1 package (.4 ounce) buttermilk salad
   dressing mix
⅓ cup safflower oil

**1.** Preheat the oven to 250°F.

**2.** Combine the popcorn, Goldfish, Cheerios, pretzels, Oysterettes, and cashews in a large bowl.
**3.** Combine the salad dressing mix and oil in a small bowl. Add the dressing to the dry ingredients and toss well.
**4.** Spread the mixture on an ungreased baking sheet and bake for 15 minutes.
**5.** Spread in a single layer on paper toweling to cool, and store in an airtight container.

"*A*zalea and Eola and all their family believed that true civilization existed only in Charleston and the low country, that thin strip of alluvial soil about forty miles in from the sea: plantation country . . ."
**Why We Never Danced the Charleston,** *Harlan Greene*

# PARTY MIX

There are endless variations of the basic party mix recipe; this is the one we like best.

*— Elizabeth Keeslar Cochran (Mrs. Edward H. Cochran, Jr.)*

---

*Yield: 11 cups*

---

¼ cup (½ stick) butter or margarine
1¼ teaspoons seasoned salt
2 tablespoons Worcestershire sauce
2 cups Cheerios cereal
2 cups Corn Chex cereal
2 cups Wheat Chex cereal
2 cups Rice Chex cereal
1 cup thin pretzel sticks
1 cup Cheese Tid-Bits
1 cup mixed nuts

**1.** Preheat the oven to 250°F.
**2.** Melt the butter in a large roasting pan. Stir in the seasoned salt and Worcestershire, then add the Cheerios, Corn Chex, Wheat Chex, Rice Chex, pretzels, Cheese Tid-Bits, and mixed nuts, stirring until evenly coated.
**3.** Bake for 1 hour, stirring every 15 minutes. Cool on paper toweling and store in an airtight container.

# INNOVATIVE CRACKERS

No one will believe how these tangy snacks are made, and nothing could be easier.

*— Merle Sparkman Tamsberg (Mrs. William Templeton Tamsberg)*

---

*Yield: 6 cups*

---

1 tablespoon dill weed
1 tablespoon garlic powder
1 package (.4 ounce) buttermilk salad
    dressing mix
1 package (.4 ounce) blue cheese
    dressing mix
2 cups vegetable oil
3 packages (7½ ounces each) oyster
    crackers

**1.** Combine the dill weed, garlic powder, dressing mixes, and oil in a blender and blend until smooth.
**2.** Place the oyster crackers in a shallow plastic container with a lid. Pour the dressing over the crackers and stir well. Cover and let stand overnight, stirring frequently.

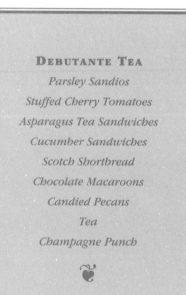

**DEBUTANTE TEA**

*Parsley Sandios*

*Stuffed Cherry Tomatoes*

*Asparagus Tea Sandwiches*

*Cucumber Sandwiches*

*Scotch Shortbread*

*Chocolate Macaroons*

*Candied Pecans*

*Tea*

*Champagne Punch*

## INDIAN SNACK

This highly portable hors d'oeuvre is great for picnics and boating parties.

— *Lucie Hall Maguire (Mrs. Robert O. Maguire)*

*Yield: 4 to 5 cups*

1 can (small) Chinese noodles
2 cups Rice Chex cereal
1 package (6 to 8 ounces) salted
    cashew nuts
½ cup sweetened coconut, toasted
1 teaspoon curry powder
¼ teaspoon ground ginger
¼ cup melted butter or margarine
1 teaspoon soy sauce

**1.** Preheat the oven to 300°F.
**2.** In a small roasting pan combine the noodles, cereal, cashews, and coconut. Sprinkle on the curry powder and ginger, then the butter and soy sauce. Mix well.
**3.** Cover the pan and bake for approximately 2 hours, until lightly browned. Uncover the pan for the last 30 to 40 minutes. Store in an airtight container.

## HERB PITA PIECES

Pita pieces may be eaten as snacks by themselves or used as crackers for spreads and dips.

— *Sallie Conner Lesemann (Mrs. A. R. Lesemann III)*

*Yield: About 5 dozen*

8 pita pockets
1 cup butter, melted
1 teaspoon dried oregano
1 teaspoon dried marjoram
1 teaspoon dried basil
1 teaspoon parsley flakes
2 cloves garlic, minced

**1.** Preheat the oven to 300°F.
**2.** Separate the pita pockets, forming two thin rounds. Break the rounds into cracker-size pieces.
**3.** Combine the melted butter, oregano, marjoram, basil, parsley, and garlic in a small bowl and brush the pita pieces with the herb butter.
**4.** Place on a baking sheet and bake until crispy, about 30 minutes.

> "Why this dearth of dining-out places? Back in 1938 there were not many tourists to cater to. And for natives the food at home and at the hospitable tables of friends was so special why should anyone be interested in dining out, except for an occasional dinner at Henry's?"
>
> **Charleston: A Golden Memory,** *Charles R. Anderson*

# MARINATED BLACK OLIVES

This simple preparation is surprisingly tasty.
— *Elizabeth Dennis Alexander (Mrs. Thomas W. Alexander, Jr.)*

---
*Yield: 8 to 10 servings*

---

*1 large can (6 ounces) ripe olives,
including liquid*
*1 clove garlic, peeled*
*¼ cup vegetable oil*

**1.** Combine the olives and liquid, garlic, and vegetable oil in a small bowl and cover and refrigerate for 24 hours.
**2.** Drain the olives, reserving the liquid, and set aside.
**3.** In a small saucepan heat the marinade. Place the olives in a bowl, pour over the marinade, and serve warm, with toothpicks.

# AHMAH'S PICKLED OKRA

"Ahmah" is the name my brother gave our grandmother, Jane Pursley Smith, when he was learning to talk, and it has stuck. Her pickled okra is a favorite with cocktails.
— *Beverly Smith Hutchison (Mrs. Leonard L. Hutchison)*

---
*Yield: 5 pints*

---

*5 pint jars, rings, and lids*
*2 pounds okra*
*5 pods hot pepper*
*5 cloves garlic*
*4 cups white vinegar*
*½ cup water*
*6 tablespoons salt*
*1 tablespoon celery or mustard seed*

**1.** Sterilize the jars by washing them in the dishwasher and drying them on the "hot" setting.
**2.** Wash the okra and pack in the hot, sterilized jars. Place 1 pepper pod and 1 clove garlic in each jar.
**3.** Bring the vinegar, water, salt, and celery or mustard seed to a boil in a medium-size saucepan. Pour the hot mixture over the okra, and seal the jars with a ring and lid.
**4.** In a large pot, bring enough water to a boil to completely cover the jars. Reduce the heat to a simmer (180°F), submerge the jars in the water to completely cover the tops, and leave for 10 minutes. Remove the jars and store for 8 weeks before serving the pickled okra.

# MRS. FOXWORTH'S BLOODY MARYS

Colonel and Mrs. E. D. Foxworth "adopted" my husband when he arrived at The College of Charleston. They housed him, fed both of us, and taught us to be gracious hosts; and Mrs. Foxworth gave me her recipe for the best Bloody Marys ever! We make them by the gallon for brunches and for tailgate parties at football games or the Charleston Cup. Be warned—the longer they sit, the hotter they get.

*— Connor H. Gantt (Mrs. John M. Gantt, Jr.)*

*Yield: 1 gallon*

*1 can (46 ounces) V-8 vegetable juice*
*1 tablespoon Worcestershire sauce*
*1 teaspoon celery salt*
*1 teaspoon celery seed*
*½ cup fresh lemon juice, or to taste*
*½ teaspoon Tabasco sauce, or to taste*
*2 cups vodka*

Combine all of the ingredients in a 1-gallon jug. Refrigerate until ready to serve.

# COLLINS MIX

This recipe was given to me by Gayle Brown Clyburn. It is good plain or as a mixer with vodka, gin, or rum.

*— Ellen Graham Brown*
*(Mrs. Jack Brown)*

*Yield: 1 gallon*

*2 cups sugar*
*1 can (6 ounces) frozen orange juice*
*concentrate, undiluted*
*¾ cup Rose's lime juice*
*4 egg whites, lightly beaten*
*1 quart ReaLemon juice*

Combine all of the ingredients in a 1-gallon pitcher or jug. Fill with water to make a full gallon. Shake or stir well.

## COLONEL AIKEN SIMONS' MINT JULEP

Having ready as many thin highball glasses as necessary, proceed as follows:

Take a pitcher or jug of suitable size and place therein a teaspoonful of sugar for each julep to be mixed, add just enough water to dissolve the sugar: about an equal volume of water to the sugar will do if you stir enough. Then pour in a whiskey glass of spirits for each julep and stir up with the syrup. Select 4 or 5 fine sprigs of mint and put them into the mixture. Whether this mint is to be crushed or is controversial and depends on the strength of the mint and the taste of individuals. Crush the mint and let stand awhile.

Then fill each glass with broken ice, taking care not to get the outside of the glass wet as that would interfere with frosting. Divide the contents of the pitcher among the glasses and stir each vigorously. The ice will have subsided and the glasses must be filled up with ice and again stirred briskly. The frost by this time has formed a thick white coating on the glass, so the glass should be handled cautiously to avoid marring the frost which is the pride and joy of a Julep Artifex. Then choose very fine sprigs of mint for the garnishing; stick one in each glass and serve.

*Albert Simons,*
*from* **Charleston Receipts**

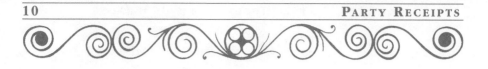

# CHAMPAGNE COCKTAIL

Years ago I visited the wonderful Oustau de Baumanière in Provence, France, with three generations of my family. We were so taken with their delicious Champagne cocktails that we came home and experimented until we reached an approximation of the real thing.

— *Cathy Huffman Forrester* (Mrs. Darryl Forrester)

*Yield: 6 to 8 cocktails*

2 tablespoons Cognac
2 tablespoons sweet vermouth
1 tablespoon Grand Marnier liqueur
1½ teaspoons orange Curaçao liqueur
1 bottle (750 ml.) Champagne, chilled
6 to 8 small sugar cubes
6 to 8 drops Angostura bitters
6 to 8 orange slices or 6 to 8
    strawberries, for garnish

**1.** Chill 6 to 8 Champagne glasses, depending on how many people you wish to serve.
**2.** Combine the Cognac, vermouth, Grand Marnier, and Curaçao in a large pitcher and mix well. Pour in the Champagne and stir until the "fizz" is gone.
**3.** Place a sugar cube in the bottom of each glass and dot each cube with 1 drop of the bitters. Crush the sugar cube and pour in the Champagne. Stir to combine, and garnish each cocktail with an orange slice or a strawberry.

# JOHN MOTT'S IRISH COFFEE

Our friend John Mott makes this beverage once a year at the Flint City Club. His wife, Patricia McGrail Mott, is a member of the Junior League of Flint, Michigan.

— *Amy Tomblinson Schultz* (Mrs. Frank Carl William Schultz III)

*Yield: 1 serving*

1 rounded teaspoon light brown sugar
1½ ounces Jameson Irish Whiskey
1 to 1½ cups hot brewed coffee
½ pint heavy or whipping cream
2 tablespoons confectioners' sugar

**1.** Place the brown sugar in the bottom of a glass Irish coffee mug. Add the whiskey and stir until blended.
**2.** Fill the mug with the coffee until the mixture comes to ½ inch from the rim. Mix carefully.
**3.** Whip the cream with the sugar in a medium-size bowl until it barely forms peaks. Lay dollops of the cream mixture on top of the coffee. Sip the coffee through the cream.

# FROZEN SHERRY PUNCH

This recipe was given to me by my mother, Nancy Dinwiddie Hawk.

— *Penny Hawk Wilson* (*Mrs. Stanley M. Wilson*)

*Yield: 1¼ gallons*

*1 gallon medium sherry*
*4 cans (12 ounces each) frozen*
  *lemonade concentrate, undiluted*
*1 lemonade can water*

**1.** Combine all ingredients thoroughly in a large bowl or pot.
**2.** Transfer to five 1-quart freezer containers and freeze for at least 24 hours. The mixture will be slushy.
**3.** To serve, spoon into wineglasses.

# SOUTHERN COMFORT PUNCH

My mother, Barbara H. Mulvey, reports that her bridge club loves this punch!

— *Mary Mulvey Smith* (*Mrs. Kurtz Smith*)

*Yield: 1 gallon*

*2½ cups Southern Comfort*
*¾ cup fresh lemon juice*
*2 cans (6 ounces each) frozen*
  *lemonade concentrate, undiluted*
*2¼ liters 7UP, chilled*
*Maraschino cherries (optional)*

**1.** Combine the Southern Comfort, lemon juice, and lemonade concentrate in a pitcher or bowl. Chill.
**2.** Just before serving, transfer the mixture to a punch bowl and add the 7UP. If you wish, keep cold with an ice ring colored with red food coloring and dotted with maraschino cherries.

*M*any occasions call for a combination of tea party and cocktail party. Set up a tea table or tray in another room or at the opposite end of the room from the bar. The food should be planned to complement both kinds of beverage.

# UNCLE OTTO SPARKMAN'S PUNCH

Uncle Otto Sparkman learned how to make this punch from his father, Edward Heriot Sparkman, who was born at Birdfield Plantation near Georgetown and fought in the 7th South Carolina regiment during the Civil War. Uncle Otto made this punch for many debutante parties and weddings in this century. It may be prepared days or even weeks ahead of serving time.

*— Helen Garvin Ingle (Mrs. J. Addison Ingle)*

*Yield: 30 servings*

1 pound sugar cubes
1½ quarts hot green tea
Juice of 12 lemons
1 pint peach brandy
1 quart Jamaican rum
1 or 2 quarts bourbon
1 or 2 liters club soda (depending on quantity of bourbon)

**1.** Place the sugar cubes in a large bowl and pour over the hot tea. Stir well.
**2.** Add the lemon juice, peach brandy, rum, and bourbon and mix well. Refrigerate.
**3.** Just before serving, transfer the mixture to a punch bowl and add the club soda.

# BARBARA'S BASIC PUNCH

This recipe, given to me by my mother, Barbara Stroupe Elliott, may also be used as the base for a cocktail. Just add 1 cup of Amaretto, freeze to a slushy consistency, and serve as a daiquiri. Great to pass at parties!

*— Monica Elliott Hudgens (Mrs. R. Edward Hudgens III)*

*Yield: About 4 quarts*

2 cans (46 ounces each) pineapple juice
3 cans (6 ounces each) frozen lemonade concentrate, undiluted
8 cans (6 ounces each) water
1 can (46 ounces) orange juice
2 tablespoons almond extract
2 tablespoons vanilla extract
2 liters ginger ale, chilled

Combine all the ingredients except the ginger ale in a large bowl or pot and chill. Just before serving, transfer the mixture to a punch bowl and add the ginger ale.

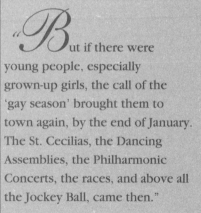

"*B*ut if there were young people, especially grown-up girls, the call of the 'gay season' brought them to town again, by the end of January. The St. Cecilias, the Dancing Assemblies, the Philharmonic Concerts, the races, and above all the Jockey Ball, came then."

**Charleston:**
**The Place and the People,**
*Mrs. St. Julien Ravenel*

# MARGARITA PUNCH

This punch may be served in a punch bowl over ice or in ice-filled cups or glasses.

— *Merrie Summer McNair*
*(Mrs. David H. McNair)*

*Yield: ½ gallon*

*2 pounds sugar*
*4 cups water*
*1 pint Tequila*
*2 ounces Cointreau or triple sec liqueur*
*2 cups fresh lemon juice*
*3 tablespoons orange extract*

Combine the sugar and water in a large saucepan and boil until the sugar is dissolved. Let cool and add the remaining ingredients. Chill.

# KATHY'S VALENTINE MIMOSA

This has been a hit as a before-dinner drink at my annual Valentine's Day party—and one year I served it on St. Patrick's Day with green cherries instead of red. For those who prefer a nonalcoholic drink, this one can be served with ginger ale substituted for the Champagne.

— *Kathleen Kennerty Rackley*
*(Mrs. Charles Gary Rackley)*

*Yield: About 1 gallon*

*1 can (6 ounces) frozen orange juice*
*concentrate, undiluted*
*1 can (46 ounces) unsweetened*
*pineapple juice*
*2 bottles (750 ml. each) extra dry*
*Champagne, chilled*
*1 jar (10 ounces) red maraschino*
*cherries*

**1.** Prepare the orange juice according to the package instructions.
**2.** Combine with the pineapple juice in a large bowl or pot, and chill.
**3.** When ready to serve, pour in the Champagne. Serve in wineglasses with a cherry in the bottom of each.

"*We* were in Hibernian Hall, that white Ionian temple at the foot of Chalmers Street, at some ball, maybe even our grandest of the season, the St. Cecilia . . . And what with all the candles on the walls and the old gaslight fixtures above us and some of the old gowns, you could almost believe it was the nineteenth century."

**Why We Never Danced the Charleston,** *Harlan Greene*

# WHITE GRAPE SPLASH

Using grenadine in this punch gives it a lovely color for Christmas parties. Sliced strawberries, cherries, and pineapple may be placed in the ice mold for additional color.

*— Elaine Meyer Bergmann (Mrs. J. Robert Bergmann)*

---
*Yield: 1¼ gallons*

---

*2 quarts white grape juice*
*2 liters ginger ale*
*¾ cup grenadine or 1 bottle (750 ml.)*
   *Champagne or dry white wine*

Combine all the ingredients in a large bowl or pot. If you wish to make an iced ring mold, fill an 8-inch or 10-inch ring mold with some of the punch mixture and freeze until solid. (If you are using Champagne in the punch, be sure to allow the mold to freeze overnight.) Serve in a chilled punch bowl with ice or a ring mold.

# EGGNOG

No holiday buffet is complete without a bowl of eggnog.

*— Bradford Simmons Marshall (Mrs. Charles K. Marshall)*

---
*Yield: 12 servings*

---

*6 eggs, separated*
*2 cups sugar*
*¼ cup rum*
*2 cups bourbon*
*2 cups heavy or whipping cream*
*2 cups milk*
*Grated nutmeg*

**1.** Beat the egg yolks well in a medium-size bowl and set aside. Beat the egg whites in a large bowl until stiff, then add the sugar.
**2.** Fold the egg yolks into the egg white and sugar mixture until thoroughly combined.
**3.** Stir in the rum, bourbon, cream, and milk. Beat well.
**4.** Pour into a punch bowl and sprinkle the nutmeg on top.

*"*Thick cream, a pint of madeira, half a pint of sack, three lemons, and near a pound of double refined sugar. You squeeze the juice of the three lemons and put into your wine. Then grate off the yellow rind, and put that in. Then add all that to your cream and sugar. Take your syllabub whipper—*"*

**Syllabub,**
*Patricia Colbert*

# HOLIDAY FRUIT PUNCH

This is the traditional beverage at my mother's Christmas gatherings.
— *Amy Carswell Willis*
*(Mrs. Thomas L. Willis)*

*Yield: 3 quarts*

*2 pounds (total) red, green, and blue-black grapes*
*½ pineapple, peeled, cored, and cubed*
*3 cups white wine*
*3 cups cranberry juice cocktail*
*3 tablespoons fresh lemon juice*
*3 tablespoons sugar*
*1 liter club soda, lemon-lime soda, or Champagne*

**1.** Divide 1 to 1½ pounds of the grapes into small clusters of all colors. Fill a ring mold with the clusters, barely cover with water, and freeze until solid.
**2.** Halve and seed, if necessary, the remaining grapes. Place in a large plastic container along with the pineapple. Add the white wine, cranberry juice cocktail, lemon juice, and sugar. Cover and chill for at least 2 hours or overnight.
**3.** At serving time, dip the ring mold in hot water for 10 seconds, then remove the ice ring and place it in a punch bowl. Pour in the fruit-wine mixture and add the soda or Champagne. Ladle the fruit and punch into cups.

# CHAMPAGNE PUNCH

We serve this punch for celebrations of all kinds. Notice that the first step must be done the day before serving.
— *Jennifer Wertz Hendricks*
*(Mrs. Ralph Martin Hendricks, Jr.)*

*Yield: 1½ gallons*

*2 quarts lemonade*
*1 can (46 ounces) pineapple juice*
*1 can (6 ounces) frozen lemonade concentrate, undiluted*
*2 bottles (750 ml. each) dry Champagne, chilled*
*Fresh pineapple wedges (garnish)*

**1.** The day before you plan to serve the punch, freeze the 2 quarts of lemonade in one or two bundt pans or ring molds (it is sometimes helpful to have a back-up ring in the freezer to add during the course of the party).
**2.** Just before serving, combine the pineapple juice and lemonade concentrate in a large pitcher or bowl.
**3.** Place the frozen lemonade ring in the punch bowl. Pour over the pineapple-lemon juice mixture and then add the Champagne. Garnish with the pineapple wedges.

# CHILLED MINT TEA

This is a refreshing alternative to plain iced tea for summer gatherings.

— *Stacey Tollison Griffith* (Mrs. Stephen A. Griffith)

*Yield: ½ gallon*

2 cups water
3 family-size tea bags
10 fresh mint leaves
½ cup sugar
1 can (6 ounces) frozen lemonade
    concentrate
1 can (6 ounces) frozen orange juice
    concentrate

**1.** Bring the water to a boil in a large saucepan and add the tea bags and mint leaves. Simmer for 10 minutes. Remove the tea bags.
**2.** Add the sugar to the hot tea and stir until dissolved.
**3.** Prepare the lemonade and orange juice according to package instructions and stir into the sweetened mint tea. Refrigerate the mixture overnight.

### MRS. WILLIAM HUGER'S ORANGE CORDIAL

50 oranges
4 pounds sugar
1 gallon whiskey

Peel oranges very thin. Put peels in the gallon of whiskey and let them soak for 6 weeks. Pour off whiskey and then make a syrup of 4 pounds of sugar with just enough water to keep sugar from burning. While *hot*, add to whiskey and stir.

*Mrs. William S. Popham (Louisa Stoney),*
*from* Charleston Receipts

# COFFEE CREAM

Don't let the gelatin in this recipe fool you; the mixture remains fluid. Devotees of coffee ice cream will love this "punch."

— *Ruth Tisdale Geer* (Mrs. Benjamin Owen Geer)

*Yield: 5 servings*

½ envelope unflavored gelatin
1 pint cream (very fresh)
5 cups strong coffee
1 cup sugar

**1.** Place the gelatin in a medium-size bowl and cover with some of the cream.

**2.** Bring the remaining cream, the coffee, and the sugar to a boil in a medium-size saucepan.
**3.** Pour the gelatin mixture into the coffee mixture and stir well. Bring to a boil.
**4.** Pour the mixture into a bowl and let it cool, stirring from time to time. When cool, pour into cups.

# HOT MULLED CIDER

This favorite cold-weather drink is a holdover from the days when Charleston had more wintry days. We used to enjoy standing around the fireplace after a day of sailing, sipping this zesty refresher. To turn it into a nonalcoholic hot buttered rum, use brown sugar instead of white and add a small amount of rum flavoring and butter to each mug before pouring in the cider mixture.

— ***Helen Smith Warren***
*(Mrs. John H. Warren III)*

*Yield: 1¼ quarts*

*⅓ cup sugar*
*3 sticks cinnamon*
*1 orange, thinly sliced*
*2 teaspoons whole cloves*
*1 lemon, thinly sliced*
*1 cup water*
*1 quart apple cider*

Place all the ingredients except the cider in a saucepan, bring to a boil, and boil for 5 minutes. Add the cider and heat just to boiling. Serve in mugs.

# HOT BURGUNDY AND CIDER

For a nonalcoholic alternative, substitute 3 cups of grape juice for the wine in this recipe.

— ***Sandra Pettersen Jackson***
*(Mrs. William Andrew Jackson)*

*Yield: 1¼ gallons*

*1 gallon apple cider*
*2 tablespoons fresh lemon juice*
*4 cinnamon sticks*
*3 to 4 whole cloves*
*¾ cup sugar*
*1 bottle (750 ml.) Burgundy wine*

**1.** Heat the cider, lemon juice, cinnamon sticks, cloves, and sugar in a large pot. Stir until the sugar dissolves. Heat to a boil and remove from the heat.
**2.** Add the wine and place the mixture in a Crock Pot to keep it warm during the serving period.

American Classic Tea, the only tea grown in America, comes from a plantation on Wadmalaw Island near Charleston. Its tea bushes are descended from plants brought to this country more than 100 years ago from China, India, and Ceylon.

# WASSAIL

This traditional Christmas drink may be served as is or with a little brandy added to each cup.

*— Hope Gazes Grayson*
*(Mrs. J. Michael Grayson)*

---

*Yield: 2 quarts*

---

*2 quarts apple juice*
*1 stick cinnamon*
*½ orange, sliced*
*½ lemon, sliced*
*5 whole cloves*

Place all the ingredients in a large pot and simmer for 15 to 20 minutes. Serve immediately.

---

### FLIP

This refreshing drink was in vogue in England in the 18th century and was brought to Carolina when settled by the Lords Proprietors. A flip glass is small at the bottom and gradually widens to the top. It holds about a quart.

*4 jiggers whiskey*
*4 egg yolks*
*4 teaspoons sugar*
*1 quart rich milk*
*Nutmeg to taste*

Beat yolks, sugar, and seasoning together. Add milk and whiskey. Shake well with crushed ice, strain and serve in stemmed glasses with a dash of nutmeg on top. 8–10 servings.

**Miss Ellen Parker,**
*from* **Charleston Receipts**

---

# SPICED HOLIDAY TEA

I like serving this hot drink for holiday parties or on chilly nights in any season. The recipe was given to me by my sister, Kristin Wray Wilda.

*— Devon Wray Hanahan*
*(Mrs. William O. Hanahan III)*

---

*Yield: 3¼ quarts*

---

*7 cups water*
*1½ cups sugar*
*5 tea bags*
*1 can (6 ounces) frozen orange juice*
*    concentrate, plus 1 can water*
*4 tablespoons fresh lemon juice*
*4 cups water*
*5 cinnamon sticks*
*1 tablespoon whole cloves*
*Lemon slices or cinnamon sticks*
*    (optional garnish)*

**1.** Bring the 7 cups of water and the sugar to a boil in a large saucepan and cook until the sugar dissolves. Add the tea bags. Remove from the heat and steep for 5 minutes; remove the tea bags.
**2.** Add the orange juice concentrate and 1 can of water and the lemon juice.
**3.** In a separate pan, combine the 4 cups of water, the cinnamon sticks, and the cloves. Simmer, covered, for 20 minutes, strain, and add to the tea mixture.
**4.** Serve hot, garnished with lemon slices or cinnamon sticks.

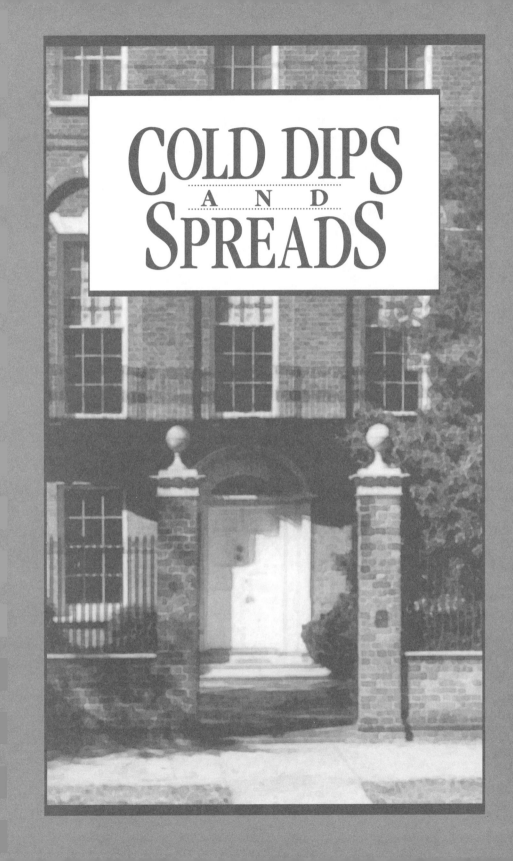

# COLD DIPS AND SPREADS

## FRUIT RAINBOW

For an easy, eye-catching hors d'oeuvre, arrange slices of fruit and cheese in a large arc (rainbow) on a silver tray.

*1½ pounds extra sharp Cheddar cheese*
*1 Granny Smith apple, cored*
*1 McIntosh (or other red) apple, cored*
*1 pear, cored*
*1 navel orange*

Cut the cheese, apples, and pear into ⅛-inch slices. Peel the orange and divide into sections. Alternate slices of cheese with each of the fruits: for example, orange, cheese, green apple, cheese, red apple, cheese, pear, cheese.

**Julia Ann Rice**

# TRINA'S PIMIENTO CHEESE

The Grand Marnier gives a nice lift to this variation on a favorite Charleston recipe.

— *Sarah Payne Maddox*

---

*Yield: About 3 cups*

---

*1½ teaspoons Dijon mustard*
*1 jar (4 ounces) chopped pimientos, drained*
*¼ teaspoon cayenne pepper*
*½ cup mayonnaise*
*¼ cup Durkee sauce*
*3 tablespoons Grand Marnier liqueur*
*2 cloves garlic, minced*
*1 pound sharp Cheddar cheese, grated*

Combine all the ingredients except the cheese in a large bowl and mix well. Add the cheese and mix until blended. Refrigerate overnight. Serve with crackers or slices of French bread, or as a stuffing for celery stalks.

# CHEDDAR CHEESEY SPREAD

Serve this spread on crackers or on bread slices (crusts removed) that have been cut in quarters. It's also great on celery sticks.
— *Elizabeth L. Boineau*

*Yield: About 1½ cups*

12 ounces extra sharp Cheddar
  cheese, grated
4 ounces cream cheese, at room
  temperature
4 ounces blue cheese, crumbled
½ cup mayonnaise
¼ cup freshly grated Parmesan cheese
2 tablespoons grated onion
Dash of Worcestershire sauce
Dash of Tabasco sauce
Salt and pepper, to taste

Combine all the ingredients in the bowl of a food processor and process until smooth. Refrigerate until serving time.

# MOCK BOURSIN

This makes a wonderful holiday gift. One idea for packaging is to fill small lotus bowls from your local import shop.
— *Laura Strader Riley*
*(Mrs. Charles W. Riley III)*

*Yield: About 3 cups*

16 ounces cream cheese, at room
  temperature
1 carton (8 ounces) whipped butter
2 cloves garlic (or to taste), minced
½ teaspoon salt
½ teaspoon Beau Monde Seasoning
¼ teaspoon dried thyme leaves
¼ teaspoon dried basil leaves
¼ teaspoon dried chives
¼ teaspoon dried marjoram leaves
1 teaspoon dried dill weed

Combine all the ingredients in a large bowl and mix until blended. Refrigerate until ready to serve.

# MAUI CHEESE BLOCK

The pineapple-mustard topping has a sweet and tangy flavor that goes well with the plainness of the cream cheese.
— *Susan Scott Waters* *(Mrs. Philip Waters)*

*Yield: About 1½ cups topping*

6 ounces pineapple preserves
6 ounces Dijon mustard
2 tablespoons horseradish sauce
8 ounces cream cheese

Combine the pineapple preserves, mustard, and horseradish sauce in a medium-size bowl and mix well. Place the cream cheese on a serving plate and pour some of the pineapple mixture over the cheese. Serve with crackers.
**Note:** There will be pineapple topping left over to use another time or with additional blocks of cream cheese.

# BLUEBERRY MANDARIN CHEESE LOAF

I like to include a sweet hors d'oeuvre in my party menus. This one is especially good served on Swedish ginger snaps.

— *Margaret Edwards Lee* (Mrs. Douglas B. Lee)

*Yield: 12 to 14 servings*

16 ounces cream cheese, at room
  temperature
1 can (11 ounces) mandarin
  oranges, drained
Blueberry chutney, homemade or
  commercial

**1.** Place the cream cheese and mandarin oranges in the bowl of a food processor and process until smooth.
**2.** Place the mixture in the center of a serving plate and shape into a loaf (or whatever shape you wish). Place in the refrigerator until chilled and firm.
**3.** To serve, pour chutney over the loaf. Serve with ginger snaps.

# GRANDMA'S FABULOUS CHEESE RING

This colorful hors d'oeuvre is perfect for a Christmas party.

— *Monti Mengedoht Hanger* (Mrs. Walter Clark Hanger)

*Yield: 15 to 20 servings*

3 cups grated sharp Cheddar cheese
½ cup chopped pecans
1 small onion, grated
¼ cup mayonnaise, or enough to
  moisten
1 jar (8 ounces) strawberry jam

**1.** Line a 1-quart ring mold with plastic wrap.
**2.** Combine the cheese, pecans, onion, and mayonnaise in a medium-size bowl and mix well. Press the mixture into the prepared mold. Refrigerate until firm, several hours or overnight.
**3.** Unmold the ring onto a serving platter. Spoon the strawberry jam into a small container and place it in the center of the ring mold. Serve with crackers.

# ISLAND CHEESE BALL

Chopped dates may be substituted for the raisins in this recipe, and a quarter cup of drained crushed pineapple makes a nice addition.

— *Vicki Kornahrens Robinson (Mrs. Neil C. Robinson, Jr.)*

*Yield: 10 to 12 servings*

¼ cup chopped raisins
¼ cup dark rum, preferably Meyers's
8 ounces cream cheese, at room
   temperature
1 teaspoon curry powder, or to taste
1 cup chopped pecans or macadamia
   nuts
1 cup shredded coconut, toasted
Mango or peach chutney
Ginger snaps, preferably thin

**1.** Place the raisins and rum in a small saucepan and cook over low heat until most of the rum has evaporated, 10 to 12 minutes.
**2.** Place the cream cheese, curry powder, nuts, raisins, and remaining rum in a large bowl and blend well.
**3.** Shape the mixture into a ball and roll in the coconut. Refrigerate or serve immediately. Place the ball on a serving plate, pour chutney over it, and serve with ginger snaps.

# EASY CHEESE BALL

This cheese ball is easy to make, easy to serve, and easy to eat!

— *Rhondy Valdes Huff (Mrs. Charles M. Huff)*

*Yield: 6 to 8 servings*

½ pound sharp Cheddar cheese,
   grated
¼ cup chopped green olives
¼ cup chopped red onion
½ cup mayonnaise
½ cup chopped walnuts or pecans

**1.** Mix together the cheese, olives, and onion in a medium-size bowl. Add just enough mayonnaise to bind the ingredients.
**2.** Form the cheese mixture into a ball. Roll the ball in the chopped nuts, pressing firmly so that the nuts will adhere to the surface. Chill or serve immediately with crackers.

The best Melba toast is homemade. Start with dry thin-sliced bread; remove the crusts and cut into circles, squares, or triangles. Bake in a 250°F oven until the toasts are crisp and a light golden brown.

# PINEAPPLE CHEESE BALL

The cool pineapple flavor makes this an appealing summer hors d'oeuvre.

— *Dale Baynard Frampton (Mrs. Henry W. Frampton III)*

---

*Yield: 8 to 12 servings*

16 ounces cream cheese, at room
   temperature
1 can (8 ounces) crushed pineapple,
   drained well
2 cups chopped pecans
¼ cup chopped green pepper
2 tablespoons chopped onion
1 tablespoon seasoned salt

**1.** Combine the cream cheese, pineapple, 1 cup of the pecans, the green pepper, onion, and seasoned salt in a large bowl and mix well.
**2.** Shape the mixture into a ball and roll in the remaining cup of pecans. Refrigerate overnight and serve with crackers.

# LIBBY'S CHRISTMAS GIFT

We look forward to this gift from our friend Libby James every Christmas.

— *Rebecca Player Bonner (Mrs. Robert Cunningham Bonner)*

---

*Yield: 2 cheese balls*

16 ounces cream cheese, at room
   temperature
½ pound sharp Cheddar cheese,
   grated
2 teaspoons Worcestershire sauce, or
   more, to taste
2 teaspoons grated onion
Cayenne pepper, to taste
1 cup chopped pecans or walnuts

**1.** Cream together the cheeses in a large bowl. Add the Worcestershire, onion, and cayenne and mix well.
**2.** Shape the mixture into 2 balls and roll each in the chopped nuts, to coat. Serve with crackers.

*A* block of cream cheese forms the base for endless hors d'oeuvre possibilities. Top the block with any of the following — and you will think of many more:

❦ Hot pepper jelly
❦ Pickapeppa Sauce
❦ Chutney
❦ Black or red caviar
❦ Guava paste

# FILLED EDAM

Advance preparation is needed for this cheese spread. The mixture has to "age" for a week.

— *Frida Moore Raley (Mrs. Charles H. Raley, Jr.)*

*Yield: 15 servings*

1 round (1½ pounds) Edam cheese,
  wax coating removed
1 cup (2 sticks) butter, at room
  temperature
3 teaspoons paprika
1 teaspoon dry mustard
½ cup brandy
3 tablespoons sherry

**1.** Cut off the top of the cheese round and scoop out the inside, leaving a ¼-inch shell. Grate the cheese removed to form the cavity and place it in a large bowl.
**2.** Add the butter to the bowl and work it into the grated Edam. Add the remaining ingredients and mix well.
**3.** Spoon the mixture into the Edam shell. Replace the top, cover with plastic wrap, and refrigerate for 1 week. Bring the cheese to room temperature before serving. Serve with party pumpernickel bread.

# LAYERED CHEESE PÂTÉ

I like to serve this cheese loaf on a bed of spinach leaves, garnished with cherry tomatoes—a particularly festive look at holiday time.

— *Lynn Orvin Kornya (Mrs. Theodore E. Kornya)*

*Yield: 8 to 10 servings*

16 ounces cream cheese, at room
  temperature
1¼ teaspoons dried Italian seasoning
¼ teaspoon freshly ground pepper
½ cup grated Gruyère cheese
¼ to ½ cup finely chopped pecans
¼ cup chopped fresh parsley
3 ounces blue cheese, crumbled
Spinach leaves, for garnish
Cherry tomatoes, for garnish

**1.** Line a small loaf pan with plastic wrap.
**2.** Place the cream cheese, Italian seasoning, and pepper in the bowl of an electric mixer and mix until smooth.

**3.** Spread one-third of the cream cheese mixture in the bottom of the loaf pan.
**4.** Top the cream cheese with a layer of the Gruyère, then a layer of chopped pecans.
**5.** Add another third of the cream cheese mixture, then a layer of parsley and a layer of blue cheese. Top with the remaining cream cheese mixture, pressing firmly to remove air pockets.
**6.** Cover with plastic wrap and refrigerate for at least 8 hours.
**7.** To serve, make a bed of spinach leaves on a serving plate, unmold the pâté, and garnish the plate with cherry tomatoes. Serve with crackers.

# CLEMSON BLUE CHEESE AND OLIVE PASTE

My husband, Dr. Wayne L. King, deserves the credit for this recipe. It can be served in a bowl surrounded by thinly sliced French bread or made into canapés by spreading the French bread slices in advance, garnishing each with a piece of olive.

—*Jeannie Nissen King (Mrs. Wayne L. King)*

*Yield: 10 to 12 servings*

8 ounces cured black olives
   (Calamata, for example), pitted
4 cloves garlic, mashed
¼ cup chopped pecans or walnuts
6 tablespoons olive oil or more, as
   needed
¾ pound Clemson blue cheese or
   Roquefort or Gorgonzola
French bread

**1.** Place the olives, garlic, nuts, and olive oil in the bowl of a food processor and process with on/off pulses until the mixture is finely chopped and blended.
**2.** Add the blue cheese and pulse until blended to a smooth consistency. The paste should be somewhat "moist" from the oil. Add more olive oil by the teaspoon, if necessary. Refrigerate until 15 minutes before serving (the paste will keep for up to a week in the refrigerator).

# STILTON AND PORT WINE SPREAD

A simple and elegant hors d'oeuvre. It is great spread on Melba toast or crackers or on slices of apples and pears.

— *Bowe Moorman Pritchard (Mrs. Edward K. Pritchard III)*

*Yield: 1 cup*

8 ounces Stilton cheese
Salt and freshly ground pepper,
   to taste
2 tablespoons unsalted butter, melted
1 tablespoon Port wine
Apple and pear slices (optional)

**1.** Crumble the cheese into a small bowl. Season lightly with salt and pepper. Add a small amount of the butter and mix gently.
**2.** Gradually add the port until the mixture becomes a smooth, spreadable paste. Transfer the paste to a small serving dish or decorative pot. Refrigerate until shortly before serving time.

# LOW-CALORIE DIP

Your guests will thank you for paying attention to calories and fats—and for making such a tasty dip.
— *Sarah R. S. Stender, M.D.*

*Yield: About 3 cups*

1 pint cottage cheese
1 cup grated Cheddar cheese
2 tablespoons grated green bell pepper
2 tablespoons grated onion
2 tablespoons prepared horseradish
3 tablespoons mayonnaise
Salt and freshly ground pepper, to
    taste

Combine the ingredients in a medium-size bowl and mix well. Refrigerate until ready to serve. Serve with crackers and/or raw vegetables.

# YOGURT DILL DIP

This is a refreshing, tangy dip that is excellent with raw vegetables. It's better when prepared a day before serving, to allow the flavors to meld.
— *Florence Wilson Miles*
*(Mrs. William L. Miles)*

*Yield: 2 cups*

1 cup plain yogurt
1 cup mayonnaise
½ teaspoon garlic powder
½ teaspoon onion powder
½ teaspoon fresh lemon juice
2 tablespoons chopped fresh dill
    (or 2 teaspoons dried dill weed)

Combine the ingredients in a medium-size bowl and mix until smooth. Chill for several hours or overnight before serving.

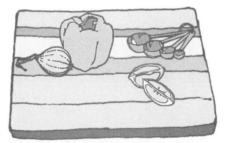

### SAGA CHEESE AND HONEY MUSTARD

Pour your favorite bottled honey mustard over a wedge of Saga Blue cheese and serve with crackers.

*Madge McCrady Hallett*
*(Mrs. James W. G. Hallett)*

# AVOCADO DIP

When you have ripe avocados, this is a nice alternative to guacamole.
— *Sarah Payne Maddox*

---

*Yield: About 1 cup*

---

1 large avocado, peeled, halved, and
    seed removed
2 tablespoons chopped scallions
    (green onions)
1 tablespoon fresh lemon juice
¾ cup mayonnaise
1 teaspoon sugar
1½ teaspoons Worcestershire sauce
¼ teaspoon hot pepper sauce

Place all the ingredients in the bowl of a food processor or in a blender and blend until smooth. Chill and serve with your favorite chips.

"*I*n ante-bellum times, despite transportation problems, Charleston and the Lowcountry had formed a single community, the same families moving in and out of the city with the seasons and with the changing priorities of their lives, very much as in England at the same period. This dual sense of place, merging rural and urban, survived at least in feeling right on down to the late 1930's, the world we came to know and cherish."

**Charleston: A Golden Memory,**
**Charles R. Anderson**

# BEAU MONDE DIP

Men love this hearty hors d'oeuvre. Because it has its own container, it "travels" well.

— *Randolph Waring Berretta (Mrs. Robert E. Berretta)*

---

*Yield: 2⅔ cups*

---

1⅓ cups sour cream
1⅓ cups mayonnaise
2 teaspoons dill seed
2 teaspoons Beau Monde Seasoning
2 teaspoons minced onion
2 teaspoons chopped fresh parsley or
    parsley flakes
1 round loaf rye bread

**1.** Combine the sour cream, mayonnaise, dill seed, Beau Monde, onion, and parsley in a medium-size bowl and mix well.
**2.** Cut a slice off the top of the loaf of bread. Remove the inside of the loaf to form a cavity large enough to hold the dip and cut the removed bread into bite-size pieces. Pour the dip into the cavity and surround the loaf with the pieces of bread.

# GINGER DIP

This dip is good served with any kind of fresh vegetable or fruit.
— *Margaret Lee McIntyre McCormack (Mrs. David B. McCormack)*

---

*Yield: 2 cups*

---

1 cup mayonnaise
1 cup sour cream
¼ cup finely chopped onion
¼ cup minced parsley
¼ cup chopped water chestnuts
1 to 2 tablespoons minced candied
    ginger
2 cloves garlic, minced
1 tablespoon soy sauce

Combine the mayonnaise and sour cream in a medium-size bowl. Add the remaining ingredients and mix well. Cover and refrigerate until chilled.

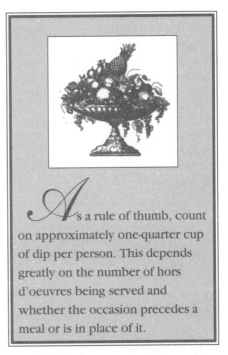

*A*s a rule of thumb, count on approximately one-quarter cup of dip per person. This depends greatly on the number of hors d'oeuvres being served and whether the occasion precedes a meal or is in place of it.

---

# HORSERADISH DIP

From roast beef to raw veggies—this dip can be used for everything.
— *Penny Barnes Parker (Mrs. James Howard Parker)*

---

*Yield: 1 cup*

---

1 egg
1 tablespoon fresh lemon juice
½ teaspoon salt
¾ cup vegetable oil
3 tablespoons bottled horseradish
1 tablespoon prepared mustard
½ teaspoon white pepper
½ teaspoon dried dill weed

**1.** Combine the egg, lemon juice, and salt in the bowl of a food processor or in a blender and process until smooth.
**2.** With the machine running, pour in the oil in a very thin stream and process until the mixture is thick and smooth.
**3.** Transfer the mixture to a medium-size bowl and stir in the horseradish, mustard, white pepper, and dill weed. Refrigerate for several hours.

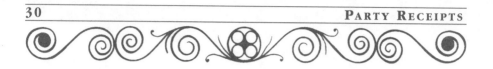

# CAVIAR AND ARTICHOKE SPREAD

Prepare this hors d'oeuvre at least a day before serving, to allow the flavors to blend. Water crackers, or other plain crackers, are the best accompaniment.

— *Caroline Green Baarcke* (Mrs. Charles F. Baarcke, Jr.)

---

*Yield: 16 to 20 servings*

---

*8 hard-cooked eggs, chopped*
*4 tablespoons mayonnaise*
*2 cans (14 ounces each) artichoke hearts, drained and chopped*
*8 scallions (green onions), chopped*
*8 ounces cream cheese, at room temperature*
*⅔ cup sour cream*
*6 ounces caviar, drained*

**1.** Combine the eggs and the mayonnaise in a medium-size bowl and blend well. Spread in the bottom of a 9-inch quiche dish. Top with a layer of the artichoke hearts and then a layer of scallions.

**2.** Combine the cream cheese and sour cream in a medium-size bowl and spread this mixture over the green onions. Top with the caviar. Cover with plastic wrap and refrigerate until ready to serve.

---

# CAPONATA

A favorite hors d'oeuvre at our Sullivan's Island beach house—especially with the adults.

— *Elizabeth St. John Weinstein* (Mrs. Victor Weinstein)

---

*Yield: About 2½ cups*

---

*Olive oil*
*1 medium eggplant, diced (about 2½ cups)*
*1 medium onion, chopped*
*½ to ¾ cup chopped celery*
*1 can (4¼ ounces) chopped black olives, drained*
*1 can (15 ounces) tomato sauce*
*Salt and freshly ground pepper, to taste*
*2 tablespoons red wine vinegar*
*3 tablespoons drained capers*
*1 tablespoon sugar*

**1.** Heat ¼ cup olive oil in a sauté pan. Add some of the eggplant (you will need to sauté it in batches, adding more oil as needed) and sauté until browned. Remove the eggplant and set aside.

**2.** Adding more oil if necessary, sauté the onion and celery in the same pan. Add the olives, tomato sauce, salt and pepper, and the sautéed eggplant.

**3.** Simmer, covered, for 30 minutes. Add the vinegar, capers, and sugar and simmer for an additional 15 minutes.

**4.** Cool to room temperature and serve in pastry cups or with crisp crackers.

## MAMOO'S CUCUMBER SPREAD

This easy preparation may be used as a spread with crackers or as a dip for raw vegetables.

— *Tyler Small*

---
*Yield: 8 to 10 servings*

---

8 ounces cream cheese, at room
    temperature
1 medium cucumber, peeled, seeded,
    and grated
½ teaspoon garlic powder
Paprika

Combine the cream cheese, cucumber, and garlic powder. Place in a small bowl, sprinkle with paprika, and serve with crackers or vegetables.

## CUCUMBER DIP

You need to start this dip the day before serving it—the "processing" of the cucumbers is worth the advance planning.

— *Jeremy Kramer Paul* (Mrs. Hugh Hadaway Paul)

---
*Yield: 10 to 12 servings*

---

2 large unpeeled cucumbers
½ cup vinegar
2 teaspoons salt
½ teaspoon garlic salt
16 ounces cream cheese, at room
    temperature
¾ cup mayonnaise

**1.** Grate the unpeeled cucumbers into a small bowl and add the vinegar, salt, and garlic salt. Stir the mixture, cover the bowl, and refrigerate the cucumbers overnight.
**2.** The next day, drain off the liquid, transfer the cucumbers to a sieve, and press out the excess liquid.
**3.** Mix together the cream cheese and mayonnaise in a medium-size bowl until well blended, add the cucumbers, and stir to combine.
**4.** Serve the dip with crackers or raw vegetables.

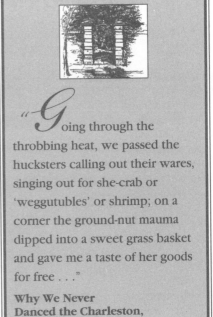

"*G*oing through the throbbing heat, we passed the hucksters calling out their wares, singing out for she-crab or 'weggutubles' or shrimp; on a corner the ground-nut mauma dipped into a sweet grass basket and gave me a taste of her goods for free . . ."

**Why We Never
Danced the Charleston,
*Harlan Greene*

# PARSLEY-HERB DIP

This recipe comes from my sister, Jane Greely Cowan.

— *Marian Greely Knott* (Mrs. David Knott)

### Yield: 1½ cups

1 small clove garlic
½ teaspoon salt
1 cup packed parsley leaves
1 scallion (green onion), including
    green part, cut in 1-inch pieces
1 cup mayonnaise
½ cup sour cream or plain yogurt
1 teaspoon chopped fresh thyme
    leaves or ½ teaspoon dried thyme
    leaves
¼ teaspoon freshly ground pepper

**1.** Place the garlic and salt in the bowl of a food processor and process until the garlic is minced. Add the parsley and scallion and process until the parsley is finely chopped.
**2.** Add the mayonnaise, sour cream, thyme, and pepper and process until the mixture is smooth. Refrigerate until ready to serve. Serve with raw vegetables.

# PLANTATION EGGPLANT DIP

Serve this dip with pita triangles that have been slowly toasted until crisp.

— *Franny Rivers Slay* (Mrs. Brian R. Slay)

### Yield: 45 servings

1 large eggplant, cut in half
    lengthwise
¼ cup olive oil
1 large red onion, chopped
2 cloves garlic, pressed
2 medium tomatoes, peeled, seeded,
    and finely chopped
2 tablespoons fresh lemon juice
⅛ teaspoon cayenne pepper
6 small rounds pita bread, separated
    and cut in triangles

**1.** Preheat the oven to 400°F. Oil a baking sheet.
**2.** Place the eggplant halves cut side down on the prepared baking sheet.

Bake until soft when pricked with a fork, about 45 minutes. Cool slightly, then peel off the skin and discard it.
**3.** Chop the eggplant into small pieces and place in a medium-size bowl.
**4.** Heat the olive oil in a large heavy frying pan over medium heat. Add the onion and garlic and cook until soft but not brown, about 5 minutes.
**5.** Mix in the eggplant, tomatoes, lemon juice, and cayenne and cook over low heat until the mixture has thickened, about 10 minutes. Let cool. Cover and refrigerate until well chilled. Serve with toasted pita triangles.

# OLIVE SPREAD

Serve this dip with crackers or use it as a spread for finger sandwiches. The recipe is easily doubled.

— **Kinloch Howell Smith**
(Mrs. Frank Smith)

---

*Yield: 3 cups*

---

4 hard-cooked eggs, cut in half
1 cup green olives stuffed with
    pimiento
1 cup pecans
1 very small onion, chopped
1 teaspoon seasoned salt
¾ cup mayonnaise

**1.** Place the eggs, olives, pecans, onion, and seasoned salt in the bowl of a food processor or in a blender and process until finely chopped, but not smooth.
**2.** Transfer the mixture to a large bowl, and gradually add the mayonnaise until the desired consistency is reached. Refrigerate until ready to use.

# BILL'S HUMMUS

A very garlicky hummus created by my dear friend Judy Werrell's husband, who is a wonderful cook! If your spouse has some, you'd better too, in self-defense.

— **Laura Morgan Waggoner** (Mrs. Geoffrey Howe Waggoner)

---

*Yield: About 2½ cups*

---

2 cups cooked garbanzo beans
⅔ cup tahini (sesame paste)
¾ cup fresh lemon juice
5 cloves garlic, or to taste
1 teaspoon salt
2 tablespoons olive oil (optional)
1 pound pita bread, cut in wedges

**1.** Combine the garbanzo beans, tahini, lemon juice, garlic, and salt in the bowl of a food processor and process until smooth (the mixture will look grainy).
**2.** Transfer the mixture to a serving dish, make a pool of olive oil in the center of the dip (if you wish), and serve with the pita wedges.

# PERFECT SPINACH SPREAD

A spicy dish that's a favorite among the men.

— *Ginger Wells Lee* (Mrs. Gary W. Lee)

### Yield: About 2 cups

1 pound spinach, washed and tough
   stems removed
1¼ cups sour cream
1 clove garlic, crushed
½ teaspoon salt
1 teaspoon fresh lemon juice
¼ teaspoon white pepper
4 drops Texas Pete sauce
1 teaspoon bottled horseradish

**1.** Wash the spinach and cook with
the water clinging to the leaves in a
sauté pan over medium heat for about
7 minutes. Drain well and chop.

**2.** Place the spinach, sour cream, garlic, salt, lemon juice, white pepper,
Texas Pete, and horseradish in the
bowl of a food processor and pulse 4
or 5 times, until the mixture contains
flecks of green and white.

**3.** Transfer the mixture to a medium-
size bowl and chill, covered, for 4 to 5
hours. Serve with small chunks of
bread or potato chips.

# SHRIMP SPREAD

This is my attempt to copy an old family recipe called "shrimp and olives" from
the family of my best childhood friend, Olive Veach Broody. As each daughter of
the family married, she was given the secret recipe. Though the family generously
made the spread for me on many occasions, they would never divulge the recipe.
By now I like my own version even better!

— *Caroline Cummings Rhodes* (Mrs. Malcolm M. Rhodes)

### Yield: About 4 cups

16 ounces cream cheese, at room
   temperature
Juice of 1 lemon
½ teaspoon Worcestershire sauce
⅛ teaspoon garlic powder
¼ cup mayonnaise
1 jar (10 ounces) green salad olives
   with pimientos, drained and diced
1 pound small shrimp, cooked,
   peeled, deveined, and diced
Parsley sprigs or lemon curls, for
   garnish

**1.** Place the cream cheese, lemon
juice, Worcestershire, and garlic powder in a large bowl and cream together
until smooth, using an electric mixer.
Add the mayonnaise and mix well.

**2.** Pat dry the olives and shrimp and
fold into the cheese mixture. Transfer
the mixture to a plate and form into
the shape of a ring mold. Cover with
plastic wrap and refrigerate overnight.
Garnish the plate with parsley or
lemon curls and serve the mold with
crackers.

# QUICK VEGGIES WITH CURRY DIP

When you're too busy to spend time cleaning and cutting raw vegetables, turn to tinned delicacies—hearts of palm and artichoke hearts. The dip may be made the day before you plan to serve it.

*— Kathleen Bullard Adams*

---
*Yield: 8 servings*
---

1 cup mayonnaise
1 cup sour cream
1 tablespoon chopped fresh parsley
1 teaspoon dried dill weed
1 teaspoon Beau Monde Seasoning
1 teaspoon curry powder
1 tablespoon minced scallion (green onion)
1 can (14 ounces) hearts of palm, drained and sliced into 1-inch pieces
1 can (14 ounces) artichoke hearts, drained and cut in quarters

**1.** Make the dip: Combine the mayonnaise, sour cream, parsley, dill weed, Beau Monde, curry powder, and scallion in a medium-size bowl and mix well. Chill.

**2.** Transfer the dip to a serving dish, place it on a platter, and surround it with the hearts of palm and artichoke hearts.

# SALLIE'S CURRY VEGETABLE DIP

This recipe was given to me by Sallie Smith Shisko. I like to serve it in a hollowed-out red cabbage set on a platter, surrounded by mounds of raw vegetables. It's wonderful not only for cocktail parties but for picnics.

*—Jane Craver Izard*

---
*Yield: About 2 cups*
---

1 carrot, peeled and finely grated
1 small onion, peeled and finely grated
2 tablespoons vinegar
1 cup mayonnaise
1 cup cottage cheese
1 teaspoon salt
1 teaspoon curry powder

Place all the ingredients in the bowl of a food processor or in a blender and process until smooth. Refrigerate until ready to serve.

*G*inger snaps as a base for cocktail spreads make a nice change from crackers, particularly when served with fruit or chutney flavors.

## SHRIMP AND CHUTNEY DIP

My mother-in-law, Julia Ravenel Dougherty, gave me this recipe. The dip is best made the day before you plan to serve it.

— *Martha Tate Dougherty*
*(Mrs. Park R. Dougherty)*

---

*Yield: About 3 cups*

---

1 cup chopped cooked, peeled, and
    deveined shrimp
16 ounces cream cheese, at room
    temperature
½ cup sour cream
1 teaspoon curry powder, or to taste
¼ teaspoon garlic powder
¼ cup Major Grey's chutney, chopped
2 tablespoons milk, as needed

Combine all the ingredients except the milk in a medium-size bowl and mix well. Add milk to thin the mixture, if necessary. Refrigerate overnight.

## SHRIMP BUTTER

I like to serve this with wheat or sesame crackers. I put the Shrimp Butter in a bowl and let the guests spread their own.

— *Jane Grote Hipp*
*(Mrs. Van Hipp, Jr.)*

---

*Yield: About 2 cups*

---

8 ounces cream cheese
¾ cup (1½ sticks) butter, at room
    temperature
2 cans (7 ounces each) shrimp,
    drained
Juice of 1 lemon
1 tablespoon chopped onion
4 tablespoons mayonnaise

Place all of the ingredients in a blender or the bowl of a food processor and blend until smooth. Serve with crackers.

## JODY'S SHRIMP SPREAD

So easy, and always a hit!

—*Jody Blackwell Anderson* (Mrs. Ivan Verner Anderson, Jr.)

---

*Yield: 1 cup*

---

3 ounces cream cheese, at room
    temperature
2 tablespoons mayonnaise
1 teaspoon prepared horseradish
1 tablespoon catsup
1 can (7 ounces) tiny broken shrimp,
    drained
½ cup finely diced celery

**1.** Combine the cream cheese, mayonnaise, horseradish, and catsup in a medium-size bowl and blend with a fork.

**2.** Add the shrimp, mash, and continue to blend with a fork. Add the celery and mix well. Refrigerate until ready to serve (can be made a day ahead). Serve with crackers.

### SOUSED FISH

This is from an old book of Maria Bachman, the wife of my great-grandfather, the Rev. John Bachman. It was she who painted many of the backgrounds for Audubon's famous paintings.

Sprinkle any fish with salt and pepper as if you were going to fry it. Then boil the fish in vinegar instead of water. Season with cloves, mace, pepper and Worcestershire sauce. Put fish and sauce into mould. The bones will all become soft, and the whole will turn out in a form like jelly.

*Mrs. Lionel K. Legge (Dorothy Porcher),*
*from* **Charleston Receipts**

# CHUNKY SEAFOOD DIP

Versatility is the key to this dip, depending on how many people you wish to serve and the kinds of shellfish on hand. A pint of cooked scallops may be used in addition to or instead of the crabmeat. The dominant flavors of the sauce should be cucumber and sour cream, so add mayonnaise sparingly.

*— Amy Gibson Morrison*

---
*Yield: About 30 servings*
---

1 pound cooked, peeled, and
   deveined shrimp, chopped
1 pint lump crabmeat
1 jar (6 ounces) marinated artichoke
   hearts, drained and chopped
1 large cucumber, peeled, seeded,
   and chopped
1 to 2 cups sour cream (for desired
   consistency)
Up to 1 tablespoon mayonnaise

Combine all the ingredients in a large bowl and refrigerate until serving time. Serve in pastry shells or with crackers.

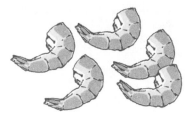

# GARLIC SHRIMP BALL

This works equally well as a cocktail spread or a sandwich filling.

*— Sarah Gregorie Miller (Mrs. Charles E. Miller)*

---

*Yield: 15 to 20 servings*

---

*1 ½ pounds shrimp, cooked, peeled, and deveined*
*2 hard-cooked eggs, mashed (optional)*
*4 tablespoons mayonnaise*
*¼ teaspoon garlic powder*
*Salt and freshly ground pepper, to taste*
*Parsley sprigs, for garnish*

**1.** Place the shrimp in the bowl of a food processor and process until finely ground. Transfer to a large bowl and add the eggs, mayonnaise, garlic powder, and salt and pepper.
**2.** Shape the mixture into a ball, place it on a serving plate, and garnish with parsley sprigs. Serve with crackers.

---

# COLD ISLAND CRAB

My mother, Mary Ellen Long Way, was asked by a friend to create a cold crab dip for her son's wedding rehearsal. It has been a favorite for over ten years and is great for large parties.

*— Ellen Way Dudash (Mrs. Stephen Dudash)*

---

*Yield: 50 servings*

---

*1 pound claw crabmeat, picked over and shells discarded*
*1 pound white crabmeat, picked over and shells discarded*
*1 tablespoon fresh lemon juice*
*2 scallions (green onions), finely chopped*
*1 large bunch parsley, finely chopped*
*2 stalks celery, finely chopped*
*1 medium green bell pepper, finely chopped*
*12 ounces cream cheese, at room temperature*
*1 teaspoon ground mace*
*1 teaspoon ground thyme*
*1 teaspoon coarsely ground pepper*

*½ teaspoon garlic salt*
*¼ teaspoon salt*
*1 tablespoon drained capers*

**1.** Place the crabmeat in a medium-size bowl, sprinkle with the lemon juice, and set aside.
**2.** Place the scallion, parsley, celery, green pepper, and cream cheese in a large bowl and combine well. Add the mace, thyme, pepper, garlic salt, and salt and stir to combine.
**3.** Lightly fold the crabmeat and lemon juice into the cheese mixture and add the capers (the mixture should be very light—not packed). Transfer to a serving dish and accompany with crackers.

# CRAB LOUIS DIP

Easy, easy, easy! That's why I love this recipe—given to me by my mother, Patricia Colligan Hancock.

*— Kathleen Hancock*

---
*Yield: 2 cups*
---

½ cup chili sauce
½ cup mayonnaise
1 clove garlic, minced
½ teaspoon dry mustard
1 tablespoon prepared horseradish
1 tablespoon Worcestershire sauce
¼ teaspoon Tabasco sauce
½ teaspoon salt
2 hard-boiled eggs, finely chopped
8 ounces flaked crabmeat, picked over and shells discarded

**1.** Combine the chili sauce, mayonnaise, garlic, dry mustard, horseradish, Worcestershire, Tabasco, and salt in a medium-size bowl and mix well.
**2.** Add the egg and crabmeat and stir gently to combine. Refrigerate for 2 or 3 hours before serving.

# CRAB SPREAD

Here is my version of a recipe I was served at The Greenbrier Cooking School.

*— Louisa Pritchard Hawkins*
*(Mrs. J. David Hawkins)*

---
*Yield: 2 cups*
---

1 pound crabmeat, picked over and shells discarded
¼ cup sour cream
¼ cup mayonnaise
2 tablespoons fresh lemon juice
2 to 3 tablespoons drained capers
1 tablespoon celery seed
Freshly ground pepper, to taste

Combine the ingredients in a medium-size bowl and stir to blend well. Serve immediately on crackers.

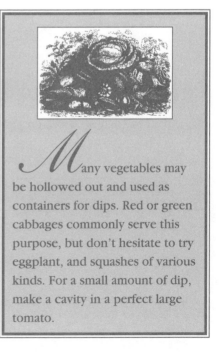

Many vegetables may be hollowed out and used as containers for dips. Red or green cabbages commonly serve this purpose, but don't hesitate to try eggplant, and squashes of various kinds. For a small amount of dip, make a cavity in a perfect large tomato.

## FRESH SALMON SPREAD

Fresh salmon makes a big difference in this easy and delicious spread.

— *Charlotte Small Bavier (Mrs. Robert N. Bavier, Jr.)*

---
*Yield: About 2 cups*
---

1 pound fresh salmon fillets or steaks
8 ounces cream cheese, softened
2 scallions (green onions), finely
    chopped
1 tablespoon prepared horseradish
½ teaspoon salt
Dash of cayenne pepper
2 tablespoons fresh lemon juice
1 teaspoon Worcestershire sauce
Minced parsley, for garnish

**1.** Poach the salmon in a frying pan in simmering water until it flakes easily, 8 to 10 minutes. Remove from the water and pat dry.
**2.** Combine the cream cheese, scallions, horseradish, salt, cayenne pepper, lemon juice, and Worcestershire in a medium-size bowl and mix well.
**3.** Flake the salmon into the cream cheese mixture and combine well. Refrigerate for several hours or overnight.
**4.** Transfer the spread to a serving dish and sprinkle with the parsley. Serve with crackers.

## SMOKED SALMON BALL

The salmon ball may be served on a variety of "toasts"—Melba, rounds of French bread, or mini bagels.

— *Sarah Holt Trible (Mrs. Waring Trible, Jr.)*

---
*Yield: 10 to 12 servings*
---

1 package (3 ounces) Nova Lox or
    smoked salmon, chopped
8 ounces cream cheese, at room
    temperature
1 medium red onion, chopped
2 tablespoons snipped fresh dill
    (or 1 tablespoon dried dill weed)
1 red onion, cut into thin rings
3 tablespoons capers
Dill sprigs, for garnish

**1.** Combine the salmon, cream cheese, chopped onion, and snipped dill in a medium-size bowl and mix well. Shape into a ball, wrap in plastic wrap, and refrigerate for at least 2 hours.
**2.** When ready to serve, cover a serving tray with the onion rings and sprinkle over the capers. Place the salmon ball on the bed of onion and capers, garnish with dill sprigs, and serve with toasts.

# LOW-CALORIE SALMON SPREAD

This tasty, healthful mixture can be made into a dip or a spread with a slight difference in procedure. Serve it with your favorite crackers.

*— Ann Smith FitzGerald (Mrs. Claude B. FitzGerald)*

---
*Yield: About 1½ cups*
---

*¼ cup low-fat cottage cheese*
*2 tablespoons olive oil*
*1 can (7½ ounces) red salmon, drained, picked over, and bones removed*
*¼ cup plain yogurt*
*4 tablespoons finely chopped green bell pepper*
*2 tablespoons finely chopped onion*
*1 tablespoon dried dill weed*
*2 teaspoons White Wine Worcestershire sauce*
*¼ teaspoon Tabasco sauce*

**1.** To make a dip: Combine all the ingredients in the bowl of a food processor and process to the desired consistency for dipping.

**2.** To make a spread: Place the cottage cheese in the bowl of a food processor and process until creamy. Transfer to a medium-size bowl and mash in the olive oil, salmon, and yogurt. Fold in the green pepper and onion. Add the dill weed, Worcestershire, and Tabasco and stir.

**3.** Refrigerate until ready to serve.

# SMOKED OYSTER ROLL

This spread is simple, quick, and scrumptious!

*— Elizabeth L. Boineau*

---
*Yield: 8 to 10 servings*
---

*16 ounces cream cheese, at room temperature*
*2 tablespoons mayonnaise*
*2 teaspoons Worcestershire sauce*
*Dash of Tabasco*
*1 tablespoon grated onion*
*¼ teaspoon garlic salt*
*Salt and freshly ground pepper, to taste*
*2 cans (3¾ ounces each) smoked oysters*
*Minced fresh parsley*

**1.** Place the cream cheese, mayonnaise, Worcestershire sauce, Tabasco, onion, and garlic salt in the bowl of a food processor and process until smooth. Add salt and pepper to taste.

**2.** Drain the oysters, rinse away the excess oil, and pat dry. Place in a shallow bowl and mash with a fork.

**3.** Spread the cheese mixture into a rectangle on a piece of plastic wrap. Spread the oysters on top of the cheese, leaving ½ inch cheese uncovered on all sides. Roll up, jelly-roll fashion, and sprinkle the top of the roll with the minced parsley. Refrigerate for 3 or 4 hours before serving.

# CHICKEN PECAN LOG

One advantage of a log is that it retains its shape as it is being consumed—and this one goes fast.

— *Ann Orlowska Kaminski* (Mrs. Alexander Kaminski)

---

*Yield: 8 to 10 servings*

---

1 whole boneless, skinless chicken breast, poached and minced
16 ounces cream cheese, at room temperature
1 tablespoon A.1. sauce
½ teaspoon curry powder
⅓ cup diced celery
2 tablespoons chopped parsley
½ cup chopped pecans

**1.** In a medium-size bowl combine the chicken, cream cheese, A.1. sauce, curry powder, celery, and parsley. Mix well.

**2.** Shape the mixture into a log, wrap in waxed paper, and chill.

**3.** Before serving, place the chopped pecans on a plate and roll the log in the nuts until it is well coated. Serve with crackers or small breads.

# PUMPERNICKEL AND CORNED BEEF SPREAD

The pumpernickel round acts as a serving dish for the spread; I usually buy an extra loaf to make additional bread cubes for dipping.

— *Betsy Mapp Clawson* (Mrs. Samuel R. Clawson)

---

*Yield: 20 servings*

---

1 round loaf pumpernickel
2 cups mayonnaise
1 tablespoon chopped chives
3 tablespoons chopped parsley
1 tablespoon dried Italian seasoning
1 tablespoon dried dill weed
1 can (12 ounces) corned beef, chopped
½ cup sour cream

**1.** Hollow out the center of the pumpernickel loaf, reserving the soft bread. Cut the bread into cubes to dip into the spread.

**2.** Place the mayonnaise, chives, parsley, Italian seasoning, dill weed, corned beef, and sour cream in the bowl of a food processor and process until smooth. Refrigerate until ready to serve.

**3.** To serve, spoon the corned beef spread into the hollowed-out pumpernickel loaf and surround with bread cubes.

# NANCY'S CHIPPED BEEF CHEESE BALL

The green pepper and Cheddar cheese make this a more interesting version of an old standby.

— *Mary Thomas West* (Mrs. Timothy Harley West)

*Yield: 8 to 10 servings*

1 jar shredded dried chipped beef, finely chopped
8 ounces cream cheese, at room temperature
1 medium onion, diced
1 medium green bell pepper, diced
1 cup grated sharp Cheddar cheese
Chopped walnuts or pecans

**1.** In a medium-size bowl combine the chipped beef, cream cheese, onion, bell pepper, and Cheddar cheese and mix well.
**2.** Form the mixture into a ball and roll in the chopped nuts to cover.

# LEFTOVER SMITHFIELD HAM SPREAD

If you don't have Smithfield ham leftovers, any country ham will work for this recipe.

— *Hamer Dillard Salmons* (Mrs. Richard Salmons, Jr.)

*Yield: 1½ cups*

2 cups minced Smithfield ham
1 tablespoon Dijon mustard
2 tablespoons mayonnaise
2 tablespoons sour cream
2 tablespoons artichoke relish
  (available at regional specialty foods stores)

Combine the ham, mustard, mayonnaise, sour cream, and artichoke relish in a medium-size bowl and mix well. Serve chilled or at room temperature, with crackers.

Artichoke relish is one of many popular Lowcountry relishes and condiments. It is made from the Jerusalem artichoke, a tuberous plant native to the coastal region that has a texture similar to water chestnuts.

## COUNTRY HAM SPREAD

Here is a wonderful way to use leftover Christmas ham—especially for a New Year's Eve get-together.
— *Margaret M. Bristow*

*Yield: About 2 cups*

*1½ cups ground country ham*
*3 ounces cream cheese, at room temperature*
*¼ cup chopped pecans*
*1 teaspoon Dijon mustard*

Place the ham, cream cheese, pecans, and mustard in the bowl of a food processor and process until smooth. Serve with stoned wheat crackers.

Country hams are available from various parts of the South, perhaps the best known coming from Smithfield, Virginia. All country hams are salt-cured and smoked with apple, oak, and hickory woods; but since the Smithfield ham is left in the salt-cure for a year instead of the standard six months, it is saltier and drier than its cousins.

# HOT DIPS
### AND
# SPREADS

# TUSCANY CHEESE SPREAD

Even though this spread should be served on crackers, many a guest has been overheard to say "I wish I had a spoon."

— *Hibernia Cuthbert Langley*
*(Mrs. William John Langley)*

---

*Yield: 16 servings*

---

*3½ cups grated sharp Cheddar cheese*
*1 cup mayonnaise*
*¼ teaspoon cayenne pepper*
*1 tablespoon grated onion*
*1 can (8 ounces) sliced water*
*   chestnuts, drained and coarsely*
*   chopped*
*¼ cup chopped, drained sun-dried*
*   tomatoes (in oil)*
*1 tablespoon Worcestershire sauce*

**1.** Preheat the oven to 350°F.
**2.** Combine all the ingredients in a large bowl and mix well. Transfer the mixture to a 1-quart baking dish and bake until bubbly, 20 to 30 minutes. Serve with crackers.

The Charleston Cup, a November social and sporting event inaugurated in 1985, actually reestablishes the charter for the country's first jockey club, formed by Colonels William Alston, William Washington, and Wade Hampton. The cup race and accompanying tailgate parties are part of an entire week of festivities, including the Charleston Cup Steeplechase Ball.

---

# AUNTIE'S HOT CHEESE DIP

This was a favorite recipe of my late aunt, Mrs. Richard E. Lankford, from Annapolis, Maryland. It's easy to make and a hit with any crowd.
— *Robin Allen Rodenberg (Mrs. E. Adolph Rodenberg III)*

---

*Yield: Serves 10 to 12*

---

*2 cups sharp Cheddar cheese, grated*
*1 cup mayonnaise*
*6 scallions (green onions), chopped*
*Cayenne pepper or chili powder, to*
*   taste*

**1.** Preheat the oven to 350°F.
**2.** Combine all the ingredients in a medium-size bowl and transfer to an ungreased 1-quart baking dish.
**3.** Bake until bubbly, about 30 minutes. Serve with tortilla chips.

# ARTICHOKE-SPINACH DIP

I suggest baking this dip in a 1½-quart round Pyrex casserole that will fit into the liner of a chafing dish. It is best served with a sturdy cracker, such as Triscuits or Melba rounds.

— *Etta Ray Longshore Simons* (Mrs. Carlton Simons)

### Yield: 25 servings

2 cans (14 ounces each) artichoke
   hearts, drained
½ package (10 ounces) frozen
   chopped spinach
1½ cups mayonnaise
1 cup freshly grated Parmesan cheese
¼ teaspoon granulated or powdered
   garlic, or 1 finely chopped onion
½ teaspoon salt
⅛ teaspoon pepper
1 teaspoon fresh lemon juice

**1.** Preheat the oven to 350°F. Butter a 1½-quart casserole.
**2.** Place the artichoke hearts in the bowl of a food processor and process only until chopped.
**3.** Cook the spinach according to package instructions, drain well, and squeeze to remove excess moisture.
**4.** Combine the artichoke, spinach, mayonnaise, Parmesan cheese, garlic, salt, pepper, and lemon juice in a large bowl and mix well. Transfer to the prepared casserole and bake until bubbly, about 35 minutes. Serve hot, preferably in a chafing dish with a warmer.
**Note:** The dip may be refrigerated for up to two days or may be frozen and thawed, before baking.

# THREE-CHEESE DIP

Every time I serve this dip I end up handing out the recipe.

— *Therese Trouche Smythe* (Mrs. George B. Smythe)

### Yield: 30 servings

8 ounces sharp Cheddar cheese,
   grated
3 cans (4 ounces each) chopped
   green chilies, drained (or half
   chilies and half jalapeños)
3 cups sour cream
8 ounces mild Cheddar cheese,
   grated
8 ounces Monterey Jack cheese,
   grated

**1.** Preheat the oven to 375°F. Butter an 8 x 8-inch baking dish.
**2.** Make a layer of one-third of the sharp Cheddar cheese in the bottom of the baking dish and top with layers of one-third of each of the remaining ingredients, in the order listed. Repeat the layering twice, to make three layers of each ingredient.
**3.** Bake until the cheese is melted and the center is set, about 30 minutes. Serve with crackers.

# BANDIT'S HOT SEAFOOD ARTICHOKE DIP

Bandit is a venerable blond cocker spaniel owned by Helene Blackwell of Florence, South Carolina. A true connoisseur of all food, Bandit particularly loves the aroma of this dip. As a result, it was served to a group of "Florentine" ladies who came to celebrate Bandit's fourth birthday, in 1982. It remains a hit at parties, testimony to Miss Bandit's discriminating sense of smell. (It's possible that she has given it a taste test, too!)

— *Hayden Blackwell Quattlebaum (Mrs. Donald A. Quattlebaum)*

*Yield: About 4 cups*

2 cans (14 ounces each) artichoke
  hearts, drained and chopped
2 cups mayonnaise
2 cups freshly grated Parmesan
  cheese
1½ cups chopped shrimp, or half
  shrimp and half crabmeat
½ cup dry seasoned bread crumbs

**1.** Preheat the oven to 325°F. Butter a 1½-quart casserole.
**2.** Combine the artichoke hearts, mayonnaise, Parmesan cheese, and shrimp in a large bowl and mix well. Transfer to the prepared casserole and top with the bread crumbs.
**3.** Bake until bubbly, about 30 minutes. Serve with assorted crackers.


# SPINACH DIP

This recipe was given to me by my mother-in-law, Mrs. Winfield M. Baldwin.

— *Lynell Gaudier Baldwin (Mrs. Robert M. Baldwin)*

*Yield: About 3½ cups*

2 packages (10 ounces each) frozen
  chopped spinach
¼ cup margarine
2 tablespoons unbleached all-purpose
  flour
½ cup evaporated milk
½ cup spinach liquid
6 ounces jalapeño pepper cheese,
  grated
½ teaspoon freshly ground pepper
½ teaspoon celery salt
½ teaspoon garlic salt
½ teaspoon Worcestershire sauce

**1.** Preheat the oven to 350°F. Butter a

1-quart round baking dish.
**2.** Cook the spinach according to package instructions and drain well, reserving ½ cup liquid.
**3.** Melt the margarine in a heavy saucepan over low heat. Add the flour and cook for 3 minutes, stirring constantly; do not brown. Add the evaporated milk and spinach liquid and continue to cook, stirring, until the mixture thickens.
**4.** Add the cheese, pepper, celery salt, garlic salt, and Worcestershire and stir until the cheese melts. Fold in the spinach. Transfer the mixture to the prepared casserole and bake until it starts to bubble, about 15 minutes. Serve with tortilla chips.

# VIDALIA ONION DIP

Since Vidalia onions are only available in spring and early summer, you may have to substitute another variety—just make sure they are sweet onions.
— *Martha Laird Sullivan*
*(Mrs. Martin Roberts Sullivan)*

---

*Yield: 8 to 10 servings*

1 cup chopped Vidalia onions
1 cup mayonnaise
1 cup grated sharp Cheddar cheese

**1.** Preheat the oven to 350°F. Butter a 1½-quart baking dish.
**2.** Combine all the ingredients in a medium-size bowl and mix well. Transfer to the prepared baking dish and bake until bubbly, about 20 minutes.
**3.** Serve with toast triangles or crackers.

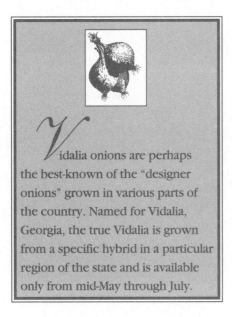

idalia onions are perhaps the best-known of the "designer onions" grown in various parts of the country. Named for Vidalia, Georgia, the true Vidalia is grown from a specific hybrid in a particular region of the state and is available only from mid-May through July.

# HOT BROCCOLI DIP

"Elegant and easy" describes this no-fuss dip. My Aunt Martha has it on her buffet table every Christmas.
— *Irene Doris Sulkowski*
*(Mrs. John Sulkowski)*

---

*Yield: About 4 cups*

1 medium onion, grated
½ pound fresh mushrooms, sliced
½ cup margarine
1 can (10¾ ounces) condensed cream of mushroom soup, undiluted
2 packages (10 ounces each) frozen chopped broccoli, cooked and drained
1 roll (6 ounces) garlic cheese, cut into chunks
3 to 4 drops Tabasco sauce
2 teaspoons fresh lemon juice
1 teaspoon Worcestershire sauce

**1.** Sauté the onion and mushrooms in the margarine in a heavy saucepan over low heat, until soft but not brown. Remove from the heat and stir in the soup.
**2.** Add the broccoli, cheese, Tabasco, lemon juice, and Worcestershire. Return to the heat and cook over low heat, stirring, until the cheese melts. Serve hot from a chafing dish, accompanied by large corn chips.

## BLUFFTON DEVILED CRAB DIP

Originally made in Bluffton, South Carolina, with blue crab from the May River, this recipe was given to me by Karen Clarno Davis.

— *V. Ashley Davis*

*Yield: 12 to 15 servings*

1 large onion, finely chopped
2 stalks celery, finely chopped
½ green bell pepper, finely chopped
Dab of bacon grease or butter
1 pint backfin blue crab, picked over
    and bones removed
½ cup catsup
2 tablespoons Shed Sauce
1 tablespoon prepared mustard
1 cup Ritz cracker crumbs
2 eggs
2 tablespoons Worcestershire sauce
Salt and freshly ground pepper, to
    taste
½ cup cornflakes cereal
2 tablespoons butter, at room
    temperature

**1.** Preheat the oven to 350°F. Butter a 2-quart baking dish.
**2.** Place the onion, celery, and bell pepper in a microwave-safe bowl with a dab of bacon grease or butter and sauté for 5 minutes on high power in a microwave oven.
**3.** Add the crabmeat, catsup, Shed Sauce, mustard, cracker crumbs, eggs, Worcestershire, and salt and pepper and mix well.
**4.** Transfer the mixture to the prepared baking dish and sprinkle with the cornflakes. Dab with the butter and bake until bubbly, 20 to 30 minutes. Serve with assorted crackers.

## HOT CRAB SPREAD

This quick and easy spread is especially good served on Melba rounds.

— *Denise Howell Darling*
*(Mrs. Stephen E. Darling)*

*Yield: 12 to 15 servings*

1 pound crabmeat, picked over and
    shells removed
6 hard-cooked eggs, chopped
1 cup mayonnaise
¾ cup milk
1 cup grated sharp Cheddar cheese

**1.** Preheat the oven to 350°F. Butter a 1-quart casserole.
**2.** In a medium-size bowl combine the crabmeat, chopped eggs, mayonnaise, and milk and mix well. Place the mixture in the prepared casserole, top with the grated cheese, and bake until bubbly, about 30 minutes.

"*The* first swim at Folly Beach in April, lightning over the Atlantic, shelling oysters at Bowen's Island during a rare Carolina snowstorm, pigeons strutting across the graveyard at St. Philip's, lawyers moving out of their offices to lunch on Broad Street. . ."

**The Lords of Discipline,**
*Pat Conroy*

# MY MOTHER'S CRAB DIP

Though there are many receipts for crab dip, this is the best I have ever had and is always a hit at my mother's parties. She catches and picks her own crabs, which has traditionally been a family activity for us.

*— Laura Wichmann Hipp (Mrs. G. Preston Hipp)*

*Yield: 25 servings*

6 tablespoons butter
2 large shallots, finely chopped
2 tablespoons cornstarch, dissolved in
    2 tablespoons water
1 cup half-and-half
Salt and white pepper, to taste
⅛ teaspoon nutmeg
1 pound crabmeat, picked over and
    shells discarded
¼ cup good quality sherry

**1.** Melt the butter in a heavy saucepan, add the shallots, and sauté over low heat until soft but not brown, about 3 minutes.

**2.** Add the cornstarch mixture and blend well. Slowly add the half-and-half and cook, stirring constantly, until the sauce is thick. Season with the salt and pepper and nutmeg. Fold in the crabmeat, heat through, and remove from the heat.

**3.** Just before serving, add the sherry. Serve in a chafing dish, with patty shells.

# LAZY MAN'S CRAB CASSEROLE

The "lazy man" who deserves credit for this recipe is my father, Colonel Eugene Dewey Foxworth, Jr.

*— Christine Louise Foxworth*

*Yield: 10 to 12 servings*

½ cup (1 stick) butter
2 tablespoons chopped onion
1 tablespoon chopped green bell
    pepper
1 pound crabmeat, picked over and
    shells discarded
1 cup mayonnaise
1 tablespoon Worcestershire sauce
12 Ritz crackers, crushed
Butter

**1.** Preheat the oven to 350°F. Butter a 7 x 11-inch baking dish.

**2.** Melt the butter in a small frying pan and add the onion and green bell pepper. Sauté until tender but not brown, about 5 minutes.

**3.** Combine the crabmeat, mayonnaise, and Worcestershire in a medium-size bowl. Add the butter, onions, and green bell pepper and mix well.

**4.** Place the crab mixture in the casserole, top with the crushed crackers, dab with butter, and bake until brown and bubbling, about 30 minutes. Serve with a choice of crackers.

# EDISTO CRAB DIP

This versatile dip can be served either hot or cold. I often serve it hot in a chafing dish surrounded by small patty shells.

— *Eleanor Vest Howard (Mrs. John Ball Howard)*

---

*Yield: 6 servings*

---

*8 ounces cream cheese, at room temperature*
*½ cup mayonnaise*
*1 tablespoon fresh lemon juice*
*½ teaspoon Worcestershire sauce*
*1 teaspoon unbleached all-purpose flour*
*Dash of cayenne pepper*
*½ pound fresh or frozen backfin crabmeat, picked over and shells discarded*
*⅓ cup slivered almonds, toasted*
*Salt, to taste*

**1.** Beat the cream cheese in a medium-size bowl until smooth. Add the mayonnaise, lemon juice, Worcestershire, flour, and cayenne pepper and mix until well blended.

**2.** Fold in the crabmeat and almonds. Add salt to taste.

**3.** Serve cold or heat in a heavy saucepan over low heat, stirring constantly, and transfer to a chafing dish. Serve with Melba toast, crackers, or, if hot, patty shells.

# ALMOST CRAB DIP

I don't remember where I got this recipe, but it has been in and out of my card file many times over the years.

— *Meggett Barnwell Lavin*

---

*Yield: 10 to 12 servings*

---

*2 cans (6⅛ ounces each) white tuna, drained*
*8 ounces cream cheese, cut in chunks*
*Juice of ½ lemon*
*1 small onion, finely chopped*
*1 to 2 shakes Worcestershire sauce*
*1 teaspoon curry powder, or more*
*Salt and freshly ground pepper, to taste*

**1.** Mash the tuna in a small bowl.

**2.** Place the tuna and cream cheese in a medium-size saucepan and cook over low heat, stirring, until the cheese has melted and the mixture is almost smooth.

**3.** Add the lemon juice, onion, Worcestershire, curry powder, and salt and pepper. Cook over low heat, stirring frequently, until the onion softens, about 10 minutes. Transfer to a chafing dish and serve with water crackers or pâte à choux puffs.

# Easy Hot Crab Dip

This is my favorite crowd-pleaser for cocktail parties.

*— Elisa Norton Cooper*
*(Mrs. Richard T. Cooper)*

---

*Yield: 15 to 20 servings*

---

2 rolls (6 ounces each) garlic cheese
4 tablespoons butter
1 can (6½ ounces) crabmeat, drained
1 can (6 ounces) sliced mushrooms, drained

**1.** Melt the cheese and butter in the top of a double boiler over simmering water.
**2.** Stir in the crabmeat and mushrooms. Transfer to a chafing dish and serve with Melba rounds.

# Hot Crab Dip

My mother has passed this recipe along to me—it's a big hit at parties.
*— Toni Austelle Rhett*

---

*Yield: 6 to 8 servings*

---

8 ounces cream cheese
½ cup (1 stick) butter
1 pound white crabmeat, picked over and shells discarded
1 small onion, finely chopped
Tabasco sauce, to taste
Garlic salt, to taste
Cayenne pepper, to taste
3 tablespoons white wine or sherry
1 teaspoon Beau Monde Seasoning
1 cup grated sharp Cheddar cheese (use more to stretch the recipe)

Melt the cream cheese and butter in the top of a double boiler over simmering water. Add the remaining ingredients and stir to combine. Heat through and transfer to a chafing dish.

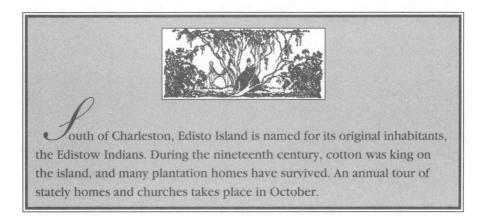

*S*outh of Charleston, Edisto Island is named for its original inhabitants, the Edistow Indians. During the nineteenth century, cotton was king on the island, and many plantation homes have survived. An annual tour of stately homes and churches takes place in October.

# HOT SHRIMP DIP

Shrimping season is the best time to make this "goodie."
— *Elizabeth Lamb Tollens* (Mrs. Peter J. Tollens)

*Yield: 6 to 8 servings*

*8 ounces cream cheese, cut in chunks*
*¼ cup mayonnaise*
*1 teaspoon grated onion*
*1 teaspoon mustard*
*1 teaspoon sugar*
*3 tablespoons sherry*
*½ pound cooked, peeled, and deveined shrimp or 1 can (7 ounces), drained*
*Salt, to taste*
*Garlic powder, to taste*
*½ cup slivered almonds*

**1.** Preheat the oven to 325°F. Butter a 1-quart soufflé dish.
**2.** Melt the cheese in the top of a double boiler over simmering water, stirring constantly. Transfer to a blender.
**3.** Add the mayonnaise, onion, mustard, sugar, sherry, shrimp, salt, and garlic powder and stir until just blended.
**4.** Transfer the mixture to the prepared soufflé dish, sprinkle with the almonds, and bake until brown and bubbly, 30 minutes.

# SHRIMP DIP WITH TOMATOES AND CHEESE

This recipe is a family treasure that has never before been written down.
—*Jean Simmons Rivers* (Mrs. Charlie Rivers)

*Yield: 12 to 15 servings*

*1½ pounds cream cheese, cut into chunks*
*1 cup cottage cheese*
*1 large tomato, peeled, seeded, and diced*
*1 onion, minced*
*1½ tablespoons chopped hot green chili peppers*
*2½ pounds cooked, peeled, and deveined shrimp, cut in bite-size pieces*
*1 can (7 ounces) shrimp, drained and mashed*

Place the ingredients in the top of a double boiler over simmering water in the order given above and blend thoroughly. Cook until the cream cheese is melted, and serve immediately with crackers.

*O*ld Bay Seasoning is a spice mixture made in Baltimore called for in many southern seafood and poultry recipes. It contains celery salt, mustard, pepper, bay leaves, cloves, pimiento, ginger, mace, cardamom, cassia, and paprika.

# TONY'S CRAB-CLAM DIP

"Tony" is our friend Anthony H. Payne from Roanoke, Virginia.

— *Ellen Graham Brown* (Mrs. Jack N. Brown)

### Yield: 18 servings

2 bottles (8 ounces each) clam juice
16 ounces cream cheese, cut in
  chunks
2 tablespoons grated onion
2 tablespoons dry sherry
White pepper, to taste
Cayenne pepper, to taste
2 cans (6½ ounces each) chopped
  clams, undrained
1 pound backfin crabmeat, picked
  over and shells discarded

**1.** Heat the clam juice in a large saucepan. Add the cream cheese and continue cooking over low heat, whisking to form a thick, smooth mixture.
**2.** Add the onion, sherry, white pepper, and cayenne pepper and mix well. Add the chopped clams and their juice and mix well. Gently fold in the crabmeat. Stir, over low heat, until heated through.
**3.** Serve in a chafing dish, accompanied by large corn chips.

# CLAM POT

The "pot" for this dip is a round loaf of sourdough bread. Be sure to save it to reheat the next day—a real treat.

— *Jane Grote Hipp* (Mrs. Van Hipp, Jr.)

### Yield: 12 to 16 servings

3 cans (6½ ounces each) minced
  clams (drain two cans and reserve
  the liquid from the third)
16 ounces cream cheese, at room
  temperature
2 teaspoons chopped chives
2 teaspoons Worcestershire sauce
½ teaspoon salt
2 teaspoons fresh lemon juice
6 drops Tabasco sauce
1 tablespoon minced fresh parsley
2 large round loaves sourdough
  bread
Paprika, for garnish

**1.** Preheat the oven to 250°F.
**2.** Place the clams, reserved liquid, cream cheese, chives, Worcestershire, salt, lemon juice, Tabasco, and parsley in a blender and blend until smooth.
**3.** Cut the top off one of the loaves of bread, set it aside to use as a lid, and remove some of the inside of the loaf to form a cavity large enough to hold the dip. Cut the bread removed from the cavity into pieces for dipping. Cut the second loaf into pieces.
**4.** Pour the clam mixture into the cavity of the first loaf, replace the lid, and wrap tightly in heavy aluminum foil. Place on a baking sheet and bake for 3 hours.
**5.** Wrap the bread pieces in aluminum foil and place in the oven with the clam pot for the last 30 minutes of baking time.
**6.** Place the clam pot on a warm tray, remove the lid, sprinkle the dip with paprika, and surround with the bread pieces.

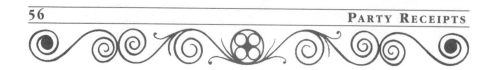

## "WHIMPIES"

Another name for this recipe might be Third Generation Sloppy Joes. "Whimpies" were served on the Mississippi River by my grandmother, Virginia Niemeyer, aboard the *Nancy Lee I*, *II*, and *III*. The tradition has been continued by my mother, Nancy Stone, as my parents cruise the Intracoastal Waterway in the *Nancy Lee IV*.

This is a versatile dish that can be served from a chafing dish and spooned onto cocktail rolls as an hors d'oeuvre or piled onto hamburger buns for lunch or supper.

— ***Melissa Stone Crosby*** (*Mrs. David M. Crosby*)

---

*Yield: 8 to 10 servings*

*2½ pounds lean ground beef*
*2 large onions, chopped*
*¼ cup chopped green bell pepper*
*(optional)*
*1 cup V-8 vegetable juice or tomato*
*juice*
*⅔ cup catsup*
*2 tablespoons sugar*
*¼ cup white vinegar*
*2 tablespoons Worcestershire sauce*

**1.** In a large frying pan or Dutch oven cook the meat and vegetables over medium heat until the meat is browned and the vegetables are tender, about 30 minutes.

**2.** Stir in the V-8, catsup, sugar, vinegar, and Worcestershire and simmer, uncovered, over low heat for 2 hours. The mixture will resemble spaghetti sauce. (Remove the lid during the last half hour of cooking if it seems too thin.)

**3.** The sauce will keep for several days in the refrigerator, freezes well, and may be reheated in the microwave.

---

*O*ne of Charleston's primary exports over the years has been the dance that captured the mood and imagination of the Roaring Twenties. No one is quite sure exactly how the dance got started, but it was based on a "Geechie step" popular in the black community and transported north by migrating laborers. Its popularity was cemented by the Broadway musical *Runnin' Wild*, in 1923, with music by James P. Johnson.

# LOWCOUNTRY HOT DIP

This is a delicious hot dip, devised by my husband. Serve it with large corn chips or crackers.

— *Martha Laird Sullivan* (Mrs. Martin Roberts Sullivan)

*Yield: 8 to 10 servings*

½ cup finely chopped onion
½ cup finely chopped green bell
   pepper
5 scallions (green onions), chopped
1 tablespoon butter
1 tablespoon Worcestershire sauce
½ teaspoon garlic salt
16 ounces cream cheese, at room
   temperature
1 cup mayonnaise
¾ cup chopped pecans
1 jar (5 ounces) dried beef, chopped
1 large round of bread

**1.** Preheat the oven to 325°F.
**2.** Sauté the onion, bell pepper, and scallions in the butter in a small frying pan over low heat until the vegetables are soft but not brown, about 5 minutes.
**3.** Transfer to a large mixing bowl and add the Worcestershire, garlic salt, and cream cheese and mix well. Add the mayonnaise, pecans, and dried beef and mix well.
**4.** Cut a slice off the top of the loaf of bread, to serve as a lid. Remove enough of the inside of the loaf to form a cavity large enough to hold the cream cheese mixture.
**5.** Pour the mixture into the cavity, replace the lid, wrap the loaf completely in aluminum foil, and place it on a baking sheet. Bake for 1 hour.

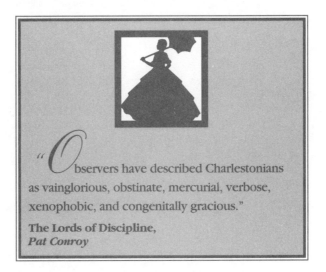

"*O*bservers have described Charlestonians as vainglorious, obstinate, mercurial, verbose, xenophobic, and congenitally gracious."

**The Lords of Discipline,**
*Pat Conroy*

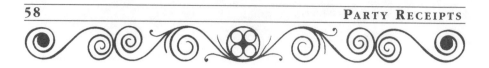

# DAWHOO HIGHLIGHT

I made this up for the annual St. Michael's Church oyster roast, and it was a big hit. The dip is named for our farm, Dawhoo, on the Dawhoo River near Edisto Island, south of Charleston, and making it helps me use up some of the great quantities of venison we have in the freezer.

— *Ruth Ellen Conway Smythe* (Mrs. David McCord Smythe)

*Yield: 10 servings*

*1 pound homemade venison sausage
   (or mild or hot bulk pork sausage)*
*8 ounces cream cheese*
*1 can (10 ounces) diced Rotel
   tomatoes*
*Red pepper flakes, to taste*

**1.** Preheat the oven to 350°F.
**2.** In a large frying pan, brown the sausage over medium heat and drain off the fat. Add the cream cheese, tomatoes, and red pepper flakes. (Add the red pepper flakes gradually; it does not take much.)
**3.** Transfer the mixture to a 3-quart casserole and bake, uncovered, for 30 minutes, stirring occasionally. Alternatively, cook the mixture in the frying pan on top of the stove over medium heat for 30 minutes, stirring frequently.
**4.** Serve the dip hot, with tortilla chips.

# HORS D'OEUVRES

# LIVER PÂTÉ

The rosemary in this simple-to-make pâté gives it a distinctive flavor.

*— Melissa Tuttle Fox (Mrs. Charles M. Fox)*

---

*Yield: 2 cups*

---

1 pound chicken livers
1 cup chicken broth
½ cup chopped onions
¼ teaspoon dried rosemary
½ cup (1 stick) butter, at room
   temperature
6 slices bacon, cooked and crumbled
Freshly ground pepper, to taste
¼ teaspoon salt
¾ teaspoon dry mustard

**1.** Place the chicken livers, chicken broth, onions, and rosemary in a small saucepan and simmer until the livers are tender, approximately 15 minutes. Cool the livers in the broth. When the livers are cool, drain off the broth and reserve it.

**2.** Place the butter, bacon, ¼ cup of the chicken broth (strained), livers, pepper, salt, and mustard in a blender or the bowl of a food processor. Blend until smooth.

**3.** Refrigerate the mixture in a covered serving dish, overnight. Serve with crackers or bread points.

# COUNTRY PÂTÉ

Serve this pâté with a selection of cocktail breads and a side dish of mustard.

*— Courteney Tucker*

---

*Yield: 12 to 20 servings*

---

1 pound ground beef
1 pound chicken livers
½ jar (3 ounces) capers, drained
¼ cup bourbon
½ teaspoon salt
½ teaspoon freshly ground pepper
¼ teaspoon ground ginger
Dash of Worcestershire sauce
Dash of Tabasco sauce
1 clove garlic, pressed

**1.** Preheat the oven to 400°F. Butter a 9 x 5 x 3-inch loaf pan.
**2.** Place the ground beef, chicken livers, capers, bourbon, salt, pepper, ginger, Worcestershire, Tabasco, and garlic in the bowl of a food processor and process until smooth.

**3.** Pour the mixture into the pan and bake for 1 hour. Let cool and then refrigerate. Slice as thinly as possible and cut into squares the size of cocktail bread. Serve cold.

"*I* walk down Stolls Alley and down Church and Longitude Lane, and the old buildings, the lovely gardens and passageways, unfold in their magic color for me . . ."

**The Golden Weather,** *Louis Rubin*

# HATTIE'S PÂTÉ

My grandmother was a member of a luncheon club in Louisville, Kentucky, and her friend Hattie's pâté was a favorite of the group.

— *Merrie Summer McNair (Mrs. David H. McNair)*

*Yield: 12 to 20 servings*

1 can (10½ ounces) beef consommé
1 package unflavored gelatin
2 cans (4¼ ounces each) liver pâté
  (Sells)
4 ounces cream cheese, at room
  temperature
1 teaspoon fresh lemon juice
1 teaspoon dried dill weed
1 teaspoon sherry
Dash of Worcestershire sauce
Dash of Tabasco sauce

**1.** Place the soup in a small saucepan and bring to a boil. Add the gelatin and stir until it is dissolved. Pour one-quarter of the mixture into a 1-quart mold and place in the refrigerator to set.
**2.** Place the liver pâté in a medium-size bowl and pour in the remaining soup mixture. Stir in the cream cheese, lemon juice, dill weed, sherry, Worcestershire, and Tabasco and mix well.
**3.** When the consommé in the mold is set, pour the liver mixture on top of it and refrigerate overnight. Unmold and serve with crackers.

# MOLDED TUNA PÂTÉ

Your guests won't know what kind of fish they're eating in this pâté often made by my mother, Elizabeth Bishop Tiller.

— *C. Elizabeth Tiller*

*Yield: About 3½ cups*

1 can (3 ounces) chopped
  mushrooms, drained, and
  liquid reserved
1 envelope unflavored gelatin
½ cup boiling water
2 cans (6⅛ ounces each) tuna,
  drained
½ cup Green Goddess salad
  dressing
½ cup pitted ripe olives
¼ cup fresh parsley leaves

**1.** Oil a 1-quart mold.
**2.** Place the liquid from the mushrooms in a blender. Sprinkle over it the gelatin and let soften for 1 or 2 minutes. Pour in the boiling water, cover, and blend for about 10 seconds on low speed, then 20 seconds on high speed.
**3.** Add the mushrooms, tuna, salad dressing, olives, and parsley. Cover and blend on high speed until well mixed.
**4.** Pour the mixture into the prepared mold and refrigerate, covered, until firm, about 3 hours. Unmold onto a platter and serve with Melba toast.

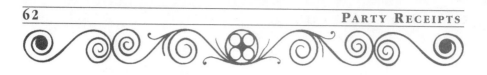

# CAVIAR MOLD

This recipe, given to me by Elizabeth Jones Bissell, is somewhat involved, but the result is worth the effort. It can be made ahead and refrigerated for up to two days. The best accompaniment is Melba toast, preferably homemade.

*— Patricia Jones*

### Yield: 4 cups

¼ cup water
1 envelope unflavored gelatin

#### Avocado Layer

2 medium avocados, peeled, pitted, and puréed
1 large shallot, minced
2 tablespoons fresh lemon juice
2 tablespoons mayonnaise
½ teaspoon salt
Dash of freshly ground pepper
Generous dash of Tabasco sauce

#### Egg Layer

4 hard-cooked eggs, finely chopped
½ cup mayonnaise
¼ cup minced fresh parsley
1 large scallion (green onion), minced
½ teaspoon salt
Dash of freshly ground pepper
Generous dash of Tabasco sauce

#### Sour Cream Layer

1 cup sour cream
¼ cup minced onions

#### For Garnish

Red lumpfish caviar
Black lumpfish caviar
Golden lumpfish caviar

**1.** Oil a 7-inch springform pan.
**2.** Combine the water and gelatin in a glass measuring cup and let stand for 5 minutes. Set the cup in a small pan and fill the pan with boiling water to reach 1 inch up the side of the cup. Heat over medium heat until the gelatin is completely dissolved, stirring, about 5 minutes.
**3.** Make the avocado layer: Combine all the ingredients in a medium-size saucepan and stir in 2 tablespoons of the dissolved gelatin. Cook over low heat, stirring constantly, until the gelatin is just melted, about 5 minutes.
**4.** Spoon the mixture into the prepared pan, spreading it evenly to the edge of the pan, and cover and refrigerate for 30 minutes.
**5.** Make the egg layer: Combine all the ingredients in a medium-size bowl and stir in 1 tablespoon plus 1 teaspoon of the dissolved gelatin. Spoon on top of the chilled avocado layer, spreading it evenly to the edge of the pan. Cover and refrigerate.
**6.** Make the sour cream layer: Combine the sour cream, onion, and the remaining dissolved gelatin in a small bowl and mix well. Spoon over the egg layer. Cover and refrigerate until set, at least 8 hours.
**7.** To serve, remove the sides of the pan and garnish the mold with the caviar, alternating the colors in whatever pattern you choose. Place the pan on a serving tray and accompany with Melba toast.

# FERNE'S STUFFED CELERY

My mother *always* served stuffed celery and black olives on Thanksgiving.
— *Dorsey Glenn Condon* (Mrs. Clarence M. Condon III)

---

*Yield: 30 pieces*

---

1 bunch celery, washed and trimmed
8 ounces cream cheese, at room
    temperature
¼ cup mayonnaise
2 teaspoons fresh lemon juice
½ teaspoon salt
¾ cup chopped pecans

**1.** Cut the celery into 2- to 3-inch
pieces. Place in a medium-size bowl of
ice water and refrigerate for at least an
hour.
**2.** Place the cream cheese, mayonnaise, lemon juice, and salt in a medium-
size bowl and use a hand mixer to
cream the mixture until fluffy, adding
more mayonnaise if necessary. Stir in
the pecans.
**3.** Drain the celery and pat dry with
paper towels. Fill each piece of celery
with a generous amount of the cream
cheese mixture. Chill before serving.

# MARINATED BROCCOLI AND CAULIFLOWER

Though the cool contrast of green and white is appealing, other vegetables may be
substituted for part of the broccoli or cauliflower.
— *Marty Rankin Bonds* (Mrs. Jonathan R. Bonds)

---

*Yield: 8 servings*

---

1 cup vinegar
1 tablespoon dried dill weed
1 tablespoon sugar
1 tablespoon seasoned salt
1 teaspoon garlic salt
1 teaspoon salt
1 teaspoon freshly ground pepper
1¼ cups vegetable oil
1 bunch broccoli, trimmed and
    broken into florets
1 head cauliflower, trimmed and
    broken into florets

**1.** To make the marinade, combine
the vinegar, dill weed, sugar, seasoned
salt, garlic salt, salt, and pepper in a
medium-size bowl. Gradually whisk in
the oil.
**2.** Place the broccoli and cauliflower
florets in a large bowl or plastic container with a lid, pour over the marinade, cover, and refrigerate for at least
6 hours.
**3.** Drain off the marinade and serve
the vegetables in a bowl with toothpicks.

## CUCUMBER WHEELS

This is an old recipe from my Grandmother Van Every, who received it from relatives in St. Catherines, Ontario. It makes a light summer hors d'oeuvre, served with mint juleps or vodka collinses.

— *Elizabeth Van Every Risher*

---
*Yield: About 80 canapés*
---

4 large cucumbers, unpeeled, cut in
   ¼-inch slices
9 ounces caviar, drained
2 lemons, cut in half
3 hard-cooked eggs, chopped
6 scallions (green onions), finely
   chopped
Parsley, for garnish

**1.** Place a small amount of caviar on top of each cucumber slice and sprinkle with lemon juice.
**2.** Place the eggs and scallions in separate small dishes and place in the middle of a serving tray. Arrange a "wheel" of cucumber slices around the dishes. Decorate the tray with parsley sprigs. Refrigerate until ready to serve (no more than an hour).

## CAVIAR BITES

These are an elegant "bite" before the theater or symphony—delicious with Champagne cocktails.

— *Croft Whitener Lane* (Mrs. Hugh Lane, Jr.)

---
*Yield: 24 leaves*
---

8 ounces crème fraîche
¼ cup minced scallions (green
   onions)
¼ cup snipped fresh dill
1 tablespoon fresh lemon juice
4 ounces caviar, drained
24 leaves Belgian endive (about
   2 heads)

**1.** Combine the crème fraîche, scallions, dill, and lemon juice in a small bowl and stir to combine. Gently fold in the caviar. Refrigerate until ready to serve (no more than 3 hours).
**2.** Arrange the endive leaves on a serving plate. Fill the root end of each leaf with a spoonful of the caviar mixture. Serve immediately.

> ### HANNUKAH PARTY
>
> *Liver Pâté*
>
> *Mushroom and Artichoke Hearts in Honey Mustard Vinaigrette*
>
> *Smoked Salmon Ball*
>
> *Plantation Eggplant Dip*
>
> *Marinated Eye of Round with Horseradish Sauce*
>
> *Hot Potato Latkes with Cran-Apple Relish (your own recipe)*
>
> *"Whatsits"*
>
> *Grandma's Nuthorns*
>
> *Champagne Punch*
>
> *Spiced Holiday Tea*

# MUSHROOMS AND ARTICHOKE HEARTS IN HONEY MUSTARD VINAIGRETTE

Two popular flavors—balsamic vinegar and honey mustard—are combined in this recipe, to make a very tasty marinade.

*— Priscilla Hinde Wendt (Mrs. Robertson H. Wendt, Jr.)*

---

*Yield: 8 to 10 servings*
*(about 1 quart)*

---

*⅓ cup balsamic vinegar*
*1 tablespoon honey*
*1 tablespoon Dijon or stone-ground*
*mustard*
*½ teaspoon salt*
*⅛ teaspoon pepper*
*⅔ cup vegetable oil*
*1 pound small to medium-size fresh*
*mushrooms*
*1 can (14 ounces) artichoke hearts,*
*drained and halved*

**1.** Prepare the vinaigrette: Combine the vinegar, honey, mustard, salt, and pepper in a small bowl and mix well. Add the vegetable oil and mix well.
**2.** Clean the mushrooms and cut off the ends of the stems. Place the mushrooms and artichoke hearts in a 1-quart dish. Pour over the vinaigrette and toss lightly to coat. Refrigerate for 3 to 5 hours, tossing occasionally.
**3.** To serve, drain off the marinade and pass with toothpicks.

# MARINATED MUSHROOMS

An easy "do-ahead" that is always popular.

*— Jean Simmons Rivers (Mrs. Charlie Rivers)*

---

*Yield: 10 servings*

---

*1 pound small fresh mushrooms,*
*cleaned and stems removed*
*½ cup olive oil*
*½ cup beer*
*2 tablespoons fresh lemon juice*
*2 tablespoons minced onion*
*1 tablespoon chopped fresh parsley*
*¼ teaspoon dried oregano leaves*
*¼ teaspoon dried thyme leaves*
*¼ teaspoon dried basil leaves*
*½ teaspoon salt*
*¼ teaspoon freshly ground pepper*
*1 clove garlic, minced*

**1.** Place the mushrooms in a shallow bowl. Add the remaining ingredients to the bowl in the order given and toss lightly. Let marinate in the refrigerator for no less than 6 hours, preferably overnight.
**2.** Serve chilled or at room temperature, after draining off the marinade. Pass with toothpicks.

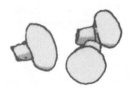

# OKRA FLOWERS

The procedure for assembling these "flowers" may sound tricky, but the process is not really complicated and takes very little time.

— *Pamela McMillan McKinney* (Mrs. Patrick W. McKinney)

---

*Yield: 28 "flowers"*

¾ *pound sliced boiled ham*
6 *ounces cream cheese, at room temperature*
1 *jar (16 ounces) pickled okra (available in specialty stores and some supermarkets)*

**1.** Spread each slice of ham with a thin layer of cream cheese.
**2.** Cut the ends and tips from the okra pods (they may be saved for a salad). Place two pods, wide end to narrow end, at one edge of each slice of ham. Starting at that end, roll each slice as for a jelly roll. The cream cheese will keep the roll together.
**3.** Cut each roll into slices ¼ to ½ inch thick. The slices will resemble flowers.

*O*kra is the most distinctively southern of all vegetables, with a flavor resembling, in one way or another, asparagus, artichoke hearts, and eggplant. Though some consider cooked okra "slimy," raw okra has a pleasant crispness and is often pickled. Okra pods are available frozen, and often fresh, in supermarkets in many parts of the country.

---

# MERRY TOMATOES

My mother's Christmas buffet is considered incomplete without Merry Tomatoes.

— *Susan Scott Waters* (Mrs. Philip Waters)

---

*Yield: 20 servings*

30 to 40 cherry tomatoes, stems removed
1 cup vodka
1 teaspoon celery salt
¼ cup lemon pepper seasoning

**1.** Place the tomatoes in a serving bowl or dish. Pour the vodka over the tomatoes. (Each tomato should be partially submerged in the vodka.

Depending on the serving bowl, you may need to use more than 1 cup.)
**2.** In a small bowl combine the celery salt and lemon pepper seasoning, mixing well. Place the bowl of seasoning next to the bowl of tomatoes along with a small container of toothpicks. Guests are to spear a tomato with a toothpick and then dip it in the seasoning mixture.

# ROASTED RED PEPPERS

My husband, Dr. Wayne L. King, devised this recipe; it is easily scaled up or down.
— *Jeannie Nissen King* (Mrs. Wayne L. King)

---
*Yield: 6 servings*
---

4 red or yellow bell peppers
4 cloves garlic, peeled, halved, and
  crushed with a knife blade
4 anchovy fillets, cut in half
2 tablespoons pine nuts, toasted or
  sautéed in olive oil until brown
1 tablespoon chopped fresh oregano
  leaves
Freshly ground pepper, to taste
Olive oil
Thinly sliced French bread

**1.** Preheat the broiler.

**2.** Roast the peppers, following the instructions given below. Cut into ¼-inch strips.
**3.** Select a 2-cup crock and place the ingredients in layers in the following order: strips of pepper, 2 pieces halved, crushed garlic, 2 pieces anchovy, nuts, oregano, and pepper. Repeat until all ingredients are used.
**4.** Pour a sufficient amount of olive oil over the ingredients to cover all the layers and cover the crock. Refrigerate until a few hours before serving, for up to one week. Serve at room temperature on the French bread.

# TANGY TOMATOES

An additional tip—drain the tomatoes upside down on a paper towel after the pulp has been removed.
— *Karen Powers Arterburn* (Mrs. James N. Arterburn)

---
*Yield: 18 servings*
---

½ cup finely chopped ham
¼ cup Roquefort cheese, crumbled
¼ cup sour cream
¼ teaspoon fresh lemon juice
Dash of freshly ground pepper
36 cherry tomatoes

**1.** In a small bowl combine the ham, cheese, sour cream, lemon juice, and pepper.
**2.** Cut the tops from the tomatoes and scoop out most of the pulp, reserving for another use. Spoon ½ teaspoon of the ham and cheese mixture into each tomato shell. Serve chilled.

To roast red peppers, place them on a baking pan 2 to 3 inches from the heat and broil until the skin becomes charred, turning to expose all surfaces. Place the charred peppers in a plastic bag, seal, and let steam for 15 to 20 minutes. Remove the peppers from the bag, peel, and remove the seeds.

# STUFFED CHERRY TOMATOES

Using a pastry bag to fill the tomatoes gives a decorative look to the finished product.

— *Brenda Morris Kerrison* (Mrs. William Legare Kerrison)

### Yield: 48 tomatoes

48 cherry tomatoes
16 ounces cream cheese, at room
　temperature
2 tablespoons snipped fresh dill
2 scallions (green onions), minced
　(include some of the top)
1 teaspoon fresh lemon juice

**1.** Using a sharp knife, cut the round bottom off each of the tomatoes, so they will sit firmly on a tray. Working from the stem end of each tomato, use a melon baller to remove the pulp.

**2.** Place the tomatoes cavity side down on a wire rack, with paper toweling underneath, to drain. Chill.
**3.** Place the cream cheese in a medium-size bowl and add the dill, scallions, and lemon juice. Mix well.
**4.** Place the cream cheese mixture in a pastry bag with a star tip and pipe it into the tomato cavities.

# DEVILED EGGS WITH ANCHOVY

The anchovy paste in these stuffed eggs makes them special. They are favorite picnic fare for our family.

— *Eleanor Cain Stutler* (Mrs. James Boyd Stutler)

### Yield: 24 deviled eggs

2 dozen hard-cooked eggs
⅔ cup mayonnaise
⅓ cup Durkee sauce
¾ tube (1¼ ounces) anchovy paste
1 medium onion, finely grated
¼ teaspoon white pepper
Salt, to taste
Capers or sliced green olives, for
　garnish

**1.** Peel the eggs, cut in half, and remove the yolks.
**2.** Transfer the yolks to a large bowl and mash with the mayonnaise and Durkee sauce until smooth. Add the anchovy paste, grated onion, pepper, and salt.
**3.** Mound some of the yolk mixture in the cavity of each egg white. Garnish with capers or sliced green olives. Chill before serving.

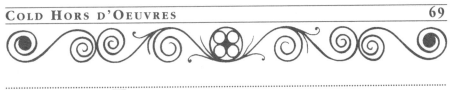

## DEVILED EGGS

These go fast, so I usually double the recipe.

— *Sara Quick Gilchrist*

| Yield: 16 deviled eggs |
| --- |

8 hard-cooked eggs
3 tablespoons mayonnaise
1 tablespoon prepared mustard
½ teaspoon Worcestershire sauce
1 teaspoon Durkee sauce
2 tablespoons minced sweet pickles
2 tablespoons sweet pickle juice
1 tablespoon cider vinegar
Salt and white pepper, to taste
Paprika, for garnish

**1.** Peel the eggs, cut in half, and remove the yolks. Place the yolks in a medium-size bowl and mash with a fork. Add the mayonnaise, mustard, Worcestershire, Durkee sauce, pickles, juice, vinegar, and salt and pepper. Mix until the yolks are smooth.
**2.** Stuff the cavities of the egg whites with the yolk mixture and sprinkle with paprika. Chill before serving.

## TEXAS CAVIAR

Black-eyed peas are said to bring luck and have become traditional New Year's fare. Here is a way to serve them as an hors d'oeuvre—perhaps for a New Year's Eve buffet. The recipe comes from my father, Harvey W. Tiller.

— *C. Elizabeth Tiller*

| Yield: 15 servings |
| --- |

2 cans (16 ounces each) black-eyed peas, rinsed and well drained
½ cup red wine vinegar
⅓ cup vegetable oil
¼ cup minced onion
1 tablespoon minced seeded green chilies, or more, to taste
1 large clove garlic, minced
½ teaspoon salt
½ teaspoon sugar
¼ teaspoon freshly ground pepper
2 tablespoons chopped pimiento, for garnish

**1.** In a large bowl combine the peas, vinegar, oil, onion, chilies, garlic, salt, sugar, and pepper. Cover and refrigerate for at least 2 days or up to 2 weeks.
**2.** Before serving, drain off the marinade. Transfer the "caviar" to a serving bowl and garnish with the pimiento.

*H*ard-cooked eggs cut crosswise instead of lengthwise for "deviling" are more decorative, and easier for the guest to handle. Cut a small slice off the bottom of each half so it will sit firmly on the platter or tray.

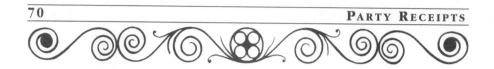

# PEARS WITH BLUE CHEESE

The cheese mixture may be prepared in advance and spread on the pears just before serving. The flavors are perfect with a nice white wine. If you do not have access to Clemson blue cheese, Stilton or another top quality blue cheese may be substituted.

— *Misty Stieglitz Boling* (Mrs. Donald Berkley Boling, Jr.)

*Yield: 16 pieces*

4 ounces cream cheese, at room
    temperature
4 to 5 ounces Clemson blue cheese
4 ripe red Bartlett pears, unpeeled
Fresh lemon juice

**1.** Combine the cream cheese and blue cheese in a small bowl and mix until smooth.
**2.** Stem, quarter, and core the pears. Sprinkle with lemon juice to prevent browning.
**3.** Spread generous amounts of the cheese mixture on each pear quarter. Arrange the pears on a serving plate, tray, or basket.

# EGGS IN A SAUSAGE BLANKET

We discovered "Scotch Eggs" on a trip to England several years ago but were unable to obtain a recipe. This is my version, which my friends and family love.

— *Mary Louise Kidder Gadsden* (Mrs. C. Deas Gadsden)

*Yield: 18 to 20 servings*

1 dozen hard-cooked eggs
3 pounds ground sausage meat,
    uncooked
4 raw eggs
3 packages (3 stacks) Ritz crackers
½ cup vegetable oil
Parsley, for garnish

**1.** Peel the eggs and leave them whole.
**2.** Using your hands, cover the outside of each hard-cooked egg completely with about ¼ pound of the sausage, patting the outside smooth and being careful that the egg retains its shape.
**3.** Beat the 4 raw eggs in a small bowl. Crush the crackers between two sheets of waxed paper with a rolling pin.
**4.** Dip each egg in the beaten eggs, coating well, and then roll in the cracker crumbs until well coated.
**5.** Heat the oil in a deep-fat fryer or iron frying pan until hot but not smoking. Place the eggs in the oil and cook, turning, until the sausage is cooked through, about 8 minutes. Remove from the oil, drain on paper toweling, cool, and refrigerate.
**6.** When the eggs are cold, cut each one into four wedges with a sharp knife. Place on a serving plate, garnish with clumps of parsley, and serve cold.

# FETA CHEESE WITH OLIVE OIL AND FRESH BASIL

Feta cheese does not slice very neatly, so don't worry if there are crumbs.
— *Mary Bennett Morrison* *(Mrs. Hagood Morrison)*

### *Yield: 6 servings*

1 pound feta cheese
¾ cup olive oil
10 or 12 fresh basil leaves, cut in
   small pieces

**1.** Cut the cheese into slices and arrange on a serving plate.
**2.** Heat the olive oil in a small saucepan over low heat until it is warm, not hot.
**3.** Drizzle the olive oil over the cheese slices. Sprinkle the basil over the cheese. Serve immediately with wheat crackers.

*T*he annual Charleston Collection fashion show fundraiser is a chance for League members, friends, and the public to put away more serious pursuits for an afternoon of good food and fashion. A Champagne reception and luncheon precede the show, for which League members are models.

# CALLIE'S SUMMERTIME SAGA

This topping works equally well spooned over toasted slices of French bread as an appetizer or over pasta for a first course or main dish. The recipe comes from Callie Hartzog White.
— *Amy Solomon Waring* *(Mrs. Bradish J. Waring)*

### *Yield: 10 to 12 servings*

1 pound fresh tomatoes, peeled,
   seeded, and chopped
1 cup chopped fresh basil leaves
4 large cloves garlic, minced
1 teaspoon olive oil
1 pound Saga blue cheese, crumbled
1 loaf French bread

**1.** Place the tomatoes, basil, garlic, olive oil, and cheese in a large bowl and stir to combine. Let sit at room temperature.
**2.** Cut the French bread into ¼-inch slices and toast them.
**3.** Place the tomato-cheese mixture in a serving dish and surround with the toasted French bread.

## CURRY CHICKEN SALAD

Mound this salad on a bed of lettuce and serve with crackers for an hors d'oeuvre or stuff it into small pita pockets for lunch.

— *Laura Nowell Vardell*

---
*Yield: 2 cups*
---

1 whole boneless, skinless chicken
    breast, cooked and minced
2 stalks celery, chopped
1 red apple (unpeeled), cored and
    chopped fine
¼ cup raisins
4 tablespoons mayonnaise
2 tablespoons milk
2 teaspoons curry powder

**1.** In a medium-size bowl combine the chicken, celery, apple, and raisins.
**2.** In a small bowl mix the mayonnaise and milk until smooth and stir in the curry powder.
**3.** Pour the mayonnaise mixture over the chicken mixture and blend well.

## MARINATED PORK TENDERLOIN

A great dish for a cocktail buffet, served with a variety of breads.

— *Elizabeth St. John Weinstein* (Mrs. Victor Weinstein)

---
*Yield: 12 servings*
---

**Marinade**

½ cup soy sauce
¼ cup hoisin sauce
½ cup dry sherry
¼ cup honey
¼ cup orange juice
1 tablespoon black bean sauce
4 garlic cloves, crushed
1 piece (2 inches) fresh ginger, peeled
    and grated
6 scallions, chopped
1 tablespoon dry mustard

3 pork tenderloins (2½ to 3 pounds
    total weight)
Orange slices, for garnish

**1.** Combine all the ingredients for the marinade in a shallow dish and mix well. Set aside ½ cup.
**2.** Place the pork tenderloins in the remaining marinade, cover the dish with plastic wrap, and refrigerate for 2 to 3 hours or overnight. Turn occasionally.
**3.** Preheat the oven to 350°F.
**4.** Remove the pork from the marinade and place on a rack in a roasting pan. Bake until the pork reaches an internal temperature of 170°F, about 50 minutes.
**5.** Let the meat cool completely and refrigerate, covered, for 2 to 3 hours or overnight.
**6.** To serve, slice the pork on the diagonal into ¼-inch slices. Arrange on a serving platter, pour over some of the reserved marinade, and garnish with orange slices.

# MARINATED FLANK STEAK

Here is an hors d'oeuvre that is both easy and delicious. The meat looks best served on a silver platter or tray, garnished with clumps of parsley.

— *Mary Louise Kidder Gadsden* (Mrs. C. Deas Gadsden)

---
*Yield: About 15 servings*
---

*1 flank steak (1¼ to 1½ pounds)*
*½ cup vegetable oil*
*½ cup soy sauce*
*2 cloves garlic, minced*
*Colored toothpicks*

**1.** Using a small sharp knife, lightly score the steak on both sides. Place it in a pan long enough for it to lie flat.
**2.** Pour the vegetable oil and soy sauce over the steak and sprinkle on the garlic.

**3.** To start, turn the steak several times in the marinade, then allow it to marinate in the refrigerator for at least 6 hours or overnight. Turn the steak at least twice while it is marinating.
**4.** Preheat the broiler.
**5.** Remove the meat from the marinade and broil for approximately 5 minutes on each side. Let the meat cool, refrigerate until chilled, and slice on the diagonal. Cut in bite-size pieces and place a toothpick in each piece.

# WHIPPED CREAM CHICKEN SALAD

This versatile dish can be served in pastry shells or scooped-out cherry tomatoes or used as a sandwich filling. It's sinfully rich.

— *Julia Burr Wills* (Mrs. Thomas Jackson Wills IV)

---
*Yield: About 4 cups*
---

*2 cups diced cooked chicken*
*1½ cups diced celery*
*2 tablespoons chopped parsley*
*1 teaspoon salt*
*½ teaspoon freshly ground pepper*
*1 cup mayonnaise*
*2 tablespoons fresh lemon juice*
*¼ cup heavy cream, whipped*
*½ cup chopped or sliced almonds*

**1.** In a large bowl toss the chicken with the celery, parsley, salt, and pepper. Add the mayonnaise and lemon juice and mix well. Gently fold in the whipped cream until it is well incorporated.

**2.** Refrigerate the salad for about an hour. Before serving, sprinkle with the almonds.

"There are tame Fowls of all sorts; and Great variety of wild Fowl; the sorts of wild fowl that frequent the inland parts of the Country, are Turkeys, Geese, Ducks, Pidgeons, Partridges, Brants, Sheldrakes, and Teal . . ."

**A Description of South Carolina, London, 1761**

## BEEF FILLETS IN WINE

This dish works well on a meat tray for a buffet or smorgasbord and can also be used as a main course. It must be prepared at least a day before serving.

— *Ann Whittemore Shumaker* (Mrs. Elmer Shumaker)

---

*Yield: 20 servings*

---

1 large onion, finely chopped
¼ cup celery, finely chopped
3 cloves garlic, minced
⅓ cup olive oil
1¼ cups dry red wine
1½ cups strong beef stock
1 tablespoon chopped parsley
Celery leaves
1 bay leaf, crumbled
Salt and freshly ground pepper, to
   taste
2 pounds fillet of beef
Stems of fresh mushrooms (optional)
Chopped parsley, for garnish
Toothpicks

**1.** In a frying pan sauté the onion, celery, and garlic in the olive oil until soft and golden, about 10 minutes. Add the wine and stock and cook over high heat until the liquid is reduced by one-third, about 5 minutes.
**2.** Add the 1 tablespoon chopped parsley, some celery leaves, the bay leaf, and salt and pepper.
**3.** Using a sharp knife, cut the beef into paper-thin slices.
**4.** Spoon some of the liquid into a 13 x 9-inch glass or ceramic dish. Add a layer of beef, then more liquid. Repeat the layers until all the beef is used. Cover the dish and refrigerate for 24 hours or up to 6 days.
**5.** Before serving, drain off the liquid. Roll each slice of meat jelly-roll style and secure with a toothpick. (A raw mushroom stem placed in the center of the meat slice before rolling is a delicious addition.)
**6.** Roll each fillet roll in chopped parsley.

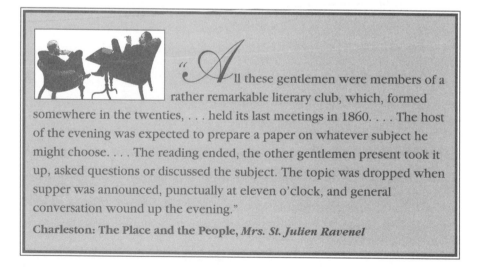

"All these gentlemen were members of a rather remarkable literary club, which, formed somewhere in the twenties, . . . held its last meetings in 1860. . . . The host of the evening was expected to prepare a paper on whatever subject he might choose. . . . The reading ended, the other gentlemen present took it up, asked questions or discussed the subject. The topic was dropped when supper was announced, punctually at eleven o'clock, and general conversation wound up the evening."

**Charleston: The Place and the People,** *Mrs. St. Julien Ravenel*

# MARINATED EYE OF ROUND WITH HORSERADISH SAUCE

Here is an easy dish for the cocktail buffet. I recommend serving the meat on Parker House rolls or any other small rolls.

*— Elizabeth S. Tucker*

---
*Yield: 30 to 40 servings*
---

*4 pounds eye of round roast*
*1 cup soy sauce*
*¼ to ½ cup gin*
*½ cup vegetable oil*
*4 cloves garlic, crushed*

### Horseradish Sauce

*1 cup heavy cream*
*1 cup mayonnaise (optional)*
*Pinch of salt*
*¼ cup prepared horseradish, or to*
*    taste*

**1.** Place the roast in a large Ziploc bag. In a small bowl combine the soy sauce, gin, oil, and garlic and mix well. Pour the marinade into the bag with the roast, close the bag well, and refrigerate for 48 hours, turning the roast several times.

**2.** When ready to cook the meat, preheat the oven to 350°F.

**3.** Pat the roast dry and bake until a meat thermometer registers medium-rare, about 1 hour. Remove the roast from the oven and immediately wrap it in foil and refrigerate (to stop the meat from continuing to cook).

**4.** To prepare the sauce, place the cream in a medium-size bowl and whip until soft peaks form. Beat in the mayonnaise and salt, then blend in the horseradish by hand. For a lighter sauce, omit the mayonnaise.

**5.** At serving time, slice the meat very thin and serve on rolls with the horseradish sauce.

---

# BEEF AND ARTICHOKE ROLL-UPS

My husband concocted this dish one night on the spur of the moment.

*— Sara Thackston Shelnutt (Mrs. David L. Shelnutt)*

---
*Yield: 48 roll-ups*
---

*4 slices bacon, cooked and crumbled*
*1 can (14 ounces) artichoke hearts,*
*    drained and chopped*
*1 cup grated Cheddar cheese*
*3 tablespoons mayonnaise*
*Garlic powder, to taste*
*1 pound sliced rare roast beef*
*Toothpicks*

**1.** Place the bacon, artichoke hearts, cheese, mayonnaise, and garlic powder in the bowl of a food processor and process until the mixture is a creamy paste (add more mayonnaise if necessary).

**2.** Cut the roast beef slices into 2-inch strips. Spread each strip with approximately 1 tablespoon of the artichoke mixture and roll up. Secure each roll with a toothpick.

# CELERY STUFFED WITH CHICKEN SALAD

I like to arrange the stuffed celery pieces on a bed of red lettuce, with mounds of olives as a garnish.

— *Kathryn Kammerling Wesson* (Mrs. Michael D. Wesson)

*Yield: 8 to 10 servings*

2 cups chopped cooked chicken
¼ cup chopped slivered almonds
1 cup mayonnaise
6 stalks celery, cut into 2-inch pieces
¼ cup crumbled cooked bacon

**1.** In a medium-size bowl combine the chicken, almonds, and mayonnaise.
**2.** Stuff the celery pieces with the chicken mixture and top with the crumbled bacon.

# STEAK TARTARE

Freshness is a must for this dish. Be sure to use very lean meat and either grind it yourself or ask the butcher to do it while you wait.

— *Marsha Hemphill Huggins* (Mrs. James Alden Huggins)

*Yield: 10 to 12 servings*

1 pound sirloin, trimmed well and
    freshly ground once
¼ cup minced onion
1 teaspoon dried tarragon
2 anchovy fillets, finely diced
1 tablespoon drained capers
1 teaspoon instant bouillon crystals,
    dissolved in 1 teaspoon water
1 egg yolk
½ teaspoon dry mustard
Salt and freshly ground pepper, to
    taste
Capers, for garnish
Minced onion, for garnish

**1.** In a large bowl combine the ground sirloin, ¼ cup minced onion, tarragon, anchovies, 1 tablespoon capers, bouillon, egg yolk, and dry mustard and mix well with a fork. Add salt and pepper to taste.

**2.** Shape the mixture into a mound on a platter and serve immediately. Serve with Melba rounds and small bowls of minced onions and capers.

"For us a special source of pleasure was Charleston's notable difference from other American cities we had known: older (founded in 1670), more complex, and above all richer in the quiet beauty of its buildings and its setting."

**Charleston: A Golden Memory,**
*Charles R. Anderson*

# HOT
# HORS D'OEUVRES

## CHEESE-STUFFED MUSHROOMS

You may prepare the cheese "stuffing" in advance and then assemble the mushrooms just before baking.

— *Misty Stieglitz Boling* (Mrs. Donald Berkley Boling, Jr.)

---

*Yield: 20 to 25 servings*

---

*8 ounces whipped light cream cheese*
*½ cup grated Jarlsburg cheese*
*4 slices bacon, cooked and crumbled*
*Garlic salt, to taste*
*Dash of Worcestershire sauce*
*1 pound fresh mushrooms, cleaned and stems removed*

**1.** Preheat the oven to 350°F. Grease a baking sheet.
**2.** Combine the cream cheese, Jarlsburg cheese, bacon, garlic salt, and Worcestershire in a medium-size bowl and mix until well blended.
**3.** Place the mushroom caps on the prepared baking sheet and stuff with the cheese mixture. Bake until bubbly, 15 to 20 minutes. Serve on a warm tray, with toothpicks.

## WILD MUSHROOMS ON PITA CRISPS

Though this hors d'oeuvre must be assembled at the last minute, the contrast between the crisp pita and the creamy mushroom filling is most appealing. Various kinds of wild mushrooms may be used, depending on what's available.

— *Cindy Henley Ball* (Mrs. Austin Ball)

---

*Yield: 12 to 15 servings*

---

*4 small rounds pita bread*
*Olive oil*
*2 cloves garlic*
*½ pound fresh mushrooms (shiitake, cremini, oyster, or domestic), sliced or chopped*
*3 tablespoons olive oil*
*1 shallot, minced*
*2 tablespoons Cognac or brandy*
*¼ cup minced fresh herbs (thyme, parsley, chives, or tarragon)*
*3 tablespoons heavy or whipping cream*
*Salt and freshly ground pepper, to taste*
*Chopped fresh herbs or enoki mushrooms, for garnish*

**1.** Preheat the oven to 450°F.
**2.** Split open the pita rounds and cut

each into 4 triangles, to make a total of 32 triangles. Place the rounds rough side up on a baking sheet and brush with olive oil. Bake until golden, about 5 minutes. Peel and cut the garlic cloves in half and rub the cut edge across the pita crisps. Set aside.
**3.** Heat the 3 tablespoons of olive oil in a frying pan over medium heat. Add the shallot, lower the heat, and cook until wilted but not brown, about 3 minutes. Add the mushrooms and cook until they begin to release moisture.
**4.** Add the Cognac and cook for 3 to 5 minutes, stirring constantly. Add the herbs, cream, and salt and pepper and heat through. Spoon a small amount of the mushroom mixture onto each pita crisp and garnish with fresh herbs or enoki mushrooms. Serve immediately.

## SPINACH SOUFFLÉ-STUFFED MUSHROOMS

These are great as an appetizer or a side dish. I use small mushrooms for hors d'oeuvres, large ones for an accompaniment.

*— Catherine Gazes*

*Yield: 12 to 18 large mushrooms;*
*24 small*

1 package (12 ounces) frozen
  spinach soufflé, thawed
Lemon pepper seasoning, to taste
Garlic powder, to taste
Salt, to taste
12 to 18 large fresh mushrooms (or
  24 small), cleaned and stems
  removed
½ cup (1 stick) butter
1½ tablespoons minced onion
Freshly grated Parmesan cheese

**1.** Preheat the oven to 375°F.
**2.** Place the soufflé in a medium-size bowl and add lemon pepper, garlic powder, and salt to taste.
**3.** Clean the mushrooms and remove the stems; reserve the stems. Melt 5 tablespoons of the butter in a small saucepan or in a microwave oven. Dip the mushroom caps in the butter and place on a baking sheet with the cavities up.
**4.** Finely mince the mushroom stems. Melt the remaining 3 tablespoons of butter in a small frying pan. Add the minced mushrooms and onion and sauté over medium heat until softened. Combine with the spinach and blend well.
**5.** Fill the mushroom caps with the spinach mixture, mounding slightly. Sprinkle with the Parmesan cheese. Bake until the filling is set and the cheese is golden, 12 to 15 minutes. Serve immediately.

"*T*he big gold and white Sèvres epergne had come down from the garret whither it went in summer when windows were open and rude winds blew; with its load of white gladioli and long trails of asparagus fern it gave a monumental festiveness to the table."

**Three O'Clock Dinner,** *Josephine Pinckney*

# IMPERIAL MUSHROOMS

This recipe combines two winners—crab imperial and fresh mushrooms.

*— Trudie Cooper Krawcheck (Mrs. Kenneth Krawcheck)*

---

*Yield: 3 dozen mushrooms*

---

*½ pound crabmeat, picked over and*
*shells discarded*
*1 tablespoon minced fresh parsley*
*1 tablespoon chopped pimiento*
*1½ teaspoons chopped, drained*
*capers*
*¼ teaspoon Dijon mustard*
*¼ teaspoon fresh lemon juice*
*½ cup mayonnaise*
*⅛ teaspoon cayenne pepper*
*½ teaspoon Old Bay Seasoning*
*Salt and freshly ground pepper, to*
*taste*
*3 dozen large fresh mushrooms,*
*cleaned and stems removed*
*Paprika, for garnish*

**1.** Preheat the oven to 375°F. Lightly grease a baking sheet.

**2.** Combine the crabmeat, parsley, pimiento, capers, mustard, lemon juice, mayonnaise, cayenne pepper, Old Bay Seasoning, and salt and pepper in a medium-size bowl and mix well.

**3.** Fill each mushroom cap with the crabmeat mixture, mounding slightly. Sprinkle with paprika. Bake on the prepared baking sheet until heated through, 8 to 10 minutes.

---

# AURELIA'S STUFFED MUSHROOMS

My aunt, Aurelia Fulton Stafford, gave me this recipe.

*— Barbara Stafford Graham (Mrs. Thomas H. Graham)*

---

*Yield: 20 servings*

---

*40 large fresh mushrooms (about 1*
*pound)*
*½ cup freshly grated Parmesan*
*cheese*
*½ cup dry bread crumbs*
*¼ cup grated onion*
*2 cloves garlic, minced*
*2 tablespoons chopped fresh parsley*
*½ teaspoon salt*
*¼ teaspoon pepper*
*½ teaspoon dried oregano leaves*
*½ cup (1 stick) butter, melted*

**1.** Preheat the oven to 350°F. Grease a baking sheet.

**2.** Clean the mushrooms and remove the stems. Chop the stems and place in a medium-size bowl with the Parmesan cheese, bread crumbs, onion, garlic, parsley, salt, pepper, and oregano. Mix well.

**3.** Place the mushroom caps on the prepared baking sheet and fill with the bread crumb mixture. Drizzle the melted butter over the mushrooms and bake until golden brown, 20 to 25 minutes. Serve hot.

# ARTICHOKE HEART FRITTERS

If you love artichokes, double the recipe, as these are habit-forming.
— *Victoria Hewitt Causey (Mrs. David Yates Causey)*

---
*Yield: 15 to 18 servings*

---

3 cans (14 ounces each) artichoke
    hearts
1 cup Italian bread crumbs
½ cup freshly grated Parmesan cheese
1 teaspoon salt
½ teaspoon pepper
3 or 4 eggs, depending on size
Oil for frying

**Garlic Butter**

1 clove garlic, minced
½ cup butter (1 stick), melted
½ teaspoon garlic salt

**1.** Drain the artichoke hearts and pat
dry with paper towels.

**2.** In a shallow bowl combine the
bread crumbs, Parmesan cheese, salt,
and pepper. In another shallow bowl
beat the eggs.
**3.** Dip each artichoke heart in the
beaten eggs and then dredge with the
bread crumb mixture. Heat enough oil
in a skillet to reach a depth of one
inch and fry the artichoke hearts until
they are golden brown, about 8 minutes.
**4.** Drain the fritters on paper towels
and place in a chafing dish. Serve hot
with the garlic butter for dipping.
**5.** To make the garlic butter, combine the garlic, melted butter, and garlic salt in a small bowl.

# SPINACH BALLS

Spinach balls are an old standby and wonderful to have on hand in the freezer.
This recipe comes from my aunt, Lillian McFetridge Wilson.
— *Susan Wilson Storen (Mrs. William Daniel Storen)*

---
*Yield: 75 spinach balls*

---

2 packages (10 ounces each) frozen
    chopped spinach
3 cups Pepperidge Farm Italian style
    stuffing, crushed
1 large onion, chopped fine
4 eggs, well beaten
½ cup (1 stick) melted butter or
    margarine
½ cup freshly grated Parmesan cheese
1¼ teaspoons garlic salt
½ teaspoon dried thyme leaves
Cayenne pepper, to taste

**1.** Preheat the oven to 325°F. Butter a
baking sheet.
**2.** Cook the spinach according to
package instructions and drain well,
squeezing out the excess water.
**3.** Place the spinach in a large bowl,
add the stuffing, onion, eggs, butter,
cheese, garlic salt, thyme, and
cayenne pepper, and mix well.
**4.** Form the mixture into ¾-inch balls
and place on the baking sheet. Bake
for 15 to 20 minutes, until golden
brown. The spinach balls may be
frozen before baking, but then will
require 25 to 30 minutes' baking time.

# SPINACH SQUARES

There are many variations of this recipe around, but I find the spinach and Monterey Jack cheese combination one of the best.

— *Joanne Gazes Ellison* (Mrs. William B. Ellison, Jr.)

---

*Yield: 24 squares*

---

4 tablespoons butter
3 eggs
1 cup unbleached all-purpose flour
1 heaping teaspoon baking powder
1 cup milk
1 tablespoon salt
White pepper, to taste
1 pound Monterey Jack cheese, grated
1 small onion, grated
2 packages (10 ounces each) frozen
    chopped spinach, thawed, drained,
    and squeezed dry

**1.** Preheat the oven to 350°F. Melt the butter in the oven in a 9 x 13-inch baking dish.
**2.** In a large bowl beat the eggs and add the flour, baking powder, milk, salt, and pepper. Mix well. Add the cheese, onion, and spinach and mix well.
**3.** Pour the mixture into the baking dish and bake for 35 minutes. Cut into small squares. Serve immediately or freeze until needed (see next page for instructions).
**4.** To reheat, place the frozen squares on a baking sheet and bake at 325°F for 12 minutes.

# HAM IN POTATO JACKETS

The success of this recipe lies in using very small potatoes and stuffing them with generous amounts of ham.

— *Kathryn Kammerling Wesson* (Mrs. Michael D. Wesson)

---

*Yield: 10 servings*

---

10 small new potatoes, with skins left
    on
¼ cup (½ stick) butter, at room
    temperature
¼ cup sour cream
1½ tablespoons prepared mustard
½ pound ham, diced
½ cup grated sharp Cheddar cheese

**1.** Preheat the oven to 350°F. Butter a 9-inch square baking dish.
**2.** In a medium-size saucepan boil the potatoes until tender in water to cover. Drain well and cool. Cut in half and scoop out approximately 2 teaspoons of potato from each half; discard or reserve for another use.
**3.** In a small bowl combine the butter, sour cream, and mustard and blend well. Place a dab of the butter mixture into the cavity of each potato half, then top with the diced ham. Sprinkle with the cheese.
**4.** Bake until the cheese bubbles, about 10 minutes. Serve hot.

Many of the hors d'oeuvres in this collection may be made ahead and frozen for later use. A good way to freeze individual morsels is to place them on a baking sheet in one layer, well separated, freeze until they are firm (two to three hours), and then package in small quantities in well-sealed plastic bags. Then you will have serving-size quantities to remove from the freezer as needed.

## CAVIAR POTATOES

These potatoes are a real crowd pleaser. They may be kept in the refrigerator for several hours before serving.

— *Janie May Clayton (Mrs. Earl Clayton)*

*Yield: 12 servings*

24 bite-size red or new potatoes
2 ounces lumpfish caviar
1 cup sour cream
1 tablespoon chopped chives

**1.** Preheat the oven to 375°F.
**2.** Place the potatoes on a baking sheet and bake for 30 minutes. Let cool.
**3.** Transfer the potatoes to a serving platter. Make a small cavity in the top of each potato and fill the cavity with lumpfish roe.
**4.** Top the roe with a dab of sour cream and garnish with the chives. Refrigerate until ready to serve.

## HOT POTATO HEARTIES

Men love these "hearties." The warm potatoes are served with small bowls of your choice of dips or toppings; I have listed just a few possibilities.

— *Elizabeth Wayne Settle*

*Yield: 10 servings*

10 small new potatoes, with skins
    left on
Melted butter
Sour cream and chives
Crumbled bacon
Grated cheese

**1.** In a medium-size saucepan boil the new potatoes in water to cover until just tender, 10 to 15 minutes. Drain and cut in half.
**2.** Serve on a heated plate or in a chafing dish over hot water. Accompany with small bowls of any or all of the following: melted butter, sour cream and chives, crumbled bacon, grated cheese.

# ZUCCHINI ROUNDS

The mayonnaise-and-cheese mixture may also be put on pieces of party rye and broiled, but the zucchini base makes a nice difference.

*— Diane Simms Marshall (Mrs. Fields D. Marshall)*

---
*Yield: 40 rounds*
---

*2 medium zucchini (about 1 pound)*
*½ cup freshly grated Parmesan cheese*
*½ cup mayonnaise*
*½ teaspoon dried basil leaves*

**1.** Preheat the broiler.
**2.** Slice the zucchini into approximately 40 ¼-inch rounds.
**3.** In a small bowl combine the Parmesan cheese, mayonnaise, and basil and mix well. Spread each zucchini round with the mayonnaise mixture. Place the rounds on a baking sheet.
**4.** Broil until tops are golden brown, about 1 minute. Serve immediately.

*A*s much a refuge as a party is the occasion when homeowners whose houses are "on tour" meet for food and drink to kill time and stay out of the way. The spring Festival of Houses and Gardens is sponsored by Historic Charleston Foundation, and the fall Candlelight Tours are a project of The Preservation Society.

# MARINATED CHICKEN WINGS

Arrange these wings on a large platter, and watch them disappear. Be sure to have plenty of napkins available.

*— Carol Adams Jackson*

---
*Yield: 6 to 10 servings*
---

*3 pounds chicken wings*
*½ pound dark brown sugar*
*1 cup soy sauce*
*2 tablespoons garlic powder*

**1.** Cut off and discard the tip of each wing, then cut the rest of the wing into two pieces. Place in a large shallow baking pan.
**2.** In a medium-size bowl combine the brown sugar, soy sauce, and garlic powder, and mix well. Pour the mixture over the chicken wings, cover, and refrigerate for 24 hours.
**3.** Preheat the oven to 350°F.
**4.** Bake the chicken for 20 minutes in the marinade. Drain off the marinade and place the wings on a large baking sheet.
**5.** Just before serving, preheat the broiler, broil the wings for 5 minutes, turn, and broil for an additional 5 minutes or until they reach the desired crispness. Serve hot.

# MICROWAVE MARINATED WATER CHESTNUTS

This recipe is a favorite of Amy Irick, a former member of our League who has transferred to Atlanta.

— *Anne Farish (Merit) Justice*

---
### Yield: 4 servings
---

1 can (8 ounces) water chestnuts
½ cup soy sauce
¼ cup brown sugar
7 slices bacon, cut in thirds
1 large green bell pepper, seeded and
    cut in ¾-inch squares
Wooden toothpicks

**1.** Drain the water chestnuts and prick each one several times with a fork.
**2.** Place the water chestnuts in a small bowl and pour over the soy sauce. Cover and let marinate for 30 minutes.
**3.** Wrap a piece of bacon around each water chestnut, placing a square of green bell pepper between the water chestnut and the bacon. Secure with a toothpick.
**4.** Place the water chestnuts on a microwave broiling pan, sprinkle with the brown sugar, and microwave on full power for 2½ minutes. Turn the water chestnuts and continue to microwave for an additional 2½ minutes. Drain on paper toweling and serve hot.

---

# SWEET POTATO BALLS

These are particularly good with nonalcoholic drinks—hot cider on a chilly day, for instance. To put them firmly into the sweets category, serve with a caramel sauce for dipping.

— *Irven Myer Stevenson (Mrs. Thomas C. Stevenson III)*

---
### Yield: 3 dozen balls
---

3 cups cooked and mashed sweet
    potatoes
3 tablespoons melted butter
½ cup brown sugar
¾ cup broken pecans
1 teaspoon vanilla
2 tablespoons sherry or bourbon
Dash of cinnamon
1 egg
Crushed cornflakes cereal

**1.** Preheat the oven to 325°F. Lightly butter a baking sheet.
**2.** Place the sweet potatoes in a large bowl. Add the butter, brown sugar, pecans, vanilla, sherry, and cinnamon and mix well. Beat in the egg.
**3.** Form the mixture into bite-size balls and roll in the crushed cornflakes.
**4.** Place the sweet potato balls on the prepared baking sheet and bake for about 20 minutes. Serve with toothpicks.

# SPICY CHICKEN-WING DRUMETTES

These wings are good as is, or they may be served with a variety of dipping sauces. Two accompaniments I like to use are a sweet and sour sauce or a mixture of pepper flakes and salt.

— *Kathryn Jarvis Nelson* (*Mrs. Robert P. Nelson, Jr.*)

*Yield: 6 to 10 servings*

3 pounds chicken wing drumettes
   (the larger joint of the chicken
   wing)
¼ cup fresh citrus juice (lime, lemon,
   or orange)
2 cloves garlic, minced
1 tablespoon brown sugar
¼ cup vegetable oil
1 teaspoon salt
2 teaspoons dried red peppers,
   minced
1 cup peanuts
1 cup bread crumbs

**1.** Using a sharp knife, scrape the chicken meat toward the joint end of each drumette, to form a ball.

**2.** In a large bowl, combine the citrus juice, garlic, brown sugar, vegetable oil, salt, and peppers and mix well. Add the drumettes, stir to cover with the marinade, and marinate, covered, for 2 hours at room temperature or overnight in the refrigerator.

**3.** Preheat the oven to 450°F.

**4.** Place the peanuts in the bowl of a food processor and process until fine. Transfer the peanuts to a medium-size bowl, add the bread crumbs and salt to taste, and mix well.

**5.** Pour the crumb mixture onto a sheet of waxed paper and coat the drumettes with the crumbs. Place on a shallow rack in a baking pan and bake for 30 minutes, turning once. Serve hot.

### GARDEN PARTY

". . . The silver éperne's filled with flowers,
*Why she must have worked for hours!*
Delicious dainties — many choices.
And buzzing all around
The cheerful sound
Of Charleston voices."

**Elizabeth Verner Hamilton,**
*from* **Tall Houses, Tradd Street Press**

# CHAFING DISH CHICKEN

Since the pastry shells may be picked up with the fingers, it is important to cut the ingredients for the chicken filling into very small pieces.
— *Neyle Jervey Wannamaker* (Mrs. L. Banks Wannamaker III)

*Yield: 20 to 25 servings*

2 tablespoons butter or margarine
½ large onion, chopped
2 teaspoons curry powder
¼ cup diced, peeled apple
1 cup diced celery
½ cup diced green bell pepper
3 tablespoons unbleached
    all-purpose flour
1½ cups milk
Dash of hot sauce
1 tablespoon catsup
Salt and freshly ground pepper, to
    taste
4 cups diced cooked chicken
¼ cup chopped chutney, or to taste
¼ cup chopped peanuts, or to taste
Miniature pastry shells

**1.** Place the butter and onions in a large saucepan with a heavy bottom and sauté the onions over low heat until they are brown, about 10 minutes.

**2.** Add the curry powder, apple, celery, and green bell pepper and cook until the vegetables are tender, about 10 minutes.

**3.** In a small bowl combine the flour and milk to make a paste. Add the paste to the saucepan and cook, stirring constantly, for 3 to 5 minutes, until the mixture begins to thicken. Remove from the heat.

**4.** Season the mixture with hot sauce, catsup, and salt and pepper. Add the chicken, chutney, and peanuts and stir to combine. Reheat the mixture over low heat if necessary. Serve warm in a chafing dish with miniature pastry shells.

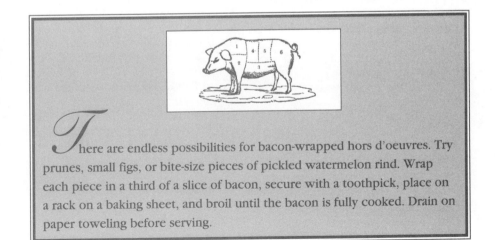

*T*here are endless possibilities for bacon-wrapped hors d'oeuvres. Try prunes, small figs, or bite-size pieces of pickled watermelon rind. Wrap each piece in a third of a slice of bacon, secure with a toothpick, place on a rack on a baking sheet, and broil until the bacon is fully cooked. Drain on paper toweling before serving.

# GRILLED ORIENTAL CHICKEN

I use this versatile dish for cocktail parties or buffet suppers, and the marinade works just as well for pork tenderloin.

*— Virginia Rossignol Lachicotte*

---

*Yield: 12 to 15 servings*

---

⅔ cup rice vinegar
2½ cups water
½ cup sugar
¼ cup plum sauce
2 tablespoons soy sauce
1 tablespoon grated fresh ginger
1 clove garlic
¾ teaspoon vegetable oil
1½ pounds boneless, skinless chicken
    breasts, cut into bite-size pieces
Bamboo skewers

**1.** Make the marinade: In a medium-size saucepan heat the vinegar, water, and sugar, stirring until the sugar dissolves. Remove the pan from the heat. Add the plum sauce, soy sauce, ginger, garlic, and oil and let cool.
**2.** Thread the chicken pieces on bamboo skewers and lay the skewers in a rectangular baking dish. Pour half the marinade over the skewers and refrigerate for two hours or more. Reserve the rest of the marinade.
**3.** Preheat the broiler or prepare the grill.
**4.** Broil or grill the chicken, turning once, until it is just done, about 10 minutes.
**5.** Remove the chicken from the skewers and place in a chafing dish. Heat the reserved marinade and pour over the chicken. Serve with toothpicks.

# BACON ROLL-UPS

These are great to make ahead and store in the freezer. I pack them in lots of twelve in Ziploc bags—ready to pull out and bake for unexpected guests.

*— Mary-Jo Mull Morgan*
*(Mrs. Milt E. Morgan)*

---

*Yield: 10 to 12 servings*

---

¼ cup (½ stick) butter or margarine
½ cup water
1½ cups herb stuffing mix
1 egg, slightly beaten
¼ pound hot sausage
⅔ pound bacon
Wooden toothpicks

**1.** Place the butter and water in a medium-size saucepan and heat over low heat until the butter has melted. (Or place the butter and water in a large bowl and melt the butter in a microwave oven.)
**2.** Remove the pan from the heat and stir in the stuffing mix. Add the egg and sausage and blend thoroughly. Chill the mixture for at least 2 hours, to make it easier to handle.
**3.** Preheat the oven to 375°F.
**4.** Shape the sausage mixture into small oblongs about the size of an unshelled pecan. Cut the bacon slices into thirds. Wrap a piece of bacon around each sausage oblong and secure with a wooden toothpick.
**5.** Place the frozen roll-ups on a baking pan with a rack and bake for 25 minutes, turning after 15 minutes. Drain on paper toweling and serve hot. (Bake frozen roll-ups for a total of 35 minutes.)

# CARLSON SWEDISH MEATBALLS

Although these tasty meatballs may be served with various dipping sauces, lingonberries in sauce is the traditional Scandinavian accompaniment. The recipe can be doubled or tripled quite successfully.

— *Mary Buckingham Carlson* (Mrs. Leif M. Carlson)

### Yield: 25 to 30 meatballs

½ cup plain bread crumbs
½ cup half-and-half
¼ pound ground veal
¼ pound lean ground pork
½ pound ground round
1 egg, beaten
½ cup milk
2 tablespoons minced onion
½ teaspoon freshly ground pepper
¼ teaspoon ground allspice
Salt, to taste
Flour
Vegetable shortening, for frying

**1.** Soak the bread crumbs in the half-and-half in a large bowl.
**2.** Combine the pork, veal, and beef and grind together twice using a food processor or meat grinder (or ask the butcher to do it). Add the ground meat, egg, milk, onion, pepper, allspice, and salt to the bread crumb mixture and combine well.
**3.** Form the mixture into balls about 1 inch in diameter and dredge lightly in flour.
**4.** Heat vegetable shortening in a frying pan over medium heat, add the meatballs in a single layer, and fry until light brown.
**5.** Drain the meatballs well and serve hot in a chafing dish, accompanied by lingonberries in sauce or other dipping sauces.

## ONION BREAD BITES

The ingredients in these morsels are sure winners; the quantities are up to you.

Thin slices white or rye bread,
    crusts removed
Chopped onions
Freshly grated Parmesan
    cheese
Butter

Cut the bread slices into squares. Top each square with chopped onions and a dab of butter. Sprinkle with grated cheese and broil until brown.

# SWEET AND SOUR SAUSAGE BALLS

The sausage balls freeze well, even combined with the sauce. Allow them to thaw before reheating.

*— Lynn Baughman Asnip (Mrs. Timothy Asnip)*

*Yield: 12 servings*

**Sausage Balls**

1 ½ pounds ground lean pork
1 pound ground cooked ham
2 cups cracker crumbs
2 eggs, well beaten
1 cup milk
Salt, to taste
Seasoned salt, to taste
1 teaspoon minced onion

**Sweet and Sour Sauce**

1 ¼ cups packed brown sugar
1 ½ teaspoons dry mustard
½ cup cider vinegar
½ cup hot water
¼ cup golden raisins

**1.** Preheat the oven to 350°F.
**2.** Make the sausage balls: Place the pork and ham in a large bowl and add the cracker crumbs, eggs, milk, salt, seasoned salt, and onion. Mix well. Using a melon baller, shape into balls. Place on a baking sheet with sides and bake for 10 minutes. Drain on paper toweling.
**3.** Make the sauce: Combine all the ingredients in a medium-size bowl.
**4.** Place the cooked sausage balls in a 9 x 13-inch baking dish, pour over the sauce, and bake at 350°F for 15 minutes. To serve, transfer the sausage balls and sauce to a chafing dish.

# CAJUN SMOKED SAUSAGE WITH MUSTARD DIP

The mustard dip served with these sausages will keep for months in the refrigerator and is a nice alternative to Dijon.

*— Lodema Richardson Adams*

*Yield: 15 to 20 servings*

½ cup dry mustard
½ cup distilled white vinegar
1 egg, beaten
1 cup sugar
3 pounds smoked sausages
Cajun seasoning
Romaine, for garnish

**1.** Make the mustard dip: In a medium-size bowl combine the dry mustard and vinegar and mix slowly. Let stand for 3 hours, stirring often.
**2.** Add the beaten egg and sugar to the mixture and stir. Transfer to a medium-size saucepan with a heavy bottom and cook over low heat, stirring frequently, until the mixture thickens. Let cool.
**3.** Preheat the oven to 425°F.
**4.** Cut the sausages into bite-size pieces. Place in a jelly-roll pan and sprinkle with the Cajun seasoning. Bake for 5 minutes.
**5.** Drain the sausage on paper toweling and place in a bowl lined with romaine lettuce. Serve with the mustard dip and toothpicks.

# COCKTAIL MEATBALLS FOR A CROWD

Try these when you need lots of a sure thing.

*— Susanne Riley Emge (Mrs. N. Keith Emge)*

### *Yield: 250 meatballs*

**Sauce**

*3 cups catsup*
*2 cups water*
*1 cup cider vinegar*
*½ cup light brown sugar*
*¼ cup chopped onion*
*3 tablespoons Worcestershire*
*    sauce*
*2 tablespoons salt*
*4 teaspoons dry mustard*
*1 teaspoon freshly ground pepper*
*12 drops Tabasco sauce*

**Meatballs**

*3 pounds ground beef*
*3 cups dried bread crumbs*
*3 teaspoons salt*
*1 teaspoon freshly ground pepper*
*2 tablespoons bottled horseradish*
*8 eggs, beaten*
*12 drops Tabasco sauce*
*6 tablespoons finely chopped onion*
*Oil for frying*

**1.** Make the sauce: Place all the ingredients in a large saucepan, bring to a boil, reduce the heat, and simmer for about 30 minutes.

**2.** Make the meatballs: In a large bowl combine the ground beef, bread crumbs, salt, and pepper.

**3.** In a small bowl combine the horseradish, eggs, Tabasco, and onion and mix well. Add to the meat mixture and mix well.

**4.** Roll the meat mixture into bite-size balls.

**5.** Preheat the oven to 250°F.

**6.** Brown the meatballs in a large frying pan or a deep fryer (do not overcook).

**7.** Drain the meatballs, transfer to one or two large flameproof casseroles or Dutch ovens, pour the sauce over, and simmer the meatballs in the sauce over low heat for 15 minutes.

**8.** Place the casseroles in the oven and bake, covered, for 2 to 2½ hours. Serve hot in a chafing dish.

---

"Iris has found the Singapore Bird cups and put three of them on the table with saucers and spoons, and sugar in the sugarbowl, where there has been no sugar for months; Alice usually spoons it out of the bag. Maybe that is why they seem to like each other, fussing over the teakettle and tea bags as if the tea were not real, the cups a tea set — those tiny gold-rimmed cups that require little girls to pinch the handles between their fingertips and take prissy lip-pursing sips of fake tea . . ."

**Dreams of Sleep,** *Josephine Humphreys*

# WILD DOVES

This recipe was developed at the Little House on Halidon Hill Plantation by a conglomeration of "cooks in the kitchen."

— *Jane Thompson Jilich* (Mrs. Jiri Jilich)

---

*Yield: 12 servings*

½ *cup olive oil, or to coat*
¼ *cup fresh lemon juice*
*Minced zest of 1 lemon*
*12 cloves garlic, sliced*
*5 or 6 sprigs fresh thyme, or 1
   teaspoon dried thyme leaves*
*1 teaspoon salt*
*1 teaspoon whole peppercorns*
*12 wild dove breasts*
*12 celery sticks, each 2 inches long*
*12 scallions (green onions), each 2
   inches long*
*6 slices bacon, cut in half*
*wooden toothpicks*

**1.** In a large bowl combine the olive oil, lemon juice, lemon zest, half of the garlic, thyme, salt, and peppercorns. Add the dove breasts and stir to coat. Let marinate for ½ hour or up to 1½ hours.

**2.** Stuff the cavity of each dove breast with a celery stick, an onion stick, and some of the remaining garlic. Wrap a piece of bacon around each breast and secure with a wooden toothpick.

**3.** Grill the breasts over very hot coals for 5 minutes. Serve hot.

---

# BOURBON BARBECUED FRANKS

My children love these. We always serve them at our Christmas drop-in.

— *Libby Shackelford Metzler* (Mrs. Timothy Metzler)

---

*Yield: 10 to 12 servings*

*1 tablespoon butter*
*2 tablespoons minced onion*
½ *cup catsup*
*1 cup currant jelly*
¾ *cup bourbon*
*1 pound cocktail franks, or standard
   frankfurters cut into bite-size
   pieces*

**1.** Melt the butter in a medium-size saucepan with a heavy bottom, add the onion, and sauté until the onion is translucent but not brown.

**2.** In a medium-size bowl, combine the catsup, jelly, and bourbon and mix well. Add to the onions and stir to combine.

**3.** Add the franks to the sauce. Simmer, uncovered, until the sauce begins to glaze, approximately 25 minutes, stirring occasionally. Serve in a chafing dish, with toothpicks.

# Dad's Grilled Dove Breasts

This is my father's traditional Thanksgiving night hors d'oeuvre. There is a dove shoot the day before Thanksgiving, and the booty is cleaned, prepared, and served the next day at the cabin. The quantities of ingredients depend on the success of the shoot.

*— Margaret M. Bristow*

*Fresh wild dove breasts*
*Bacon slices, cut in thirds*
*Italian salad dressing*
*Wooden toothpicks*

**1.** Using a sharp knife, fillet each side of the dove breast off the bone. Wrap each breast piece with a piece of bacon. Secure with a toothpick.
**2.** Place the wrapped breasts in a shallow baking pan and pour over the salad dressing. Cover and refrigerate overnight.
**3.** Prepare coals for grilling.
**4.** Remove the breasts from the marinade and place in a grill basket. Grill over hot coals until the bacon is done. Serve immediately.

### Cheesey Shoestring Potatoes

*1 can (4 ounces) shoestring*
  *potatoes*
*⅓ cup freshly grated Parmesan*
  *cheese*

Preheat the oven to 450°F. Spread the potatoes evenly on a baking sheet. Sprinkle with the cheese and bake for 4 minutes. Serve immediately.

*Jane Stoney Cook*
*(Mrs. Charles Cook IV)*

"It is said of Charleston ladies that their names appear in Charleston newspapers only three times in their lives — when they are born, when they are married, and when they die. No social function of importance except a wedding or a funeral is ever mentioned in any of its newspapers. You look in vain in their columns for the doings of names of great tradition. The esoteric cooking, the stately dinner, are therefore kept close and quiet. It is for this reason, though you have heard about the restaurants of New Orleans, you have heard little of cooking in Charleston . . ."

**Two Hundred Years of Charleston Cooking,**
*Blanche Rhett and Lettie Gay*

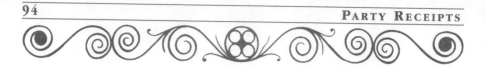

# BILLY'S MARINATED VENISON STRIPS

The marinade in this recipe, created by my husband, is also delicious for whole tenderloins of beef, pork, or venison. Just increase the marinating time to 4 to 6 hours.

*— Elizabeth Hagood Craver (Mrs. William E. Craver III)*

### Yield: 25 skewers

2 cans (10½ ounces each) beef
   consommé
¾ cup vegetable oil
½ cup soy sauce
½ cup Worcestershire sauce
1 clove garlic, minced
1 teaspoon sugar
½ teaspoon salt
2 venison tenderloins
Freshly ground pepper, to taste
Bamboo skewers

**1.** In a large bowl combine the consommé, oil, soy sauce, Worcestershire, garlic, sugar, and salt. Set aside.
**2.** Cut the venison into strips 1 inch wide, ¼ inch thick, and 2 to 3 inches long. Thread the strips onto skewers and place in the marinade; refrigerate for 2 to 3 hours.
**3.** Prepare coals for grilling.
**4.** Grill the venison for 1 to 2 minutes over hot coals (the strips should be rare). Sprinkle on pepper to taste. Serve with horseradish sauce.

# LOWCOUNTRY
# SHRIMP·CRAB
## AND OTHER
# SEAFOODS

# MOTHER'S COCKTAIL SHRIMP

A pretty presentation for this recipe is to put the shrimp in a large glass bowl set on a tray. Then surround the bowl with waxy leaves and whole lemons and limes.

— *Helen Garvin Ingle* (Mrs. J. Addison Ingle)

*Yield: 15 to 20 servings*

1¼ cups vegetable oil
¾ cup cider vinegar
8 bay leaves
2 tablespoons capers, including their juice
1½ teaspoons celery seed
Salt and freshly ground pepper, to taste
3 pounds cooked shrimp, peeled and deveined
2 medium onions, thinly sliced
2 limes, thinly sliced

**1.** Combine the vegetable oil, vinegar, bay leaves, capers, celery seed, and salt and pepper in a large bowl and mix well.

**2.** Add the shrimp, onions, and limes and toss to coat with the marinade. Chill for several hours or overnight. Drain off the marinade, remove the bay leaves, and transfer the shrimp to a serving dish. Pass with toothpicks.

"*M*ost receipts call for cooked or boiled shrimp. To cook shrimp: Wash the shrimp thoroughly and boil 4 or 5 minutes in a covered pot, using just enough salted water to cover them. As soon as they are cool, they are 'picked' or peeled. Large shrimp are cooked longer; the black line removed and the shrimp cut into pieces. Black pepper, celery, onion, or paprika can be boiled with shrimp for added flavor. Beer is sometimes substituted for water in cooking shrimp. To pick a shrimp any local person will tell you to 'pull, peel, pinch' — you pull off the heads, peel the shell off the body, and pinch the shrimp out of the tail."

***From* Charleston Receipts**

## SHRIMP IN MUSTARD SAUCE

Depending on the amount of red pepper flakes used, this can be a very spicy hors d'oeuvre. The recipe calls for marinating the shrimp for twenty-four hours, but they are even better when allowed to marinate for several days.

— *Stephanie Snowden Atkinson (Mrs. Bert Connor Atkinson)*

*Yield: 8 to 10 servings*

1½ pounds shrimp, peeled and
   deveined
¼ cup finely chopped parsley
¼ cup finely chopped onion
1 cup finely chopped celery
¼ cup tarragon vinegar
¼ cup white wine vinegar
½ cup olive oil
3 tablespoons Dijon mustard
1 to 2 teaspoons crushed red pepper
   flakes, to taste
2 teaspoons salt
Freshly ground pepper, to taste

1. Place the shrimp in a pot of boiling salted water and cook only until they begin to curl into a C. Drain and place in a large bowl that has a tight-fitting lid.
2. Combine the parsley, onion, celery, vinegars, olive oil, mustard, red pepper flakes, salt, and pepper in a medium-size bowl and mix well. Pour over the shrimp.
3. Cover the shrimp and refrigerate for at least 24 hours. Stir the mixture every several hours.
4. Drain off the marinade and serve the shrimp in a shallow dish, accompanied by cocktail forks or toothpicks.

## SHRIMP AND ARTICHOKE MARINADE

This is the first thing to go at all my cocktail parties. Simply the best!

— *M. Angela Askins*

*Yield: 12 to 15 servings*

2 pounds medium shrimp, cooked,
   peeled, and deveined
2 cans (14 ounces each) artichoke
   hearts
15 to 20 small mushrooms
¾ cup olive oil
¼ cup tarragon vinegar
2 tablespoons water
2 cloves garlic, crushed
1 teaspoon sugar
½ teaspoon freshly ground pepper
1½ teaspoons salt
1½ teaspoons dry mustard

1. Combine the shrimp, artichokes, and mushrooms in a large bowl or a large container with a lid that seals.
2. Combine the olive oil, vinegar, water, garlic, sugar, pepper, salt, and mustard in a jar with a lid. Tightly close the lid and shake the jar. Pour the mixture over the shrimp, artichokes, and mushrooms, cover tightly, and refrigerate overnight. Stir two or three times during the marinating process.
3. Drain off the marinade, place the shrimp in a serving bowl, and pass with toothpicks.

# SHRIMP WADMALAW

The original recipe comes from Jilich's on East Bay Restaurant; I have modified it for cocktail parties.

— *Jane Thompson Jilich*
*(Mrs. Jiri Jilich)*

---

*Yield: 30 servings*

---

¾ cup white wine
2 tablespoons chopped shallots
1 tablespoon sugar
¾ cup Dijon mustard
1 cup vegetable oil
1 cup olive oil
2 tablespoons sherry
Salt and freshly ground pepper, to
    taste
1 teaspoon dried dill weed
90 snow peas, blanched (about 1¼
    pounds)
90 medium shrimp (3 to 4 pounds),
    cooked, peeled, and deveined, with
    tails left on
Toothpicks

**1.** Make the sauce: Combine the wine, shallots, sugar, mustard, oils, sherry, salt and pepper, and dill weed in the bowl of a food processor. Process until combined. Refrigerate while you assemble the shrimp and snow peas.
**2.** Wrap one of the snow peas around each of the shrimp and secure with a toothpick.
**3.** Arrange the shrimp on a platter, leaving room in the center for a bowl of the sauce, for dipping.

# SHRIMP PÂTÉ

I make the pâté in a fish mold and decorate it with sliced almonds for scales and an olive slice for the eye.

— *Catherine Gazes*

---

*Yield: 10 servings*

---

3 ounces cream cheese, at room
    temperature
2 tablespoons mayonnaise
3 to 6 tablespoons butter, melted
1 small onion, minced
¼ cup minced celery
Juice of 1 lemon
Dry mustard, to taste
Salt and freshly ground pepper, to
    taste
Garlic salt, to taste
2 tablespoons brandy or sherry
1 pound shrimp, cooked, peeled,
    deveined, and mashed

**1.** Oil a 1-quart fish mold or other 1-quart mold.
**2.** Place the cream cheese in a shallow medium-size bowl, add the mayonnaise and melted butter, and beat well.
**3.** Add the onion, celery, lemon juice, mustard, salt and pepper, garlic salt, brandy, and shrimp and use a fork to blend well. Place the mixture in the prepared mold and refrigerate for 12 to 24 hours. (The pâté may also be frozen.)

# SHRIMP MOLD

If you have a shrimp mold, by all means use it for this recipe!
— *Ferdinan Stevenson Dodds* (Mrs. William Grandby Dodds)

---

*Yield: 15 to 20 servings*

---

1 pound cooked, peeled, and
   deveined small shrimp
1 cup finely chopped celery
1 medium onion, finely chopped
1 cup mayonnaise
⅛ teaspoon seasoned salt
⅛ teaspoon salt
3 drops Tabasco sauce
2 teaspoons fresh lemon juice
1 can (10¾ ounces) condensed
   tomato soup, undiluted
8 ounces cream cheese
1½ tablespoons unflavored gelatin
¼ cup cold water

**1.** Oil a 1-quart mold, preferably a shrimp mold.

**2.** Combine the shrimp, celery, onion, and mayonnaise in a large bowl. Add the seasoned salt, salt, Tabasco, and lemon juice and toss to combine.

**3.** Heat the soup in a medium-size saucepan over very low heat. Add the cream cheese and stir until it is melted.

**4.** Place the gelatin and water in a medium-size bowl and stir to dissolve the gelatin. Pour the tomato and cream cheese mixture into the gelatin and mix well.

**5.** Fold the gelatin mixture into the shrimp mixture. Pour into the prepared mold and refrigerate overnight. Unmold and serve with crackers.

# MOM'S CRAB MOLD

This recipe is a favorite from our times at Pawley's Island. We serve the mold on the porch, having caught the crabs in the creek nearby.
— *Anne Farish (Merit) Justice*

---

*Yield: 20 servings*

---

1 envelope unflavored gelatin
2 tablespoons water
½ cup undiluted condensed cream of
   mushroom soup
8 ounces cream cheese, at room
   temperature
1 small onion, grated
1½ cups crabmeat, picked over and
   shells discarded
½ cup finely chopped celery
½ cup mayonnaise

**1.** Oil a 1-quart mold.

**2.** Place the gelatin and water in a small bowl and stir to dissolve the gelatin.

**3.** Heat the soup in a medium-size saucepan. Stir in the gelatin, cream cheese, onion, crabmeat, celery, and mayonnaise and blend well. Cook, stirring constantly, until the cheese has melted.

**4.** Pour the mixture into the prepared mold, cool, and refrigerate until set, at least 2 hours. Unmold and serve with crackers.

# TUNA ANTIPASTO

This appetizer gets better the longer it sits. It should be made well ahead and will keep for a number of weeks in the refrigerator.

*— Dolores Danby James (Mrs. John M. James)*

### Yield: 6 cups

3 carrots, thinly sliced
3 large onions, chopped
3 green bell peppers, chopped
1 cup olive oil
1 can (8 ounces) tomato sauce
1 teaspoon red wine vinegar
1 bottle (20 ounces) catsup
2 teaspoons Worcestershire sauce
4 sweet pickles, chopped
2 cans (3 ounces each) mushroom
   pieces, drained
3 cans (6⅛ ounces each) white tuna,
   drained
4 bay leaves
8 to 12 peppercorns
Salt, to taste

**1.** Steam the carrots until barely tender, about 5 minutes. Set aside.
**2.** Sauté the onion and green bell pepper in the olive oil in a frying pan over low heat until the vegetables are just tender, about 5 minutes. Add the tomato sauce, vinegar, catsup, and Worcestershire sauce. Cook over low heat for 3 minutes.
**3.** Add the pickles and mushrooms and cook for 3 more minutes. Add the tuna, carrots, bay leaves, peppercorns, and salt and cook for 15 minutes. Cool and place in a jar or airtight container and refrigerate until ready to serve.
**4.** Before serving, remove the bay leaves and peppercorns. Serve in a bowl, surrounded by crackers.

## CHARLOTTE'S BROILED SOFT SHELL CRABS

*(From her San Domingan Grandmother)*

Lay crabs in shallow baking pan, tucking claws close to body. Put a teaspoon of butter on each crab; put under broiler for ten minutes; then in top oven for ten minutes. If lemon juice is liked, pour over ½ cup to each dozen crabs before cooking—use no seasoning. Salt in crabs and butter is sufficient. Can be served on toast and garnished with parsley and lemon slices.

*Mrs. W. Turner Logan, Sr. (Louise Lesesne),*
*from* **Charleston Receipts**

## SHARK BITES

Be creative with this recipe. It can be made with as much or as little fish as you need, and the marinade and tartar sauce can be doubled or tripled accordingly.

— *Courteney Tucker*

---

*Yield: 4 to 6 servings*

---

1 pound mako shark, cut in bite-size pieces
Toothpicks

**Marinade**

½ cup olive oil
¼ cup soy sauce
Juice of 1 lemon
Dash of sesame oil
¼ cup catsup
1 clove garlic, pressed
Dash of salt and pepper
Dash of Tabasco sauce and Worcestershire sauce

**Tartar Sauce** (¾ cup)

½ cup mayonnaise
⅓ cup sweet pickles, chopped
Juice of ½ lemon

**1.** Make the marinade: Combine all the ingredients in a nonmetallic bowl. Add the shark cubes and let marinate for 8 to 10 hours.
**2.** Make the tartar sauce: Combine all the ingredients in a small bowl, cover, and refrigerate until ready to serve.
**3.** Preheat the broiler. Grease a baking sheet.
**4.** Place the marinated shark cubes on the prepared baking sheet and broil until the fish flakes easily with a fork, about 4 minutes.
**5.** Place a toothpick in the center of each shark bite and serve hot, with tartar sauce.

## SEVICHE

Seviche need not be made just with scallops. Try my husband's version, and serve it in a glass bowl, surrounded by crackers.

— *Susanna Wierman Prause*
*(Mrs. W. Kent Prause III)*

---

*Yield: 10 servings*

---

2 pounds fresh (not frozen) firm-fleshed fish (bass, trout, flounder), cut in bite-size pieces
1 large ripe tomato, peeled, seeded, and chopped
1 medium onion, chopped
1 medium green bell pepper, chopped
1 tablespoon olive oil
Juice of 2 limes
3 dashes Tabasco sauce
⅛ teaspoon dried oregano leaves
⅛ teaspoon dried basil leaves
Garlic salt, to taste
Freshly ground black pepper, to taste
⅓ cup chopped fresh parsley

Combine all the ingredients in a large glass bowl, cover, and chill from 2 hours to overnight.

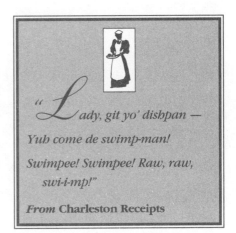

"*Lady, git yo' dishpan —*

*Yuh come de swimp-man!*

*Swimpee! Swimpee! Raw, raw, swi-i-mp!*"

**From Charleston Receipts**

# ANNANDALE BARBECUED SHRIMP

Annandale Plantation is north of Charleston, near the delta of the Santee River. These shrimp make a quick appetizer for an outdoor gathering. Always a success, they never make it to a plate!

— *Margaret Reeves Drury (Mrs. Andrew S. Drury, Jr.)*

---

### Yield: 4 servings

½ cup soy sauce
1 cup olive oil
2 cloves garlic, crushed
1 pound shrimp, peeled but with tails
    left on

**1.** Combine the soy sauce, olive oil, and garlic in a medium-size bowl. Add the shrimp, toss to coat, and refrigerate for at least an hour or as long as overnight.
**2.** Prepare coals for grilling.
**3.** Remove the shrimp from the marinade and grill, turning once, until tender, about 2 minutes per side.

"*A*t the wharf, across the narrow street, the fishermen were discharging strings of gleaming whiting and porgy. Vegetable sloops, blowing up from the Sea Islands, with patched and tawny sails, broke the flat cobalt of the inner harbor with the cross-wash of their creamy wakes."

Porgy, *Du Bose Heyward*

---

# ANGIE'S SHRIMP BITES

My grandmother, Mrs. Archibald Baker, frequently served this hors d'oeuvre to her guests.

— *Robin Allen Rodenberg (Mrs. E. Adolph Rodenberg III)*

---

### Yield: 20 shrimp bites

¼ cup catsup
¼ cup mayonnaise
¼ cup grated sharp Cheddar cheese
5 slices white bread, crusts removed
    and cut in quarters
20 cooked medium-size shrimp,
    peeled and deveined

**1.** Preheat the broiler.
**2.** Mix together the catsup, mayonnaise, and cheese in a small bowl.
**3.** Place the bread squares on an ungreased baking sheet and broil until light golden brown, about 2 minutes (watch carefully).
**4.** Remove the toasts from the oven, turn over each square, and place 1 shrimp on the untoasted side. Spoon 1 teaspoon of the cheese mixture on top of each shrimp and broil until the sauce bubbles, about 2 minutes.

# SHRIMP TARTS

I have served these on numerous occasions, and they have always been a big hit. The filled tarts can be frozen for later use.

— *Elizabeth Gantt Castles* (Mrs. Charles Guy Castles III)

---

*Yield: 24 tarts*

---

### Pastry

*1 cup plus 2 tablespoons unbleached all-purpose flour*
*¼ teaspoon salt*
*2 tablespoons freshly grated Parmesan cheese*
*½ cup (1 stick) butter or margarine, cut in pieces*
*1 small egg, lightly beaten*

### Filling

*½ cup mashed, cooked, peeled, and deveined shrimp*
*1 teaspoon Dijon mustard*
*1 tablespoon mayonnaise*
*¼ teaspoon grated onion*
*¼ teaspoon fresh lemon juice*
*Salt and freshly ground pepper, to taste*
*¼ teaspoon dried tarragon leaves*

**1.** Make the pastry: Place the flour, salt, and cheese in a medium-size bowl. Add the butter and cut in with a pastry blender or two knives, until the mixture resembles coarse bread crumbs.

**2.** Add the egg and combine well. Shape into a ball and chill for 3 to 4 hours.

**3.** Preheat the oven to 450°F.

**4.** Form the dough into balls the size of large marbles. Using your thumbs, press each ball into the cup of a bite-size muffin pan. Bake for 5 minutes, then reduce the oven temperature to 400°F and bake until golden, 8 to 10 minutes (watch carefully). Cool and remove from the pan.

**5.** Make the filling: Place the mashed shrimp in a medium-size bowl. Add the mustard and mayonnaise (just enough to hold the mixture together), grated onion, lemon juice, salt and pepper, and tarragon. Stir to combine.

**6.** Assemble: Fill 24 of the tart shells with a teaspoonful of the filling. Warm before serving.

---

"The Sea Coast is full of Islands, Sounds, Bays, Rivers, and Creeks, which are well stored with great variety of Excellent Fish: the most common whereof are, Bass, Drum, Whitings, Trouts, Herrings, Mullets, Rocks, Sturgeons, Shads, Sheepheads, Plaice, Flounders, small Turtel, Crabs, Oysters, Muscles, Cockles, Shrimps, &c."

**A Description of South Carolina,** *London, 1761*

# MRS. QUEENY'S CRABMEAT RAREBIT

"Mrs. Queeny" is my mother, Charlotte Fitzpatrick Queeny.

— *Suzanne Queeny Little (Mrs. S. Martin Little)*

---
*Yield: 6 servings*
---

6 tablespoons butter
6 tablespoons unbleached all-purpose
   flour
2 cups milk
1 pound Velveeta cheese
1 can stewed tomatoes
1 can (6 ounces) crabmeat, drained,
   or 1 pound fresh crabmeat, picked
   over and shells discarded

**1.** Melt the butter over low heat in a large saucepan with a heavy bottom.

Add the flour, combining well, and cook for 3 to 5 minutes, stirring constantly. Gradually add the milk, whisking well. Continue to cook until the mixture thickens.

**2.** Cut the cheese into chunks and add to the cream sauce. Stir to incorporate. Add the tomatoes and crabmeat and stir. Let the rarebit cool, then refrigerate it overnight.

**3.** When ready to serve, reheat in the top of a double boiler over simmering water. Serve in a chafing dish accompanied by pastry shells or crackers.

# CRAB NORFOLK

Crab Norfolk is always on the menu for my annual Christmas Eve party.

— *Janet Hall Eubank (Mrs. Manly Eubank)*

---
*Yield: 8 to 10 servings*
---

3 tablespoons butter
2 tablespoons unbleached all-purpose
   flour
½ cup chicken stock
½ cup light cream
¼ cup finely chopped onion
¼ cup finely chopped celery
1 cup fresh crabmeat, picked over
   and shells discarded
¾ pound Virginia ham, cut in ½-inch
   julienne
Salt and freshly ground black pepper,
 ·  to taste
⅛ teaspoon cayenne pepper

**1.** Melt 2 tablespoons of the butter in a medium-size saucepan with a heavy bottom over low heat. Add the flour, stirring until blended, and cook for 2 or 3 minutes. Whisk in the stock and cream and cook for another 2 minutes.

**2.** Melt the remaining tablespoon of butter in another saucepan and in it sauté the onion and celery over low heat until they are tender, about 6 minutes (do not brown). Add the crabmeat, ham, salt and pepper, and cayenne and continue cooking, stirring, until they are heated through, about 3 minutes.

**3.** Add the crabmeat mixture to the cream sauce and bring to a boil, stirring constantly. Serve in a chafing dish, accompanied by crackers.

# CHAFING DISH CRAB

This is the kind of dish every party needs—rich and delicious.
— *Rebecca Turner Riggs* (Mrs. Edward W. Riggs)

---

*Yield: 20 to 25 servings*

---

6 tablespoons butter
⅓ cup chopped scallions (green onions)
3 tablespoons unbleached all-purpose flour
2½ cups half-and-half
4 ounces cream cheese
1 pound crabmeat, picked over and shells discarded
¼ cup dry vermouth
Juice of ½ lemon
1½ tablespoons prepared horseradish
2 teaspoons Worcestershire sauce
Salt and white pepper, to taste

**1.** Melt the butter in a large saucepan with a heavy bottom; add the scallions, and sauté until they are translucent but not brown. Stir in the flour and cook over low heat, stirring, for 3 minutes. Add the half-and-half and continue stirring until the mixture has thickened.

**2.** Cut the cream cheese in chunks and add to the cream sauce; stir until melted. Add the crabmeat, vermouth, lemon juice, horseradish, Worcestershire, and salt and pepper. Stir to combine and cook only until the ingredients are heated through. Serve in a chafing dish, accompanied by pastry shells.

or hors d'oeuvre-size servings of deviled crab, collect small sea shells (to hold two or three tablespoonsful) at the beach. Clean them thoroughly and fill with the crab mixture. Pass the shells on a tray, accompanied by small forks and lots of napkins, or keep them warm on a hot tray.

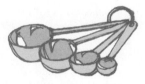

# MINI CRAB CAKES

I usually arrange the crab cakes on a tray for a cocktail buffet, but they would work equally well as a first course for a sit-down dinner.

— *Cheri Lee Burritt Yates* (Mrs. Jonathan Lucas Yates)

---
*Yield: 10 servings*

---

1 egg
*Minced garlic, to taste*
*2 teaspoons prepared mustard*
*1 teaspoon Worcestershire sauce*
*Salt and freshly ground pepper, to taste*
*1 pound backfin crab, picked over and shells discarded*
*¼ cup unseasoned bread crumbs*
*Unbleached all-purpose flour, for dredging*
*Clarified butter*
*2 tablespoons unsalted butter*
*1 teaspoon fresh lemon juice*
*1½ tablespoons chopped parsley*

**1.** Preheat the oven to 350°F.
**2.** Combine the egg, garlic, mustard, Worcestershire, and salt and pepper in a small bowl and beat well.
**3.** Place the crabmeat in a medium-size bowl. Add the egg mixture and the bread crumbs and mix well. Using your hands, form small cakes, ½ to ¾ inch thick and 1½ to 2 inches in diameter.
**4.** Flour the cakes on both sides. Heat the clarified butter in an ovenproof frying pan. Add the crab cakes and brown on one side. Turn the cakes and immediately place the pan in the oven. Bake until the undersides are brown and the cakes are heated through, 3 to 5 minutes.
**5.** While the crab cakes are baking, place the unsalted butter in a small saucepan and heat over low heat until the butter foams. Add the lemon juice and parsley.

**6.** Place the crab cakes on a platter or tray and pour over the butter sauce.

### DEVILED CRABS

*1 pound crab meat*
*12 saltines (mashed)*
*¼ pound butter*
*1 tablespoon mayonnaise*
*2 tablespoons sherry*
*Pinch dry mustard*
*Pinch minced parsley*
*1 teaspoon Worcestershire*
*Salt, pepper to taste*

Pour melted butter over cracker crumbs, saving out 4 teaspoons to put on top of the stuffed crabs. Add mayonnaise, and other seasoning, then mix in crab meat with fork to keep from breaking up. Fill 6 large backs (crab shells) generously, then sprinkle with cracker crumbs, pouring the remaining butter on top. Bake in 400° oven for 30 minutes. Serve piping hot. 6 servings.

*Mrs. Thaddeus Street*
*(Mary Leize Simons),*
*from* **Charleston Receipts**

# THAT MUSHROOM AND CRAB THING

Here is a versatile dish that can be served in small squares as an hors d'oeuvre or in larger ones for lunch or supper. It can be made without the crab and is just as delicious.

— *Caroline Clary Lesesne*

*Yield: 24 small squares*

1 pound fresh mushrooms, sliced
6 tablespoons butter
½ pound fresh crabmeat, picked over and shells discarded
6 slices white bread
4 scallions (green onions), finely chopped
2 stalks celery, finely chopped
½ green bell pepper, finely chopped
½ cup mayonnaise
¾ teaspoon salt
½ teaspoon freshly ground pepper
1 tablespoon sherry
2 eggs
1½ cups milk
½ can (10¾ ounces) condensed cream of mushroom soup, undiluted

**1.** Butter a 2½-quart casserole.
**2.** Sauté the mushrooms in 1 tablespoon of the butter in a frying pan over medium heat until they are tender and the liquid has evaporated. Remove from the pan and set aside.
**3.** Using the same pan, sauté the crabmeat in 1 tablespoon of the butter until it is heated through and coated with butter. Set aside.
**4.** Butter 3 slices of the bread on both sides with 2 tablespoons of the butter and cut into cubes. Spread the cubes in the bottom of the prepared casserole.
**5.** Combine the scallions, celery, and green pepper with the mayonnaise in

a small bowl and mix in the salt, pepper, and sherry. Pour the mixture over the bread cubes.
**6.** Butter the remaining 3 slices of bread on both sides, cut into small cubes, and spread evenly over the mayonnaise mixture. Spread the mushrooms and crabmeat over the bread cubes.
**7.** Break the eggs into a medium-size bowl, beat lightly, and add the milk. Stir to combine well. Pour over the mushrooms and crabmeat. Cover the casserole and refrigerate overnight.
**8.** Remove the casserole from the refrigerator an hour before serving. Preheat the oven to 325°F.
**9.** Spread the mushroom soup over the top of the casserole and bake, uncovered, until lightly brown and bubbling, about 50 minutes. Let sit for 10 minutes. To serve as an hors d'oeuvre, cut into small squares.

---

### HOW TO COOK CRABS

Have one inch of water in the pot in which crabs are to be cooked. Add 2 or 3 tablespoons of vinegar and salt to this. Put in crabs when water boils. Steam crabs for 25 to 30 minutes. The vinegar and steam make the crabs easy to pick. Keep clean crab shells in the refrigerator before using.

*From* **Charleston Receipts**

# DuVal's Sea Special

My grandmother, Mary B. DuVal, passed along this recipe. It has been a success at many cocktail parties over the years.

— *Molly Myers Bridges* (Mrs. Robert W. Bridges)

*Yield: 20 to 25 servings*

3 tablespoons butter (do not substitute margarine)
3 tablespoons unbleached all-purpose flour
1½ cups half-and-half
1 pound peeled shrimp, cooked, deveined, and coarsely chopped
1 pound crabmeat, picked over and shells discarded, coarsely chopped
1½ teaspoons seasoned salt
1 teaspoon white pepper
½ teaspoon paprika
¼ cup sherry

**1.** In the top of a double boiler over simmering water melt the butter and stir in the flour. Cook for 3 minutes, stirring constantly. Slowly add the half-and-half and continue cooking, stirring, until thickened.
**2.** Add the shrimp and crab and season with the seasoned salt, pepper, and paprika.
**3.** Just before serving, stir in the sherry. Transfer to a chafing dish and accompany with Melba toast.

# Mother's Shrimp and Crab in a Chafing Dish

My mother, Helen Jones, always receives rave reviews for this dish.

— *Cheri Jones Allen* (Mrs. Carl Montgomery Allen)

*Yield: 12 to 15 servings*

1 pound mushrooms, sliced
6 tablespoons butter
4 tablespoons unbleached all-purpose flour
1 can (13½ ounces) evaporated milk
1½ pounds raw shrimp, peeled and deveined
2 tablespoons freshly grated Parmesan cheese
¼ cup sherry
Mace, salt, and freshly ground pepper, to taste
1 pound crabmeat, picked over and shells discarded

**1.** Sauté the mushrooms in 2 tablespoons of the butter in a frying pan until they are tender and the liquid begins to evaporate, about 5 minutes. Remove from the pan and set aside.
**2.** Add the remaining butter to the frying pan and stir in the flour; cook for 3 minutes, stirring constantly. Stir in the evaporated milk. Add the shrimp and cook slowly, stirring constantly, until the mixture thickens and the shrimp are cooked through.
**3.** Season with the cheese, sherry, mace, salt, and pepper. Fold in the crabmeat.
**4.** Transfer the mixture to a chafing dish and serve with patty shells or Melba toast (add milk if the mixture becomes overly thick).

# LOBSTER PHYLLO TRIANGLES

These pastries keep, unbaked, in the refrigerator for two days, or they may be frozen immediately for future use.

*— Susan W. Simons*

---
*Yield: 50 pastries*
---

### Filling

*4 tablespoons unsalted butter*
*3 scallions (green onions), finely chopped*
*5 large canned tomatoes, drained, seeded, and chopped*
*1 tablespoon chopped fresh tarragon*
*Salt and freshly ground pepper, to taste*
*Meat of 1 steamed lobster (1½ pounds), finely chopped*
*2 tablespoons sweet white wine*
*1½ tablespoons flour*
*¼ cup heavy or whipping cream*

### Pastry

*1 pound phyllo dough*
*1 cup (2 sticks) unsalted butter*

**1.** Make the filling: Heat 2 tablespoons of the butter in a medium-size frying pan. Add the scallions and sauté over low heat until limp, about 2 minutes. Add the tomatoes, tarragon, and salt and pepper and simmer until slightly thick, 15 to 20 minutes.
**2.** Add the lobster meat and wine, raise the heat to high, and stir quickly to combine. Drain the mixture, reserving the liquid.

**3.** Melt the remaining 2 tablespoons of butter in another frying pan over low heat. Add the flour and cook slowly, stirring constantly, for 5 minutes (do not let the mixture brown). Add the reserved liquid and the cream and continue stirring until the mixture begins to thicken.
**4.** Combine the lobster mixture and the cream mixture and allow to cool completely.
**5.** Assemble the triangles: Melt the 1 cup butter. Brush 1 sheet of phyllo with butter. Top with 2 more sheets, buttering each. Cut the stack of sheets in half lengthwise, then cut each half crosswise into 6 parts.
**6.** Spoon 1 teaspoon of the lobster filling onto the end of each strip and fold as you would a flag, forming a triangle and tucking the end under.
**7.** Repeat the process until the phyllo and filling have been used.
**8.** Preheat the oven to 400°F. Butter baking sheets.
**9.** Place the phyllo triangles on the prepared baking sheets, brush the tops with melted butter, and bake until golden brown, about 10 minutes. Serve hot.

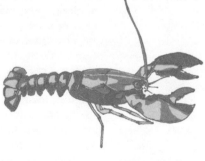

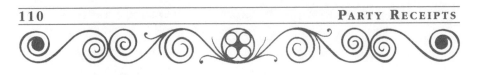

# GARLIC OYSTERS

This recipe can easily be doubled or tripled to accommodate the number of guests. As an appetizer, five or six oysters per person should be plenty, as they are somewhat rich.

— *Charlotte H. Cochran*

### Yield: 3 or 4 servings

6 tablespoons butter
2 tablespoons minced onion
2 cloves garlic, minced
½ cup chopped fresh parsley
½ cup bread crumbs
18 freshly shucked oysters on the half shell (loosen the oyster from the bottom of the shell)
½ box rock salt

**1.** Preheat the broiler. Cover a baking sheet with the rock salt.
**2.** Melt the butter in a frying pan over low heat and sauté the onions and garlic until they begin to soften but not brown, 3 to 4 minutes. Add the parsley and sauté for 1 more minute. Add the bread crumbs and combine well. Remove the pan from the heat.
**3.** Arrange the oysters on the prepared baking sheet. Top with the bread crumb mixture, using enough to completely cover each oyster.
**4.** Place under the broiler until the bread crumbs are lightly browned, about 3 minutes.

# OYSTERS IN CHAMPAGNE

There can be no more romantic and delectable combination than oysters and Champagne! This dish can be served in small pastry or puff pastry shells or, as a first course, with toast points.

— *Mitzi Grove Ball* (Mrs. Bruce D. Ball)

### Yield: About 3½ cups

3 tablespoons butter
3 tablespoons unbleached all-purpose flour
½ cup cream
1 pint shucked oysters
1 cup Champagne
Ground nutmeg, to taste
Ground allspice, to taste
Salt, to taste
White pepper, to taste
Chopped fresh parsley, to taste

**1.** Preheat the oven to 300°F. Butter a 1-quart baking dish.
**2.** Melt the butter in a saucepan with a heavy bottom over low heat. Add the flour and cook over low heat, stirring, for 3 minutes. Pour in the cream and continue cooking, stirring constantly, until the mixture begins to thicken. Remove from the heat.
**3.** Stir in the oysters, Champagne, nutmeg, allspice, salt, pepper, and parsley. Pour into the prepared baking dish and bake until bubbly, about 25 minutes.

# OYSTER PUFFS

I always think hot canapés make a party special, and nothing could be more special than hot oyster canapés.

*— Lodema Richardson Adams*

---

*Yield: 18 to 20 canapés*

*½ pound shucked oysters*
*3 ounces cream cheese, at room*
*    temperature*
*1 teaspoon onion juice*
*1 teaspoon prepared horseradish*
*4 tablespoons butter*
*18 to 20 bread rounds*
*Paprika, for garnish*

**1.** Preheat the broiler.
**2.** Drain the oysters, pat dry with paper toweling, and chop.

**3.** Place the cream cheese in a medium-size bowl and add the onion juice and horseradish; stir to combine well. Stir in the oysters.
**4.** Melt the butter in a frying pan over low heat and sauté the bread rounds on one side until they are golden brown. Remove from the frying pan, place untoasted side up on a baking sheet, and spread with the oyster mixture.
**5.** Broil until bubbly, about 3 minutes (watch carefully). Sprinkle with paprika and serve.

# CHARLESTON OYSTERS

These are marvelous for any gathering.

*— Vereen Huguenin Coen (Mrs. Richard E. Coen)*

---

*Yield: 48 oysters*

*48 shucked oysters, drained well and*
*    placed on paper toweling*
*24 slices bacon, cut in half*
*Wooden toothpicks*

**1.** Preheat the oven to 375°F.
**2.** Wrap one of the bacon pieces around each oyster and fasten with a toothpick. Arrange on a rack over a baking sheet.
**3.** Bake until the bacon is crisp, about 10 minutes. Drain briefly on paper toweling and serve hot.

---

"*I*n Charleston . . . April was the last month you could buy oysters in the city, and the restaurants began scratching them from their menus. The trawlers with their black, mended netting began moving out of Shem Creek before daylight to shrimp the fertile shorelines along the barrier islands."
**The Lords of Discipline,** *Pat Conroy*

# ZUCCHINI-TUNA CROQUETTES

This is a favorite recipe of my grandmother, Gertrude Greenspan.

— *Deborah London Ellison* (Mrs. Morris Ellison)

*Yield: 12 servings*

1 onion, grated
1 carrot, grated
1 potato, grated
2 or 3 zucchini (unpeeled), grated
1 can (6⅛ ounces) white or chunk
    light tuna, drained and flaked
1 cup matzoh meal
2 eggs
Salt and freshly ground pepper, to
    taste
Garlic powder, to taste
2 tablespoons vegetable oil

**1.** Combine the onion, carrot, potato, zucchini, tuna, matzoh meal, eggs, salt and pepper, and garlic powder in a large bowl and stir to combine well.

**2.** Heat the oil in a frying pan until hot but not smoking. Drop the zucchini mixture into the oil by teaspoonfuls and cook over medium heat until the underside is brown, about 5 minutes. Turn the croquettes and brown the other side. Remove and drain on paper toweling. Serve immediately.

# SOUTHWESTERN
## FAVORITES

# MEXI-BITES

These are great for picnics or tailgate parties!

— *Caroline Cain Hayes* (Mrs. Ronald Hayes)

*Yield: 10 to 12 servings*

*8 ounces cream cheese, at room
    temperature*
*1 can (3 ounces) green chilies,
    drained and diced*
*2 tablespoons minced onion*
*1 package (10-count) flour tortillas,
    large or small*
*Salsa*

**1.** Combine the cream cheese, chilies, and onion in a medium-size bowl.
**2.** Spread the mixture on the tortillas and roll each into a jelly-roll shape. Place in a shallow dish or pan in one layer and cover with a damp cloth. Refrigerate for at least 1 hour.
**3.** When ready to serve, slice the rolls crosswise into 1-inch pieces and serve with your favorite salsa.

# BLACK BEAN DIP

It's worth the extra effort to make this dip "from scratch." Serve it with pita triangles, crackers, or, for a special combination of flavors, banana chips.

— *Bowe Moorman Pritchard* (Mrs. Edward K. Pritchard III)

*Yield: 12 servings*

*½ pound dried black beans, picked
    over and rinsed*
*1 quart water*
*1 ham hock*
*1 bay leaf*
*2 jalapeño peppers, seeded*
*2 cloves garlic*
*½ cup minced cilantro*
*⅓ cup fresh lime juice*
*Salt and freshly ground pepper, to
    taste*

**1.** Place the rinsed beans in a large saucepan or stockpot and add the water, ham hock, bay leaf, jalapeño peppers, garlic, and cilantro. Bring to a boil, then reduce the heat and simmer, uncovered, for 1½ hours. Remove and discard the ham hock and bay leaf and let the mixture cool somewhat.
**2.** Transfer the bean mixture in batches, using a slotted spoon, to the bowl of a food processor. Add all of the lime juice and just enough of the cooking liquid to form a smooth, thick paste. Transfer the paste to a bowl and season with salt and pepper. Refrigerate until ready to use. The dip will keep in the refrigerator for two or three days.

# LINDA'S "O-LA-LA" FIESTA DIP

This is a layered dip that looks especially appetizing in a clear glass dish. If you don't have one, line any attractive container with curly lettuce leaves. The avocado mixture and the chopped vegetables may be prepared ahead; however, the dip should not be assembled until serving time.

— *Donna Smith FitzGerald*
*(Mrs. James Perdue FitzGerald)*

---

*Yield: 8 to 10 servings*

---

3 ripe avocados, peeled, halved, and
  seed removed
1 tablespoon mayonnaise
2 to 3 drops Tabasco sauce
Squeezes of fresh lemon and lime
  juice
⅛ teaspoon garlic powder
1 cup sour cream
1 jar (16 ounces) picante sauce
1 cup grated sharp Cheddar cheese
¼ to ½ cup chopped red onion
1 can (4¼ ounces) chopped ripe
  olives
1 medium tomato, peeled, seeded,
  and chopped

**1.** Mash the avocados in a shallow bowl until smooth. Add the mayonnaise, Tabasco, lemon and lime juice, and garlic powder, and mix well. Spread this mixture over the bottom of the serving dish.
**2.** Top with layers of sour cream, picante sauce, cheese, onion, ripe olives, and tomatoes, in that order. Serve immediately with tortilla chips.

# JALAPEÑO PIMIENTO CHEESE SPREAD

A combined love for pimiento cheese and Mexican food was the inspiration for this recipe, which has received rave reviews whenever I've served it. It is best made a day before you plan to serve it, so the flavors will blend.

— *Elizabeth Walker Grimball*

---

*Yield: 15 to 20 servings*

---

1 pound extra sharp Cheddar cheese,
  grated
1½ to 2 tablespoons minced canned
  jalapeño peppers
2 jars (4 ounces each) chopped
  pimientos
2 teaspoons sugar
1½ cups mayonnaise
Salt and freshly ground pepper, to
  taste

Combine all the ingredients in a large bowl and mix well. Refrigerate until ready to serve. Serve with crackers or use to stuff celery.

*P*arties for children of all ages are a particular feature of Charleston entertaining. One hostess recommends a taco party for pre-teens — set out the components on the kitchen table and let the guests have fun creating their own Tex-Mex feast.

# QUICK GUACAMOLE

Guacamole can be used as a dip or as a topping for a dinner salad. Serve it in a terra-cotta bowl for a Mexican feel, or substitute a hollowed-out round loaf of bread or a bowl made from a tortilla.

— *Evelyn Keim Beebe*

*Yield: About 2 cups*

2 ripe avocados, peeled, halved, and
    seed removed
1 large tomato, peeled, seeded, and
    diced
Juice of 1 lemon or lime
¼ cup bottled picante sauce

Mash the avocados with a fork in a medium-size bowl, leaving the mixture with some small chunks to give the dip texture. Add the tomato, lemon juice, and picante sauce and mix well. Serve with tortilla chips.
**Note:** If you do not plan to serve the dip immediately, pour the lemon juice over the top of the avocado mixture instead of mixing it in. Just before serving, stir the dip to incorporate the juice.

*A*s an alternative to serving guacamole with corn chips, surround the bowl with halved cherry tomatoes. Be sure to include a knife for spreading.

# SALSA SUPREME

Though this salsa contains several packaged products, the combination of ingredients (and the fresh tomatoes) makes the result significantly different from bottled salsa.

— *Marjorie Cantwell*

*Yield: 8 to 10 servings*

2 large tomatoes, peeled, seeded, and
    chopped
3 scallions (green onions), chopped
1 can (4¼ ounces) chopped black
    olives
1 can (7½ ounces) hot jalapeño relish
1 can (4 ounces) chopped green
    chilies (mild)
1½ tablespoons wine vinegar
3 tablespoons vegetable oil

Place the ingredients in a medium-size bowl in the order listed and mix well. Serve with tortilla chips.

# WHITE BEAN DIP

Here is a southwestern version of hummus, especially if you serve it with tortilla chips. It also makes a good dip for crudités.

*— Kimberly Martin Baldwin (Mrs. Edward Benjamin Baldwin)*

### Yield: About 2½ cups

4 cloves garlic
2 cans (15 ounces each) white kidney beans, rinsed and drained
4 tablespoons fresh lemon juice
½ cup virgin olive oil
3 teaspoons ground cumin
2 teaspoons cayenne pepper, or less, to taste
Salt and white pepper, to taste
4 tablespoons fresh cilantro leaves
Chopped cilantro, for garnish

**1.** Place the garlic in the bowl of a food processor and process until finely minced. Add the kidney beans and lemon juice and process until smooth. Add the oil, cumin, cayenne, and salt and white pepper and process to incorporate.

**2.** Add the 4 tablespoons of fresh cilantro and process for 30 seconds with on/off pulses. Transfer the dip to a bowl, cover, and refrigerate until chilled or overnight. Before serving, sprinkle with the chopped cilantro.

# FRESH CILANTRO SALSA

This recipe was given to me by Susan Proefke Brock. It may be used as a dip for tortilla chips or as an accompaniment to chalupas, fajitas, and other Mexican entrées.

*— Charlotte Nancie Quick*

### Yield: About 2½ cups

2 cloves garlic
1 large onion, quartered
1 green bell pepper, quartered and seeded
3 to 4 jalapeño peppers, seeded
6 tomatoes, peeled, seeded, and chopped, or 2 cans (16 ounces each) plum tomatoes, drained and chopped
1 cup fresh cilantro leaves
Salt and freshly ground pepper, to taste

**1.** Place the garlic in the bowl of a food processor and process until it is minced. Add the onion and peppers and process with on/off pulses until they are barely chopped.

**2.** Add the tomatoes and cilantro and process until combined but slightly chunky. Add salt and pepper. Refrigerate until ready to serve.

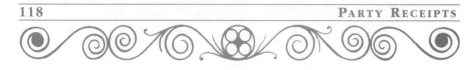

# MEXICAN PICADILLO DIP

This hearty dip is great for winter parties. It freezes well and is substantial enough to use as a taco filling. The recipe was given to me by Mr. James E. Wade, Jr.

— *Elizabeth S. Tucker*

---
*Yield: 15 to 20 servings*
---

½ pound bulk hot sausage
1 pound lean ground beef
1 teaspoon salt
Freshly ground pepper, to taste
1 can (16 ounces) diced tomatoes
3 scallions (green onions), chopped
1 jar (2½ ounces) chopped pimientos
½ cup sliced almonds
1½ cloves garlic, minced
1 can (12 ounces) tomato paste
2 jalapeño peppers, seeded and
    chopped
¾ cup golden raisins
¼ teaspoon dried oregano

**1.** In a Dutch oven brown the sausage and ground beef until cooked through. Drain off the fat, add the salt, pepper, tomatoes, onion, pimientos, almonds, garlic, tomato paste, jalapeños, raisins, and oregano. Cover the pan, bring the mixture to a boil over medium heat, reduce the heat to low, and simmer for 20 minutes.
**2.** Serve hot in a chafing dish with corn chips or taco chips.

# FRIJOLES CON QUESO

If you bake this dip in a glass or porcelain baking dish, it can be reheated in a microwave oven during the serving period or the next day.

— *Katherine Barry Catterton (Mrs. Gary Catterton)*

---
*Yield: 12 to 15 servings*
---

2 cans (16 ounces each) refried
    beans
1 can (4 ounces) chopped green
    chilies
½ teaspoon ground cumin
1 cup sour cream
2 cups grated sharp Cheddar
    cheese
2 scallions (green onions), finely
    sliced

**1.** Preheat the oven to 325°F.
**2.** Combine the beans, chilies, and cumin in a medium-size bowl. Spread the mixture in the bottom of a 2-quart casserole. Top with the sour cream, spreading it evenly from edge to edge. Spread the cheese evenly over the sour cream.
**3.** Bake until the cheese is melted, about 15 minutes. Remove from the oven and top with the sliced scallions. Serve with tortilla chips.

# PRAIRIE FIRE

Men especially love this dip. For a large party, double or triple the recipe.

*— Betsy Mapp Clawson (Mrs. Samuel R. Clawson)*

*Yield: 12 to 18 servings*

1 cup chopped onion
1 tablespoon vegetable oil
1½ cups well-drained crushed
    tomatoes (fresh or canned)
1 can (4 ounces) green chilies
1 teaspoon salt
½ teaspoon pepper
1 pound extra sharp Cheddar cheese,
    grated

**1.** Sauté the onion in the oil in a heavy frying pan over medium heat until it is soft but not brown, about 8 minutes. Add the tomato, chilies, salt, pepper, and cheese and cook, stirring, until the cheese is melted.
**2.** Serve in a chafing dish with large corn chips.

# TEXAS FRITO DIP

This is a "heavy" hors d'oeuvre—great for Super Bowl parties, tailgate parties, and other informal gatherings.

*— Alison Moore Sessoms (Mrs. Bobby D. Sessoms, Jr.)*

*Yield: 25 servings*

1 pound ground beef
6 cups chopped onion
2 bottles hot catsup
4 tablespoons chili powder
4 cups grated Cheddar cheese

**1.** Brown the ground beef and 2 cups of the onion in a large heavy frying pan over medium heat, until the meat is cooked through and the onion is soft, about 10 minutes. Drain off the fat.
**2.** Stir the catsup and chili powder into the beef and onion mixture and mix well. Cook over medium-low heat until thickened, about 10 minutes.
**3.** Transfer to a serving dish or chafing dish and sprinkle the top with some of the remaining onion and some of the cheese. The rest of the onion and

cheese can be placed in separate bowls, for the guests to help themselves. Serve the dip with large corn chips.

---

**SUPER BOWL SPREAD**

*Peanuts Caliente*

*Golden Nut Crunch*

*Fresh Cilantro Salsa with Corn Chips*

*Pumpernickel and
Corned Beef Spread*

*"Whimpies"*

*Lazy Man's Crab Casserole*

*Jalapeño Pimiento Cheese Spread*

*Marinated Broccoli and Cauliflower*

*Chocolate Chip Banana Nut Bread*

*Coffee Bars*

# CHILI DIP

Serve this hot dip with corn chips; for a gourmet touch, try the ones made with blue corn, available in specialty foods stores.

*— Anne Cogswell Burris*
*(Mrs. A. A. Burris III)*

*Yield: 8 to 12 servings*

6 ounces cream cheese, at room
  temperature
1 small onion, chopped
1 can (16 ounces) chili without
  beans
¾ cup grated Monterey Jack cheese

**1.** Preheat the oven to 350°F.
**2.** Cover the bottom of a 1-quart casserole with a layer of the cream cheese. Sprinkle the onion on top and spread a layer of chili over the onion. Top with a layer of the cheese.
**3.** Bake until bubbly, about 20 minutes.

# LAURA'S "DIET" MEXICAN DIP

Although this is not really a diet recipe, it does include ingredients that lower the calories and fat grams found in most Mexican dips. I am always asked to bring this dip to parties—it is tasty and not too spicy.

*— Laura Jenkins Thompson (Mrs. Joseph F. Thompson, Jr.)*

*Yield: About 24 servings*

2 cans (16 ounces each) refried
  beans
1 package (1¼ ounces) taco
  seasoning
1 can (4¼ ounces) chopped ripe
  olives
1 jar (8 ounces) taco sauce
2 cups plain yogurt
½ pound light Cheddar cheese,
  grated

**1.** Preheat the oven to 350°F.
**2.** Place the beans, taco seasoning, and olives in a large saucepan and cook over medium heat, stirring, until the ingredients are fully blended and the mixture is hot.
**3.** Pour the mixture into an 8 x 12 x 2-inch casserole. Spread the taco sauce over the bean mixture. Place the casserole in the freezer for 1 hour, or until the taco sauce is somewhat solid.
**4.** Layer the yogurt on top of the taco sauce and sprinkle the cheese on top of the yogurt. Bake until the cheese is melted, about 20 minutes. Serve with low-salt "light" tortilla chips.
**Note:** Instead of baking the casserole, you may heat it in a microwave oven until the cheese melts.

# MICROWAVE CHILI CON QUESO DIP

Here is a great last-minute hors d'oeuvre or quick snack for the family.
— *Carole Graves Manos*
*(Mrs. Andrew Daniel Manos)*

---

*Yield: 4 servings*

---

1 cup cubed Cheddar cheese
1 cup cubed Monterey Jack hot
    pepper cheese
¼ cup peeled, seeded, and diced
    tomato
2 tablespoons diced onion

Place all of the ingredients in a microwave-safe bowl and microwave on high power for 1 minute. Stir and microwave for 1 additional minute. Serve immediately with tortilla chips.

"*C*atfish Row, in which Porgy lived, was not a row at all, but a great brick structure that lifted its three stories about the three sides of a court. . . . The northern face, unbroken except by rows of small-paned windows, showed every color through its flaking stucco, and, in summer, a steady blaze of scarlet from rows of geraniums that bloomed in old vegetable tins upon every window-sill."

**Porgy,** *Du Bose Heyward*

# MEXICAN BEAN DIP

This dip is easy to make and always the first to go. Try it with blue corn taco chips.
— *Kristin Fischer Fary (Mrs. David J. Fary)*

---

*Yield: 10 servings*

---

2 cans (16 ounces) refried beans
2 ripe avocados, halved, peeled, and
    seeds removed
½ teaspoon fresh lemon juice
1 teaspoon crushed garlic
Salt and freshly ground pepper, to
    taste
1 cup sour cream
1 package (1¼ ounces) taco
    seasoning mix
1 cup peeled, seeded, and chopped
    tomatoes
1 cup chopped scallions (green onions)
1 cup chopped black olives
2 cups grated Monterey Jack cheese

**1.** Spread the beans in an even layer on the bottom of a 9 x 13-inch (or smaller) baking dish.
**2.** Combine the avocados, lemon juice, garlic, and salt and pepper in a small bowl and mash well. Spread the avocado mixture in a layer over the beans.
**3.** Preheat a broiler.
**4.** Combine the sour cream and taco seasoning mix in a small bowl and spread over the avocado mixture. Top with layers of tomato, onion, olives, and then cheese.
**5.** Broil until the cheese is melted, about 2 minutes. Serve with tortilla chips.

# EASY CHEESE DIP

If you want to make this dip a bit more elaborate, add a total of 1 cup of sautéed chopped green bell pepper, onion, or fresh tomatoes.

— *Cynthia Molony Masters (Mrs. Ernest L. Masters, Jr.)*

*Yield: 10 to 12 servings*

1 pound sausage meat
1 pound ground round
2 pounds Velveeta cheese, cut in
   cubes
1 can (10 ounces) Rotel whole
   tomatoes
Salt and freshly ground pepper, to
   taste

**1.** Brown the sausage and ground round in a large frying pan over medium heat and drain off the grease.
**2.** Add the cheese, tomatoes, and salt and pepper. Cook over low heat, stirring, until the cheese has melted and the liquid from the tomatoes has cooked away, about 15 minutes.
**3.** Serve hot with tortilla chips.

# HERBED CHEESE QUESADILLAS

This hors d'oeuvre may be assembled a day ahead and stored in the refrigerator. Place a layer of parchment paper or plastic wrap between each quesadilla and cover the stack with plastic wrap.

— *Cindy Henley Ball (Mrs. Austin Ball)*

*Yield: 16 quesadillas*

1 small red onion, cut in ½-inch
   slices
¼ cup olive oil, or more, as needed
2 tablespoons balsamic vinegar
1 red bell pepper, roasted, peeled, and
   diced (see page 67)
½ pound Monterey Jack cheese,
   grated
¼ cup minced fresh herbs (marjoram,
   parsley, basil, oregano)
Freshly ground pepper, to taste
8 flour tortillas

**1.** Preheat the broiler. Oil a baking sheet.
**2.** Brush the onion slices with some of the olive oil and broil on each side until lightly caramelized. Sprinkle with the vinegar. Set aside to cool.
**3.** Lower the oven heat to 400°F.
**4.** Combine the red bell pepper, cheese, herbs, and a pinch of pepper in a medium-size bowl. Chop the onion and add to the peppers and cheese.
**5.** Heat a frying pan over high heat (without oil) and cook the tortillas for a few seconds on each side to soften.
**6.** Divide the pepper and cheese mixture among four of the tortillas and top with the remaining four. Brush both sides with olive oil. Transfer to a baking sheet and bake until lightly browned, about 5 minutes. (Can be stored overnight before baking.) Cut into quarters and serve immediately.

## BLACK BEAN QUESADILLAS

These are always a big hit, even with people who claim not to be fans of Mexican food. You may want to prepare several in advance and reheat them in a 325°F oven just before serving.

*— Devon Wray Hanahan (Mrs. William O. Hanahan III)*

---

*Yield: 6 to 8 servings*

---

2 teaspoons butter or margarine, or
    more as needed
4 flour tortillas (10 inches in
    diameter)
1 can (16 ounces) black beans,
    rinsed and drained
1 medium onion, diced
1 cup shredded Monterey Jack or
    mozzarella cheese
Lettuce, for garnish
Salsa, for garnish
Sour cream, for garnish

**1.** Place one of the tortillas on a flat surface and add a single layer of beans to cover exactly one-half of the tortilla. Sprinkle one-quarter of the onions over the layer of beans. Top with a layer of one-quarter of the cheese and fold the tortilla in half to form a half-circle.

**2.** Repeat the process with the three remaining tortillas.

**3.** Melt the butter in a frying pan over low heat. Place two of the tortilla "turnovers" in the pan and cook until the bottoms are brown, 2 to 3 minutes, then flip to brown the other sides, for another 2 to 3 minutes. Repeat until all four tortillas have been cooked.

**4.** Place a bed of lettuce on a large plate. Cut each tortilla "sandwich" into 3 or 4 wedges and arrange on the lettuce. Garnish with salsa and sour cream.

*R*otel (more accurately Ro∗Tel) tomatoes are a product of the Knapp-Sherrill Company in Donna, Texas, and have become a staple throughout the South and Southwest. The tomatoes come diced or whole, seasoned with green chilies, cilantro, and other spices.

# GOAT CHEESE TORTILLAS

Serve these as a first course for a Mexican dinner party. The recipe was given to me by Callie Hartzog White.

*— Amy Solomon Waring (Mrs. Bradish J. Waring)*

*Yield: 10 or 20 servings*

10 corn or flour tortillas
1 package (8 ounces) goat cheese
   (Montrachet or chèvre)
½ pound chorizo sausage, minced, or
   breakfast sausage, crumbled and
   cooked
2 small jars jalapeño peppers, or 10
   fresh jalapeño peppers, seeded and
   chopped
Minced cilantro
Peeled, seeded, and chopped tomato
   (optional)

**1.** Preheat the broiler. Oil a baking sheet.
**2.** Fry the tortillas according to the directions on the package and set aside.
**3.** Break the cheese into chunks and sprinkle it over each tortilla. Cover the cheese with layers of sausage, cilantro, jalapeño peppers, and tomatoes, if you are using them.
**4.** Place the tortillas on the prepared baking sheet and broil until bubbly, about 3 minutes. Serve whole or cut in half, on individual plates.

# MEXICAN CRUSTLESS QUICHE

Cut in larger squares, this "quiche" works well as a luncheon or supper dish.

*— Elizabeth Crawford Hamrick (Mrs. H. Brown Hamrick)*

*Yield: 24 small squares*

8 eggs
1 pint cottage cheese
½ pound Cheddar cheese, grated
½ pound Monterey Jack cheese,
   grated
¼ cup (½ stick) butter, melted
1 can (7 ounces) green chilies
½ cup unbleached all-purpose
   flour
1 teaspoon baking powder

**1.** Preheat the oven to 350°F. Butter a 9 x 13-inch baking dish.
**2.** Combine the eggs, cheeses, butter, and chilies in a large bowl and mix well.
**3.** Combine the flour and baking powder and stir into the cheese mixture until well blended.
**4.** Pour into the prepared baking dish and bake until golden brown and set, about 45 minutes. Cut in 24 squares and serve warm or at room temperature.

# SANDWICHES
## AND
# BAKED SAVORIES

## ASPARAGUS TEA SANDWICHES

It is very important to drain off any liquid that remains after thorough mashing of the asparagus, or else the spread will be soupy.

— *Virginia Taylor Howell* (*Mrs. Roy Allen Howell III*)

*Yield: 60 tea sandwiches*

1 can asparagus (15 ounces), drained
8 ounces cream cheese, at room temperature
½ cup mayonnaise
¼ teaspoon salt
½ cup chopped pecans
1 loaf (1 pound) thin-sliced bread

**1.** In a shallow bowl, mash the asparagus until as much liquid has been absorbed as possible. Drain off remaining liquid.
**2.** Add the cream cheese, mayonnaise, salt, and chopped pecans and mix with an electric mixer until well combined.
**3.** Refrigerate until ready to use.
**4.** Spread the mixture on half the bread slices and top with the remaining slices. Trim away the crusts and cut each sandwich in quarters.

## CUCUMBER SANDWICHES

For a different look, omit the olives or substitute an equal amount of chopped pimientos.

— *Lisa Salmon Tapert* (*Mrs. Michael J. Tapert*)

*Yield: 60 tea sandwiches*

3 ounces cream cheese, at room temperature
1 tablespoon chopped scallion (green onion)
1 tablespoon chopped ripe olives
⅛ teaspoon celery salt
Dash of black pepper
Dash of garlic powder
1 loaf (1 pound) thin-sliced white bread
2 large cucumbers, peeled and sliced thin

**1.** In a small bowl combine the cream cheese, scallion, olives, celery salt, pepper, and garlic powder and mix until blended well.
**2.** Spread the cheese mixture on half the slices of bread. Top with a layer of sliced cucumbers. Place the plain bread slices on top, trim away the crusts, and cut into quarters.

# ARDEN'S "I DON'T DO FOOD" CUCUMBER SANDWICHES

People rave about these and ask for them again and again. They are so simple, and better than most cucumber sandwiches. Children will thank you for taking the "sour" out of the cucumber, using a method my friend Yoko says is common in Japan. The quantities are up to you.

*— Langborne Howard*

*Plain white bread, sliced*
*Cucumbers*
*Mayonnaise (regular or light)*
*Salt and freshly ground pepper*
*Dried dill weed or parsley*
*    flakes*

**1.** Using a jigger glass or small cookie cutter, cut rounds from the bread slices (one slice yields 3 or 4 rounds).
**2.** Cut ½ inch off the stem end of the cucumber. Put the end in place again and rub on the cut end of the cucum-ber, using a circular motion, for about one minute. A foam of bitter, sour liquid will appear at the edges.
**3.** Rinse away the foam and peel the cucumber; score it with a fork, length-wise, if desired. Cut the cucumber into thin slices.
**4.** Spread each bread round with a very thin layer of mayonnaise, scrap-ing off all excess. Place a cucumber slice on each round. Sprinkle with salt and pepper to taste and top with dill weed or parsley flakes.

# SPINACH PARTY SANDWICHES

A family secret goes public! Every time I've made these sandwiches there have been numerous requests for the recipe. Now my mother's secret recipe can be enjoyed by all.

*— Corinne Vincent Sade (Mrs. Robert Miles Sade)*

*Yield: 48 tea sandwiches*

*1 package (10 ounces) frozen*
*    chopped spinach*
*2 cups mayonnaise*
*½ cup dried minced onion flakes*
*½ cup dried parsley flakes*
*1 tablespoon fresh lemon juice*
*2 drops Tabasco sauce*
*1 large loaf Roman Meal bread*

**1.** Cook the spinach according to package directions and drain well to remove all excess moisture.
**2.** In a medium-size bowl, combine the spinach with the mayonnaise, onion, parsley, lemon juice, and Tabas-co and mix well.
**3.** Refrigerate the mixture for 2 to 3 hours, to allow the flavors to blend.
**4.** Trim the crusts from the slices of bread. Spread the spinach mixture on half the slices and top with the remaining slices. Cut each sandwich in quarters.

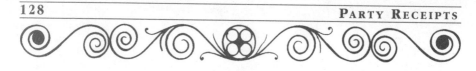

## EGG-OLIVE SANDWICHES

This recipe is a Stone family favorite, customarily served the day after Easter. Dyed eggs really do taste better.

— *Melissa Stone Crosby* (Mrs. David M. Crosby)

*Yield: 48 tea sandwiches*

12 to 14 hard-boiled eggs (depending on size)
1 jar (6 ounces) green salad olives
²/₃ to 1 cup mayonnaise
Salt and freshly ground pepper, to taste
24 slices white or whole-wheat bread

**1.** Chop the eggs until fine (the fine disc of a meat grinder works well, if available).

**2.** Chop the olives and combine the eggs and olives in a medium-size bowl.
**3.** Stir in the mayonnaise, ⅓ cup at a time, until the mixture is moist and fluffy but not soupy. Season with salt and pepper.
**4.** Trim the crusts from the bread. Spread 12 slices of the bread with the egg mixture and then cover with the plain slices. Cut in halves or quarters.

## PARSLEY SANDIOS

Wonderful for bridal showers or debutante teas, these sandwiches are even better if the filling is prepared a day ahead.

— *Ann Mapp Robinson* (Mrs. Russ Robinson)

*Yield: 60 tea sandwiches*

2 bunches parsley, stems removed
1½ pounds bacon, cooked and crumbled fine
Dash of Worcestershire sauce
1 teaspoon garlic salt
1 cup mayonnaise
1 loaf (1 pound) white or whole-wheat bread

**1.** Wash the parsley and pat dry in

paper toweling. Mince the parsley, using a knife or food processor.
**2.** In a medium-size bowl, combine the parsley, bacon, Worcestershire sauce, and garlic salt. Add mayonnaise, 1 tablespoon at a time, until the desired consistency is reached.
**3.** Trim crusts off the bread. Spread the slices with mayonnaise and cover half the slices with the parsley mixture; top with the remaining slices. Cut the sandwiches in halves or quarters.

## TOMATO SANDWICHES

Garden-ripe tomatoes and fresh basil make all the difference in these simple open-face sandwiches.

— *Marion D. Simons*

*Yield: About 40 tea sandwiches*

½ *cup sour cream*
½ *cup mayonnaise*
1 *teaspoon dried dill weed*
1 *loaf (24 ounces) sandwich bread*
2 *pounds Roma tomatoes, sliced thin*
1 *bunch fresh basil (spicy globe basil*
   *if possible), for garnish*

**1.** In a small bowl, combine the sour cream, mayonnaise, and dill weed.
**2.** Trim the crusts from the bread and cut into circles or squares just large enough to hold 1 tomato slice.
**3.** Spread the bread with the sour cream–mayonnaise mixture and top with a tomato slice. Garnish each sandwich with a piece of fresh basil.

## GINGER AND CREAM TEA SANDWICHES

Instead of serving these sandwiches in quarters, I often cut them in pretty shapes with cookie cutters.

— *Jeanne Clement*

*Yield: 60 tea sandwiches*

8 *ounces cream cheese, at room*
   *temperature*
½ *cup chopped pecans*
¼ *cup crystallized ginger, chopped*
   *fine*
*Mayonnaise*
1 *loaf (1 pound) white bread*

**1.** Cream the cream cheese in a shallow bowl and add the pecans, ginger, and enough mayonnaise to make the mixture spreadable.
**2.** Trim the crusts from the bread. Spread half the slices with the filling and top with the remaining slices. Cut into quarters or shapes.

> **"TEA TO**
> **MRS. McGOWAN,**
> **JAN. 28TH, 1898.**
>
> *49 strangers — 18 home people. 12 quarts ice cream (a very close shave). Cold tea, hot tea, coffee. 3 lbs. salted almonds, 5 lbs. sugar plums, 12 doz. small cakes (just about enough)."*
>
> **From the party notebook of**
> **Mrs. Samuel Gaillard Stoney, Sr.**
> **(Louisa Cheves Smythe Stoney)**

## CREAM CHEESE AND CARROT SANDWICH SPREAD

This spread is equally nice for morning coffee, luncheon, or teatime. Depending on the occasion, it can be used for either canapés or sandwiches.

— *M. Elizabeth Bennett Sheridan* (Mrs. John C. Sheridan)

---

*Yield: About 2 cups*

8 ounces cream cheese, at room
    temperature
½ cup finely chopped walnuts or
    pecans
1 cup grated carrots
Dash of Tabasco sauce
1 teaspoon onion juice
½ teaspoon Worcestershire sauce
Salt, to taste

**1.** Place the cream cheese in a medium-size bowl and add the nuts, carrots, Tabasco, onion juice, Worcestershire, and salt. Mix thoroughly.

**2.** Spread on crustless bread squares or rounds as canapés or cover a whole slice of crustless bread, roll up, chill, and slice into ½-inch thick rounds a half hour before serving.

## SALMON SPIRALS

For best results, carefully follow the instructions for assembling this simple hors d'oeuvre.

— *Adelaida Uribe Bennett* (Mrs. Edward G. R. Bennett)

---

*Yield: About 100 spirals*

12–14 slices thinly sliced "lite"
    pumpernickel bread
8 ounces light cream cheese, or
    boursin cheese, at room
    temperature
½ pound thinly sliced smoked salmon
Watercress sprigs, for garnish

**1.** Trim the crusts from the bread and sprinkle the slices lightly with water on both sides, to avoid breaks when rolling.

**2.** On one side of each slice, thinly spread the cheese and then cover the entire surface with one layer of salmon. If necessary, use small scraps of salmon to fill in the gaps.

**3.** Roll the bread slice jelly-roll fashion, as tightly as possible, trying not to break the bread. Place the rolls seam side down in a nonmetallic container and completely cover the top with a damp dish towel. Seal the container with plastic wrap and refrigerate for at least 2 hours.

**4.** When ready to serve, use a serrated knife to slice the rolls into spirals ¼ inch thick. Place the spirals on a serving platter and garnish with tiny sprigs of watercress.

# SPINACH AND CHEESE CANAPÉS

Cut in larger pieces, or left whole, these go well with a cream soup at lunchtime.
— *Cynthia Anne Austelle Hundley* (Mrs. Robert Walter Hundley)

*Yield: 32 canapés*

1 package (10 ounces) frozen
   chopped spinach, thawed
4 ounces mozzarella cheese, grated
4 ounces Cheddar cheese, grated
1 egg, beaten
4 English muffins
¼ cup butter, at room temperature
Garlic salt
Freshly grated Parmesan cheese

**1.** Preheat the oven to 350°F.

**2.** Thoroughly drain and dry the spinach. Place it in a medium-size bowl with the mozzarella cheese, Cheddar cheese, and beaten egg and mix well.

**3.** Split each English muffin in half and butter lightly. Sprinkle with garlic salt. Spread each half with the spinach mixture and top with Parmesan cheese.

**4.** Bake for 10 minutes, then run under the broiler to brown, watching carefully. Cut each muffin half in quarters and serve hot.

"The tea table remains a strong tradition in the Lowcountry, if only in training young ladies in comportment and etiquette. As late as 1934, when the Charleston City Directory listed only eight hotels in downtown Charleston, there were as many 'Tea Rooms.' Recipes for sugar cookies, gingerbread, and old plantation favorites such as wigs, jumbles, and marvels are passed down through the generations like the family silver."

**Hoppin' John's Lowcountry Cooking,** *John Martin Taylor*

# GUACAMOLE-BACON CANAPÉS

To add a bit of color to these canapés, I sometimes top each one with a slice of cherry tomato.

— *Melaina Clement Pate* (Mrs. Clarence W. Pate)

*Yield: 96 canapés*

24 slices thin-sliced pumpernickel bread, crusts removed
½ cup (1 stick) butter or margarine, at room temperature
10 slices lean bacon
2 large avocados, peeled, halved, and seeds removed (reserve one seed)
4 tablespoons finely minced garlic, or to taste
5 tablespoons minced onion
1 teaspoon Tabasco sauce
1 tablespoon fresh lemon juice
Salt and freshly ground black pepper, to taste

**1.** Preheat the oven to 200°F.
**2.** If the pumpernickel is not thin-sliced, roll each slice with a rolling pin, to flatten. Spread one side of each piece of bread with butter, cut into quarters, and bake until dry and crisp,
about 5 minutes. Set aside.
**3.** Fry the bacon until crisp. Drain on paper toweling, cool, and coarsely chop in a food processor. Set aside.
**4.** Mash the avocados in a medium-size bowl, leaving some chunks for texture. Add the garlic, onion, Tabasco, lemon juice, and salt and pepper and mix well. Place the reserved seed in the bowl, to keep the mixture from turning brown, and refrigerate for 1 hour.
**5.** When ready to serve, remove the seed from the guacamole, add the bacon bits, and spread the mixture on the pumpernickel toasts.

The "power" tea has become an attractive alternative to the power lunch, and teatime can be an effective setting for committee meetings at home as well as in the business world. The menu can be simple or elaborate, but be sure to offer herbal teas along with interesting caffeinated varieties.

# NIKISH

This recipe was given to me by my mother, Elizabeth Perkins Marsh (Mrs. William Kilman Marsh, Jr.). Nikish look especially attractive when they are arranged in circles on a platter, with edges overlapping a bit.

— *Robin Marsh Dallis* (Mrs. W. Alex Dallis, Jr.)

*Yield: 40 canapés*

8 ounces cream cheese, at room
   temperature
1 cup (2 sticks) unsalted butter, at
   room temperature
Anchovy paste in a tube
2 loaves (1 pound each)
   pumpernickel party bread
1 jar (10 ounces) Spanish olives
   stuffed with pimientos

**1.** Cream together the cream cheese and butter in a medium-size bowl. Squeeze in about 3 inches of the anchovy paste (or to taste) and mix until well blended.
**2.** Spread each slice of pumpernickel with the anchovy mixture.
**3.** Slice the olives as thin as possible, making sure there is a center of pimiento in each slice. Place an olive slice in the center of each piece of bread.
**4.** Refrigerate the nikish, covered. Remove from the refrigerator an hour before serving.

# HAM AND CHEESE CANAPÉS

Gruyère cheese has a subtle flavor that makes these canapés special, though if you cannot find it easily, another Swiss cheese may be substituted.

— *Elizabeth Prioleau*

*Yield: 4 to 6 servings*

½ cup ground ham
¼ pound Gruyère cheese, grated
1 tablespoon mayonnaise
1 tablespoon heavy or whipping
   cream
Pinch of cayenne pepper
¼ teaspoon dry mustard
Dash of Worcestershire sauce
Toast points or Melba rounds

**1.** Preheat the broiler.
**2.** In a small bowl combine the ham, cheese, mayonnaise, and cream and blend well. Add the seasonings and mix.
**3.** Spread the ham mixture on toast points or Melba rounds and broil until bubbly, about 3 minutes.

# HOT MUSHROOM CANAPÉS

There are several steps to this recipe, and the canapés must be prepared at the last minute; but your guests will love you!

*— Pamela Jean Edwards*

### Yield: 25 servings

*1 pound small fresh mushrooms*
*½ cup (1 stick) margarine*
*About 20 slices whole-wheat bread*
*8 ounces light cream cheese, at room*
    *temperature*
*3 egg yolks*
*½ teaspoon salt*

**1.** Clean the mushrooms and remove the stems, reserving them for another use. Dry the mushroom caps thoroughly and sauté them in 4 tablespoons of the margarine in a frying pan over medium heat until they are light brown and begin to release their juices.
**2.** Preheat the oven to 250°F.
**3.** Using a cookie cutter just slightly larger than the mushroom caps, cut rounds from the bread. Melt the remaining 4 tablespoons of margarine. Brush the bread rounds with the margarine, place on a baking sheet, and bake until golden brown, about 20 minutes.
**4.** When the mushrooms and toasts are both cool, place a mushroom cap,

*Canapés* and finger sandwiches often benefit from being made a few hours in advance of serving. Place them in a shallow container, cover with a damp cloth towel, and refrigerate for up to six hours.

rounded side up, on each toast round.
**5.** Preheat the broiler.
**6.** Beat the cream cheese in a medium-size bowl until light and fluffy. Add the egg yolks and salt and beat until smooth. Spoon the cheese mixture over each mushroom-toast round, completely covering the surface.
**7.** Place the baking sheet under the broiler, about 8 inches from the flame, and broil until the canapés are lightly browned and heated through, 10 to 15 minutes. Serve hot.

*Her* pastimes [were] the little amusements offered to widows in Charleston: unlimited christenings; a tea during the debutante season for somebody's granddaughter; one or two chamber music concerts during the Spoleto Festival . . ."

**Dreams of Sleep,** *Josephine Humphreys*

# JANE'S STUFFED BAGUETTE

The hardest part of this recipe is to resist eating the pistachios before you combine them with the other ingredients. I usually shell two or three cups in order to end up with the half cup called for in the recipe.

— *Elizabeth Chandler Jenrette* (Mrs. Joseph M. Jenrette III)

*Yield: 6 to 12 servings*

1 cup grated Swiss cheese
1 cup freshly grated Parmesan cheese
½ cup (1 stick) unsalted butter, at
    room temperature
½ cup chopped blond pistachio nuts
1 loaf freshly made French bread

**1.** In a medium-size bowl or the bowl of a food processor, mix the cheeses and butter until they are well blended. (If you use a food processor, process for about 30 seconds.) The mixture should be a thick paste; if too thick, add a little heavy cream. Stir in the pistachio nuts.

**2.** Slice the bread crosswise into three or four sections and pull out the soft insides; reserve for another use. Stuff the cavities of the bread pieces with the cheese mixture. Re-form the bread into a single loaf, wrap in foil or plastic wrap, and chill.

**3.** When ready to serve, slice the loaf into ½-inch slices.

# SHRIMP BREAD

My mother, Catherine Delord Lee, is the originator of this recipe.

— *Elizabeth L. Lee*

*Yield: About 30 slices*

16 ounces cream cheese, at room
    temperature
1 package (.6 ounce) Italian salad
    dressing mix
1 jar (4 ounces) pimiento, drained
    and chopped
1 pound cooked, peeled, and
    deveined shrimp, chopped fine
1 long loaf French or rye bread, cut
    into 4 pieces
½ cup mayonnaise
½ cup chopped parsley

**1.** Combine the cream cheese, salad dressing mix, pimiento, and shrimp in a medium-size bowl and blend well.

**2.** Hollow out the pieces of bread, and spread the entire circumference of the interior with mayonnaise. Sprinkle the parsley over the mayonnaise.

**3.** Pack the shrimp mixture into the bread. Wrap each piece in plastic wrap and chill for several hours. To serve, cut into slices approximately ½ inch thick.

# MUFFULETTA LOAF

This filling sandwich is great at picnics, tailgates, or for lunch at home, eaten on a sunny day with a cold beer.

*— Pamela A. Porter*

---

*Yield: 15 to 20 servings*

1½ cups chopped green olives
1 cup chopped black olives in oil
⅔ cup olive oil
½ cup chopped pimiento
1 teaspoon dried oregano
5 tablespoons finely chopped Italian
    parsley
1 teaspoon minced garlic
2 teaspoons fresh lemon juice
Freshly ground pepper
1 round loaf Italian bread
1 cup shredded lettuce
2 cups thinly sliced tomatoes
¼ pound thinly sliced sweet Italian
    salami (mortadella)
¼ pound thinly sliced mozzarella
    cheese
¼ pound thinly sliced pepperoni

**1.** Combine the olives, olive oil, pimiento, oregano, parsley, garlic, lemon juice, and pepper in a medium-size bowl. Cover and let marinate for 2 to 4 hours.

**2.** Cut the loaf of bread in half horizontally and pull out most of the soft bread in the center of the bottom half, making a well for the contents.

**3.** Drain the olive salad, reserving the marinade. Place half of the salad in the hollow of the bottom half of the bread, leaving a ¾-inch rim around the outside (important for easier serving).

**4.** Top the olive salad with layers of the lettuce, tomato, mortadella, mozzarella, and pepperoni, in that order. Top with a mound of the remaining olive salad and cover with the top half of the loaf of bread.

**5.** Wrap the loaf in plastic wrap, place on a flat plate or pan, and cover with another plate or pan. Place several pounds of weight (canned goods, bag of sugar, etc.) on the top pan. This will compress the loaf and make it easier to serve.

**6.** Refrigerate for at least 6 hours. To serve, cut in small wedges, as this sandwich is very rich.

---

"*P*orgy was to be found any morning, by the first arrival in the financial district, against the wall of the old apothecary shop that stands at the corner of King Charles Street and The Meeting House Road. Long custom, reinforced by an eye for the beautiful, had endeared that spot to him."

**Porgy,** *Du Bose Heyward*

# CHEESE BISCUITS

This recipe was given to me by my maiden aunt, Miss Elizabeth Robinette, and was enjoyed by many of her Middle Tennessee friends at afternoon teas.

— *Eleanor Vest Howard* (Mrs. John Ball Howard)

---

*Yield: 4 dozen*

---

½ cup (1 stick) butter (no substitutes)
½ pound sharp Cheddar cheese,
    grated
2 cups unbleached all-purpose flour
½ teaspoon salt
Cayenne pepper, to taste
2 tablespoons light cream

**1.** Preheat the oven to 350°F.
**2.** Cream the butter and cheese together in a large bowl. In a separate bowl combine the flour, salt, and cayenne pepper and mix well.
**3.** Spoon the flour mixture into the butter and cheese mixture 1 tablespoon at a time, mixing well after each addition. Add the cream and mix well.
**4.** Roll out the dough on a floured surface and cut with a small cutter (the size of a quarter or half-dollar coin). Prick each round with a fork.
**5.** Place on an ungreased baking sheet and bake until lightly browned, 10 to 12 minutes.

---

# SESAME PARMESAN THINS

These are delicious for cocktail parties, and they make wonderful gifts. Bake the thins several days ahead and store them in airtight containers.

— *Florence Wilson Miles* (Mrs. William L. Miles)

---

*Yield: About 5 dozen*

---

¼ cup sesame seeds, toasted until
    golden
4 tablespoons dried parsley, crushed
1 cup (2 sticks) butter, at room
    temperature
2 cups unbleached all-purpose flour
½ teaspoon crushed garlic
1 cup freshly grated Parmesan cheese

**1.** Combine the sesame seeds and 2 tablespoons of the parsley in a small bowl and set aside.
**2.** Cream the butter in a medium-size bowl until it is smooth. Gradually stir in the flour, using a fork, until well blended. Stir in the garlic, Parmesan cheese, and remaining 2 tablespoons of parsley and blend well.
**3.** Shape the dough into a log about 1 inch in diameter. Roll the log in the sesame/parsley mixture and refrigerate for about 20 minutes.
**4.** Preheat the oven to 350°F.
**5.** Cut the log into ¼- to ⅛-inch slices and place them on ungreased baking sheets. Bake until golden, 15 to 20 minutes. Cool on waxed paper and store in airtight containers.

## DORA'S CHEESE BENNES

This recipe lets you produce a traditional Charleston cocktail accompaniment in record time.

*—Janice Duffie Waring (Mrs. Thomas Waring)*

*Yield: About 4 dozen*

1 pound sharp Cheddar cheese,
    grated
1 box (10 or 11 ounces) piecrust mix
1 cup benne (sesame) seeds
Salt
Cayenne pepper

**1.** Preheat the oven to 350°F.
**2.** Place the cheese in a large bowl and stir in the piecrust mix. Add the benne seeds and mix well.

**3.** Shape the dough into a ball and place it on a large piece of waxed paper. Place another large piece of waxed paper on top of the ball. Roll out the dough into a flat (¼- to ⅛-inch) sheet. Use a small glass to cut the dough into circles.
**4.** Place the circles on an ungreased baking sheet and bake for 10 minutes. Remove from the oven and sprinkle lightly with salt and cayenne pepper. Return to the oven and bake for 10 minutes more, or until brown.

## HAM AND CHEESE PUFFS

These make great finger food and can be prepared in advance (up to the baking point).

*—Jane Webber Guerry*

*Yield: 40 puffs*

½ cup (1 stick) butter, at room
    temperature
1½ cups grated Cheddar cheese
⅓ cup finely chopped baked ham
¼ teaspoon Worcestershire sauce
Dash of cayenne pepper
1 cup sifted unbleached all-purpose
    flour

**1.** Preheat the oven to 350°F.
**2.** Combine the butter, cheese, ham, and seasonings in a medium-size bowl and mix well. Gradually add the flour, mixing well after each addition.
**3.** Shape the dough into a smooth ball. Break off small pieces of dough

the size of large marbles. Place the balls on a baking sheet and bake until lightly browned, 15 to 18 minutes.

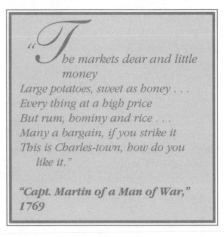

"*The markets dear and little
        money
Large potatoes, sweet as honey . . .
Every thing at a high price
But rum, hominy and rice . . .
Many a bargain, if you strike it
This is Charles-town, how do you
    like it.*"

**"Capt. Martin of a Man of War,"
1769**

*T*he "single house," essentially a Georgian house one room deep with its side facing the street, is a distinctive example of Charleston architecture. A side porch, or piazza, runs the length of the house, making an extra room for entertaining. Because of the mild climate, porch parties are possible in all but the hottest and coldest months of the year.

# ITALIAN CHEESE PUFFS

This recipe comes from my mother-in-law, Jean C. Bouch.
— ***Margaret McDonald Bouch*** *(Mrs. Timothy W. Bouch)*

### Yield: About 4 dozen

1 cup water
½ cup (1 stick) butter
½ cup plus 2 tablespoons unbleached all-purpose flour
½ cup Italian seasoned bread crumbs
½ teaspoon salt
¼ teaspoon freshly ground pepper
3 eggs
6 ounces shredded mozzarella cheese
1½ cups freshly grated Parmesan cheese

**1.** Preheat the oven to 375°F.
**2.** Place the water and butter in a medium-size saucepan and bring to a boil over medium heat.
**3.** Remove the pan from the heat and stir in the flour, bread crumbs, salt, and pepper. Cook over low heat, stirring, for 1 minute.
**4.** Transfer the mixture to a medium-size bowl. Add the eggs, one at a time, mixing well after each addition. Beat in the mozzarella cheese.
**5.** Drop the mixture by teaspoonsful on an ungreased baking sheet. Sprinkle with the Parmesan cheese. Bake until puffed and golden brown, about 15 minutes.

# CHICKEN AND WATERCRESS PUFFS

Frozen puff pastry makes it relatively easy to produce professional looking hot hors d'oeuvres. Though the filling for these puffs may be prepared in advance, they should be assembled and baked just before you plan to serve them.

— *Diane Pappas Ferrara* (Mrs. Bernard E. Ferrara, Jr.)

*Yield: About 70 puffs*

1 whole boneless, skinless chicken
    breast, cooked
1 bunch watercress, stems removed
8 ounces cream cheese, at room
    temperature
Juice of 1 small lemon
1 teaspoon dried dill weed
Salt and white pepper, to taste
1 package (17¼ ounces) frozen puff
    pastry sheets
1 egg yolk, lightly beaten (optional)

**1.** Preheat the oven to 350°F.
**2.** Cut the chicken into 1-inch pieces and place in the bowl of a food processor. Process until it resembles bread crumbs.

**3.** Add the watercress, cream cheese, lemon juice, dill weed, and salt and pepper to the food processor and process until the watercress is chopped fine and the cheese is thoroughly incorporated.
**4.** Roll out the puff pastry according to package directions. Cut the sheets into 2-inch squares.
**5.** Place 1 tablespoon of the chicken mixture in the corner of each square, leaving a ¼-inch border. Fold the pastry on the diagonal, to cover the filling. Seal the edges with a fork.
**6.** Place the turnovers on an ungreased baking sheet and bake until golden brown and puffed, about 20 minutes. To glaze, brush with beaten egg yolk before baking. Serve hot.

"*I* found Charleston a ghost town that summer. . . . Grass grew up in the streets, and every afternoon the streetcar came by, depositing my father for his dinner, which we ate at three: cold potato salad, cutlets and shrimp, tomato sandwiches, okra or green beans."

**Why We Never Danced the Charleston,**
*Harlan Greene*

# ASPARAGUS ROLL-UPS

These are the hit of every party—when passing a tray of hot roll-ups I rarely get past the first few guests. Save the bread crusts to make croutons or feed them to the birds.

*— Pamela McMillan McKinney (Mrs. Patrick W. McKinney)*

---
Yield: 35 roll-ups
---

1 loaf (1 pound) thin-sliced white
    bread
1½ cups pimiento cheese
2 cans (15 ounces) asparagus spears,
    drained
¼ cup (½ stick) butter, melted (more
    or less)

1. Preheat the oven to broil. Butter a baking sheet.
2. Using a very sharp knife, trim the crusts from the bread. Roll each slice with a rolling pin to flatten.
3. Spread a thin layer of pimiento cheese on each slice. Place an asparagus spear on one end of the bread and roll it up, jelly-roll style.
4. Place each roll-up on the baking sheet, seam side down. When they are all assembled, brush the tops with the melted butter, using more or less, according to your taste. Broil until lightly brown, watching carefully. Serve hot.

# HAM PASTRIES

My aunt, Camille Cade Raggio, used this recipe at the wedding receptions for all three of my daughters.

*—Janet Raggio Eaddy (Mrs. Winston M. Eaddy)*

---
Yield: 45 pastries
---

4 ounces cream cheese, at room
    temperature
½ cup (1 stick) butter, at room
    temperature
1 cup unbleached all-purpose flour
¼ teaspoon salt
1 can (4¼ ounces) deviled ham
1 teaspoon prepared mustard

1. Place the cream cheese and butter in a medium-size bowl and cream until well blended. Combine the flour and salt and add to the cheese and butter mixture; blend well. Chill the dough for several hours.
2. Preheat the oven to 450°F.
3. Roll out the dough on a floured surface until it is very thin. Cut rounds with a small biscuit cutter.
4. In a small bowl combine the deviled ham and the mustard and blend well. Place about ¼ teaspoonful in the center of each pastry round. Fold over pocketbook fashion (to form a half circle) and crimp the edges to seal.
5. Bake immediately, or freeze on baking sheets, place in Ziploc bags, and freeze for future use. If baking immediately, bake until golden brown, 5 to 8 minutes, watching carefully. If frozen, bake the pastries for about 10 minutes.

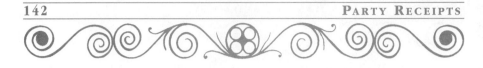

# BLACK OLIVE PARTY ROLLS

These substantial "canapés" are a big hit with the men.
— *Kathleen Hubbard Stelling* (Mrs. James Mitchell Stelling)

*Yield: 24 canapés*

1½ cups grated Cheddar cheese
1 cup chopped ripe olives
½ cup chopped scallions (green
    onions)
½ teaspoon salt
½ teaspoon chili powder
½ cup mayonnaise
1 package (8 ounces) party rolls

**1.** Preheat the oven to 450°F.
**2.** Combine the cheese, olives, onions, salt, chili powder, and mayonnaise in a medium-size bowl.
**3.** Leaving the party rolls connected, split the sheets horizontally into two rectangles and lay them on a baking sheet. Spread the olive mixture over each rectangle and bake until bubbly, 3 to 5 minutes. Cut into sections and serve hot.

# GOAT TOAST

This recipe is easily expanded or contracted; the cheese mixture can be kept in the refrigerator for a few days and used as needed.
— *Sharon Young Ward* (Mrs. David Ward)

*Yield: 6 to 8 servings*

1 loaf French bread
½ cup (1 stick) butter, at room
    temperature
Garlic powder, to taste
1 tablespoon dried basil
1½ tablespoons chopped parsley
6 ounces goat cheese, at room
    temperature

**1.** Preheat the broiler.
**2.** Slice the bread into ¼-inch slices.
**3.** In a small bowl, combine the butter, garlic powder, basil, and 1 tablespoon of the parsley. Spread the mixture on the bread slices.
**4.** Broil until barely brown, about 3 minutes. Spread with the goat cheese and broil for 1 minute. Sprinkle the tops with parsley and serve warm.

"*A*lthough Lucille gave us good daily examples of local dishes, like all Charleston cooks she came in time for breakfast but left after our two o'clock dinner, so that we were on our own for the evening meal. Genie enjoyed trying her hand at light suppers . . . making good use of the varied seafood and wide range of fruits and vegetables abounding in the market of this subtropical city by the sea."

**Charleston: A Golden Memory,**
*Charles R. Anderson*

# Vegetable Bread

This is a great hot hors d'oeuvre for an informal party—particularly a barbecue.

*— Mary Beth Molony Bunch*
*(Mrs. Mark C. Bunch)*

---

*Yield: 10 servings*

---

3 packages (10 ounces each)
    refrigerator buttermilk biscuits
½ cup (1 stick) butter or margarine,
    melted
1 onion, chopped
1 green pepper, chopped
½ cup cooked and crumbled bacon
½ cup grated Parmesan cheese

**1.** Preheat the oven to 350°F. Butter a bundt pan.
**2.** Starting with one can of biscuits, cut each biscuit into quarters, dip each piece in the melted butter, and arrange in concentric circles on the bottom of the bundt pan.
**3.** Sprinkle half of the onion, pepper, bacon, and Parmesan over the layer of biscuit.
**4.** Prepare the second can of biscuits as in step 2 and place in a layer on top of the vegetable-bacon layer. Top with the remaining vegetables and bacon.
**5.** Finish with a layer of the third can of biscuits, prepared as in steps 2 and 4.
**6.** Bake for 40 to 45 minutes. Unmold and serve hot, letting guests pull apart pieces of biscuit.

# Ham Biscuits

These are wonderful to have on hand in the freezer.

*— Rika Rich DeMasi*
*(Mrs. Alexander William DeMasi)*

---

*Yield: 36 rolls*

---

1 medium onion
1 pound ham
¾ pound Swiss cheese
1 cup (2 sticks) butter or margarine,
    at room temperature
3 tablespoons poppy seeds
1 teaspoon Worcestershire sauce
3 tablespoons prepared mustard
3 packages (8 ounces each) party
    rolls

**1.** Preheat the oven to 325°F.
**2.** Using a food processor, in separate batches chop the onion, ham, and cheese.
**3.** In a medium-size bowl combine the butter, poppy seeds, Worcestershire, and mustard and add the onion, ham, and cheese.
**4.** Split the pans of rolls in half horizontally, leaving the sheet of bottom halves in the pan. Spread each bottom with ⅓ of the ham and cheese mixture.
**5.** Top with the sheets of top halves and cut into individual servings by following the outline of the rolls. The rolls can be frozen at this time.
**6.** At serving time, cover the foil pans with aluminum foil and heat through, 25 to 30 minutes (less if not frozen).

# HERBED HAM BISCUITS

For cocktail parties, cut the biscuits in tiny rounds; for breakfast or brunch, use a 2-inch cutter. These travel well—I have been known to slip a few in my sandwich case when going fox hunting.

— *Helen Smith Warren* (Mrs. John H. Warren III)

---

*Yield: 24 biscuits*

---

2 cups unbleached all-purpose
   flour
4 teaspoons baking powder
½ teaspoon salt
½ teaspoon garlic powder
1 teaspoon dried basil
½ teaspoon dried thyme leaves
6 tablespoons vegetable shortening
⅔ cup milk
1 cup ground ham
Dijon mustard
Butter, at room temperature

**1.** Preheat the oven to 425°F.
**2.** In a large bowl, combine the flour, baking powder, salt, garlic powder, basil, and thyme. Add the shortening and cut in well with a pastry cutter until the mixture resembles cornmeal.
**3.** Make a well in the center of the mixture and pour in the milk. Mix lightly with a fork. (The mixture should form a soft ball; if it is too wet add more flour, if too dry, add more milk.)
**4.** Place the dough on a floured board (do not knead) and roll to a thickness of ¼ inch. Cut into rounds. Bake on an ungreased cookie sheet for 8 to 10 minutes. Cool on racks.
**5.** To make the filling, in a small bowl mix the ham with mustard to taste. Add softened butter until the mixture has a spreadable consistency.
**6.** Split and fill the biscuits. Serve warm or at room temperature.

---

# MEETING STREET PASTRY CUPS

This recipe predates the commercial pastries now available. I fill the pastry cups with Meeting Street Crab Meat from *Charleston Receipts* (see page x).

— *Vereen Huguenin Coen* (Mrs. Richard Coen)

---

*Yield: About 100 pastry cups*

---

4½ cups unbleached all-purpose
   flour
½ teaspoon salt
2 cups (4 sticks) butter, at room
   temperature
2 eggs, well beaten

**1.** In a large bowl combine the flour, salt, and butter with a pastry blender. Add the eggs and incorporate them well, using your hands. Form the dough into a ball, wrap in plastic wrap, and refrigerate for several hours or overnight.
**2.** Preheat the oven to 400°F.
**3.** Pinch off the dough in small amounts and press into miniature muffin tins or pastry molds. Bake until light brown, about 10 minutes. Fill with your favorite filling.

# LOU'S LOVE BISCUITS

This is a variation of a family recipe from my grandmother's family cook. It has been a standby for four generations.

— *Lynn Baughman Asnip* (Mrs. Timothy Asnip)

---

*Yield: 24 biscuits*

---

2 cups self-rising flour (unsifted)
2 teaspoons baking powder
2 tablespoons sugar
¾ cup vegetable shortening
½ to ¾ cup milk or buttermilk

**1.** Preheat the oven to 400°F.
**2.** Combine the flour, baking powder, and sugar in a medium-size bowl. Add the shortening and cut into the dry ingredients, using a fork or pastry cutter. Pour in the milk and mix lightly (do not overmix).
**3.** Turn the dough out onto a floured surface and pat into a disc about ½ inch thick. Cut with a small biscuit cutter.

**4.** Bake until just beginning to brown, 12 to 15 minutes. Serve plain or slice while hot and stuff with a small piece of country ham.

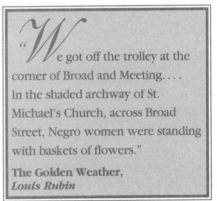

"*We* got off the trolley at the corner of Broad and Meeting.... In the shaded archway of St. Michael's Church, across Broad Street, Negro women were standing with baskets of flowers."

**The Golden Weather,**
*Louis Rubin*

---

# PARTY ROLLS

These are wonderful on the buffet table alongside a meat tray. The sweetness of the roll is a particularly delicious complement to Smithfield ham.

— *Lisa Keith Heape* (Mrs. Stephen R. Heape)

---

*Yield: 24 rolls*

---

½ cup boiling water
½ cup lard
¼ cup sugar
¾ teaspoon salt
1 package active dry yeast
½ cup warm water
1 egg, slightly beaten
3 cups unbleached all-purpose flour

**1.** Preheat the oven to 400°F.
**2.** In a large bowl, mix the boiling water, lard, sugar, and salt and allow to cool.

**3.** In a small bowl, dissolve the yeast in the warm water. Add to the mixture in the large bowl, along with the egg.
**4.** Gradually add flour to the mixture, blending well after each addition.
**5.** Refrigerate the dough, covered, for at least 2 hours.
**6.** Roll out the dough on a floured surface. Cut in 2½-inch circles. Dot each circle with butter and fold in half. Place on cookie sheets and allow to rise in a warm spot for 2 hours, covered.
**7.** Bake the rolls for 8 to 10 minutes, until lightly brown.

# MUSHROOM ROLL-UPS

These are excellent for cocktail parties since they can be made ahead and frozen.
— *Janet Raggio Eaddy* (Mrs. Winston M. Eaddy)

### Yield: About 100 roll-ups

1 pound fresh mushrooms, finely
   chopped
½ cup (1 stick) butter or margarine
6 tablespoons unbleached all-purpose
   flour
1½ teaspoons salt
1 teaspoon seasoned salt
1 cup half-and-half
2 teaspoons fresh lemon juice
1 teaspoon onion salt
1 to 1½ loaves white sandwich bread
Melted butter

**1.** Sauté the mushrooms in the butter over low heat for 5 minutes. Cool. Add the flour and blend well; add the salt and seasoned salt.
**2.** Stir in the half-and-half and cook over low heat until the mixture is thick. Remove from the heat and stir in the lemon juice and onion salt. Let cool.
**3.** Trim the crusts from the bread. Roll each slice with a rolling pin. Spread each slice with a small amount of the mushroom mixture and roll up, jelly-roll style. Place the rolls on a baking sheet and freeze until firm, about 2 hours.
**4.** Cut each roll in thirds, crosswise, place in Ziploc bags, and freeze until needed.
**5.** When ready to serve, preheat the oven to 375°F.
**6.** Place the frozen roll-ups on an ungreased baking sheet, brush with melted butter, and bake until light brown, about 15 minutes.

# BACON AND CHEESE TIDBITS

Since these tidbits must be eaten immediately after they come from the broiler, they work best for a small crowd.

—*Joanne Gilmer Cole* (Mrs. Charles T. Cole, Jr.)

### Yield: 4 to 6 servings

6 slices bread, crusts removed and
   each slice cut into 4 triangles
⅓ cup grated sharp Cheddar cheese
¼ cup mayonnaise
1 tablespoon minced onion or
   ¾ teaspoon dried instant onion
2 teaspoons prepared mustard
8 slices bacon, cooked and each
   broken into 3 pieces (or 6 slices,
   broken into 4 pieces each)

**1.** Preheat the broiler.
**2.** Place the bread triangles on an ungreased baking sheet and toast one side in the broiler (watch carefully).
**3.** Place the cheese, mayonnaise, onion, and mustard in a small bowl and mix well.
**4.** Spread the cheese mixture on the untoasted side of each bread triangle and place the triangles on a baking sheet. Top each one with a bacon piece. Broil until the cheese bubbles, 1 to 3 minutes (watch carefully). Serve immediately.

# MUSHROOM TURNOVERS

These freeze well and may be baked frozen; the cooking time will need to be increased by at least five minutes.

*— Ellen Condon*

---

*Yield: About 36 turnovers*

---

### Crust

*8 ounces cream cheese, at room temperature*
*½ cup (1 stick) butter, at room temperature*
*1½ cups unbleached all-purpose flour*

### Filling

*3 tablespoons butter*
*1 onion, finely chopped*
*½ pound fresh mushrooms, finely chopped*
*¼ teaspoon dried thyme leaves*
*½ teaspoon salt*
*2 tablespoons unbleached all-purpose flour*
*¼ cup sour cream*

**1.** Make the crust: Cream together the cream cheese and butter in a medium-size bowl. Gradually add the flour, mixing well after each addition. Shape the dough into a ball and chill for at least 30 minutes.

**2.** Make the filling: Melt the butter in a frying pan over low heat. Add the onion and cook until it is lightly brown, about 5 minutes. Add the mushrooms and cook until they begin to release their juices. Add the thyme and salt and sprinkle in the flour. Stir in the sour cream and cook until the mixture has thickened, about 8 minutes. Remove from the heat and let cool.

**3.** Preheat the oven to 450°F.

**4.** Roll out the dough on a floured surface to a ⅛-inch thickness. Using a small glass or a cookie cutter, cut the dough into rounds.

**5.** Place ½ to 1 teaspoon of the filling in the center of each round. Fold the round in half and press the edges together with a fork. Prick the top of the crust. Bake on an ungreased baking sheet until golden brown, 8 to 10 minutes. Serve hot.

---

### SHRIMP AND SALSA ROUNDS

Place a cooked shrimp (peeled and deveined) on a Melba round. Spoon over a small amount of your favorite salsa, then top with grated Cheddar cheese. Broil until the cheese melts.

*Nancy Wallace Saalfield (Mrs. John Irvin Saalfield)*

# BACON BLUE CHEESE TOAST

A quick and delicious treat for that surprise guest! The quantities may be adjusted according to the number of people you need to serve.

— *Sterling Hannah*

---
*Yield: About 2 dozen*
---

½ cup (1 stick) butter, at room
   temperature
4 ounces blue cheese, at room
   temperature, crumbled
6 slices bacon, cooked until crisp and
   crumbled
1 loaf French bread

**1.** Preheat the broiler.
**2.** Combine the butter, blue cheese, and bacon in a medium-size bowl.
**3.** Cut the bread into slices ⅓ inch thick. Toast in the broiler on one side only (watch carefully).
**4.** Spread the cheese and bacon mixture on the untoasted sides of the bread slices and broil until bubbly, 1 to 2 minutes. Serve hot.

# CHEESE BITES

To be sure the cheese bites remain hot, serve them from a warming tray or bake and pass a few at a time.

— *Lucie Hall Maguire* (Mrs. Robert O. Maguire)

---
*Yield: 6 dozen*
---

6 ounces cream cheese
1 cup (2 sticks) butter or margarine
½ pound extra sharp Cheddar cheese,
   grated
1 teaspoon dry mustard
4 egg whites, beaten until stiff but not
   dry
1 loaf unsliced white or whole-wheat
   bread, cut into cubes about 1 inch
   square

**1.** Place the cream cheese, butter, Cheddar cheese, and mustard in a heavy saucepan and heat it over medium heat, stirring constantly, until the cheeses are melted. Remove the pan from the heat and let the mixture cool slightly.
**2.** Fold in the egg whites. Spear the bread cubes with a sharp fork and dip into the cheese mixture, covering each side except the one into which the fork is stuck.
**3.** Place the cubes on a baking sheet, plain side down and not touching one another, and freeze. Transfer to a plastic bag and store in the freezer until ready to use. Do not thaw.
**4.** Preheat the oven to 400°F. Bake the frozen cubes until they are puffed and golden brown, 10 to 12 minutes.

# Jalapeño Cheese Twist

Men really seem to love this hors d'oeuvre. A round of Gouda cheese (red wax removed!) can be used instead of the jalapeño, with Dijon mustard as an accompaniment.

— *Lydia Lloyd Evans* (Mrs. A. Donald Evans)

*Yield: 6 to 8 servings*

1 package (4 ounces) refrigerator
  crescent rolls
1 jalapeño cheese round (6 to 8
  ounces)
1 egg yolk, beaten

**1.** Preheat the oven to 350°F. Top a baking sheet with foil.

**2.** Unroll the crescent roll dough on a cutting board, press together the seams, and place the cheese round in the center. Wrap the dough around the cheese, tucking in the edges.
**3.** Brush the dough with the egg yolk, place on the baking sheet (tucked-in edges down), and bake for 15 to 20 minutes, until golden brown. Place on a serving tray and surround with crackers.

# Cream Cheese and Bacon Hors d'Oeuvre

What would we do without crescent rolls?

— *Laura Anderson Moseley* (Mrs. Rod D. Moseley)

*Yield: 16 hors d'oeuvres*

8 ounces cream cheese, at room
  temperature
2 tablespoons chopped scallions
  (green onions)
1 package (8 ounces) refrigerator
  crescent rolls
8 slices bacon (uncooked)
Wooden toothpicks

**1.** Preheat the oven to 350°F. Line a baking sheet with aluminum foil.
**2.** In a small bowl combine the cream cheese and scallions until well mixed.

**3.** Cut the dough for each crescent roll in half, to form two triangles. Cut each slice of bacon in half.
**4.** Place a teaspoonful of cream cheese mixture in the center of each triangle of dough. Fold the dough over the cheese and pinch the edges together. Wrap one bacon piece around each roll and secure it with a wooden toothpick.
**5.** Place the rolls on the prepared baking sheet and bake for 15 minutes, until the bacon is crisp. Drain the rolls on paper toweling to absorb the grease. Serve hot.

# PEPPERONI BREAD

If you wish to freeze the bread to use later, bake it for only 20 minutes. Let it cool completely, then wrap it in foil and place in the freezer. To serve, thaw the rolls and heat at 375°F for 10 to 15 minutes.

— *Sandra Parks Anderson* (Mrs. Charles M. Anderson)

### Yield: 25 to 30 servings

1 package (16 ounces) Pillsbury Hot
   Roll Mix
1¼ cups hot water
2 tablespoons oil
2 teaspoons dried oregano
1 egg, lightly beaten
1½ cups freshly grated Parmesan
   cheese
7 ounces sliced pepperoni
1 cup shredded mozzarella cheese
1 cup shredded Cheddar cheese

**1.** Combine the roll mix and the yeast packet from the box in a large bowl. Pour in the water and oil, mix well, and knead for 5 minutes.
**2.** Place the bowl in a warm place, cover the dough, and allow it to rise until it is double in bulk.
**3.** Preheat the oven to 375°F.
**4.** Divide the risen dough into 2 balls. On a floured surface, roll each ball into a 10-inch round. Sprinkle each round with a teaspoon of oregano.
**5.** Combine the egg and Parmesan cheese in a medium-size bowl. Spread half the cheese mixture over each round of dough. Top each with slices of pepperoni and sprinkle with the mozzarella and Cheddar cheeses.

**6.** Roll each round into a cylinder and turn under the ends. Place seam side down on an ungreased baking sheet. Bake until the top is light brown, about 30 minutes.
**7.** Let the bread cool somewhat, and cut each roll into 10 to 15 slices. Serve in a napkin-lined basket or plate.

"*T*he bread should be thin enough to be almost revealing, well filled, the sandwich large enough for only two bites and tailored to the last degree of perfection. Stars, crescents, tigers, rabbits, and four-leaf-clover shapes may be acceptable for tea; but for cocktails — ah, ah! Thin rectangular fingers or small squares, diamonds, and rounds should be the only shapes ever seen on a tray served with drinks."

**Hors d'Oeuvre and Canapés,
*James Beard***

# SIT·DOWN
# STARTERS

# CHICKEN CONSOMMÉ WITH AVOCADO

A perfect first course for a dinner party or for summertime entertaining.

*— Susan Mikell Mills (Mrs. David N. Mills)*

---

*Yield: 4 to 6 servings*

2½ cans (14½ ounces each) chicken
  broth
2 avocados, peeled and thinly
  sliced
2 lemons, sliced
½ cup dry sherry
½ cup chopped parsley

**1.** In a large saucepan heat the chicken broth; do not let it boil.

**2.** Place slices of avocado in the bottom of each soup plate. Top with 2 slices of lemon. Pour the chicken broth over the avocado and lemon and add 1½ tablespoons of sherry to each bowl. Sprinkle chopped parsley on top.

---

# ARTICHOKE CREAM SOUP

Here is a very popular soup for special occasions—guests rave over it. No one suspects how easy it is to prepare.

*— Corinne Vincent Sade (Mrs. Robert Miles Sade)*

---

*Yield: 8 servings*

¾ cup finely chopped onion
¾ cup finely chopped celery
¼ cup finely chopped green bell
  pepper
6 tablespoons butter
6 tablespoons unbleached all-purpose
  flour
6 cups chicken broth
¼ cup fresh lemon juice
2 bay leaves
½ teaspoon ground thyme
2 cans (14 ounces each) artichoke
  hearts, drained and chopped
2 cups half-and-half
2 egg yolks, beaten
Lemon slices, for garnish
Chopped parsley, for garnish

**1.** In a large saucepan sauté the onions, celery, and green bell pepper in the butter until tender, about 10 minutes.

**2.** Add the flour and cook, stirring constantly, for 1 minute. Slowly add the chicken broth and lemon juice, stirring until blended. Add the bay leaves, thyme, and chopped artichoke hearts. Cover and simmer until thickened, about 20 minutes.

**3.** In a medium-size bowl combine the half-and-half and egg yolks and mix well. Pour a small amount of the hot soup into the egg mixture and whisk to combine. Then pour the egg mixture into the hot soup, whisking well.

**4.** Remove the bay leaves and pour the soup in batches into a blender or the bowl of a food processor. Process until smooth.

**5.** Serve immediately, garnished with the lemon slices and parsley. If you need to reheat the soup before serving, do not let it come to a boil.

## POPPY SEED CARROT SOUP

Proper presentation is what makes this soup special. Serve it in colorful bowls and garnish each serving with a tablespoon of sour cream and a sprinkling of poppy seeds.

*— Katherine E. Wimpy*

---
*Yield: 8 to 10 servings*
---

½ cup (1 stick) margarine
2 cups chopped onion
2 cans (13¾ ounces each) chicken
    broth, plus 2 cans water
1 pound carrots, thinly sliced
¾ cup long-grain rice
1 tablespoon dried thyme leaves
½ teaspoon white pepper
Salt, to taste
Sour cream, for garnish
Poppy seeds, for garnish

**1.** Melt the margarine in a large heavy saucepan and add the onions. Sauté until the onions are translucent.
**2.** Add the chicken broth, water, carrots, rice, thyme, pepper, and salt and cook over medium heat, stirring frequently, until the mixture comes to a boil. Reduce the heat to low, cover the pan, and simmer for 30 minutes, stirring occasionally.
**3.** Remove from the heat and let cool for 15 minutes. Place half of the mixture in a blender and purée until smooth. Transfer to a clean saucepan. Repeat the process with the other half.
**4.** When ready to serve, reheat over low heat and garnish with the sour cream and poppy seeds.

"The old family table-service, of course, was not suggested for sale; it was beautiful old silver-ware, wrought with the family's crest and arms, and with designs of armorial bearings and vines, huntsmen, boars, wolfhounds, and other devices from the old noble sport of forest and field, richly beat and heavily chased upon it . . ."
**The Treasure of Peyre Gaillard,** *John Bennett*

# CAULIFLOWER SOUP

The soup base for this recipe can be used with other vegetables; just eliminate the cauliflower and nutmeg. For broccoli soup substitute 1 bunch broccoli and 1 onion, chopped. To make spinach soup, use 2 packages (10 ounces each) frozen chopped spinach and 1 onion and garnish the soup with bacon bits and chopped egg.

— *Martha Ann Monroe Robertson* (Mrs. Claron A. Robertson III)

*Yield: 6 to 8 servings*

1 head cauliflower
3 cups chicken stock or broth
4 tablespoons butter
5 tablespoons unbleached all-purpose
    flour
Salt and white pepper, to taste
Dash of ground nutmeg
1 to 2 cups milk

**1.** Trim away the thick stalk of the cauliflower and chop the florets and small stems into pieces about ½ inch in diameter.
**2.** In a large saucepan bring the stock to a boil, add the cauliflower, and cook until tender, about 10 minutes. Let cool and purée in batches in a blender or food processor.
**3.** In another large saucepan melt the butter. Add the flour and cook over low heat, stirring constantly, for 3 minutes. Slowly add the cauliflower mixture, stirring to incorporate. Add the salt and pepper and nutmeg. Thin to the preferred consistency with the milk. Serve immediately or refrigerate and reheat over low heat, without letting the soup come to a boil.

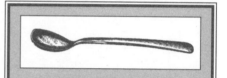

*M*any of the hearty soups in this chapter are served as starters at a favorite Charleston outdoor gathering, the oyster roast. An opportunity for the public to enjoy this tradition is the oyster roast held during the spring Festival of Houses and Gardens at Drayton Hall, an eighteenth-century plantation on the Ashley River mercifully spared the ravages of the Civil War. The house has been left unrestored and unfurnished, highlighting the beauty of the mantels, ceilings, and other details of the interior.

## CHEESEY CORN AND HAM CHOWDER

Here is a greatly embellished version of corn chowder, including the distinctly southern flavor of country ham.

*— Betsy Fant Jones*
*(Mrs. Gregory Alan Jones)*

*Yield: 8 to 10 servings*

*4 tablespoons butter*
*2½ cups shredded carrots*
*1 cup chopped onion*
*½ cup unbleached all-purpose flour*
*4 cups milk*
*3 cups chicken broth*
*2 cups chopped country ham*
*2 cups fresh corn, cut off the cob*
*1 teaspoon Worcestershire sauce*
*2 cups grated Cheddar cheese*
*1 teaspoon salt*
*1 teaspoon freshly ground pepper*

**1.** Melt the butter in a Dutch oven over low heat. Add the carrots and onions and sauté over low heat until tender but not brown, about 10 minutes. Blend in the flour and cook, stirring, for 3 minutes. Add the milk and broth and cook over low heat, stirring constantly, until the mixture has thickened.
**2.** Add the ham, corn, Worcestershire, cheese, salt, and pepper and continue to cook, stirring constantly, until the cheese has melted. Serve immediately.

**Note:** If you are not able to serve the soup immediately, reserve the cheese to add just before you reheat it; otherwise the mixture may curdle.

### COOTER SOUP

*1 large or 2 small "yellow belly"*
*    cooters (preferably female)*
*1 large onion, chopped*
*Salt to taste*
*2 teaspoons allspice*
*Red pepper to taste*
*3 tablespoons dry sherry*
*4 quarts of water*
*1 small Irish potato, diced*
*12 whole cloves*
*2 tablespoons Worcestershire*
*Flour to thicken*

Kill cooter by chopping off head. Let it stand inverted until thoroughly drained, then plunge into boiling water for five minutes. Crack the shell all around very carefully, so as not to cut the eggs which are lodged near surface. The edible parts are the front and hind quarters and strip of white meat adhering to the back of the shell, the liver and the eggs. Remove all outer skin which peels very easily if water is hot enough. Wash thoroughly and allow to stand in cold water a short while, or place in refrigerator over night.

Boil cooter meat, onion and potato in the water, and cook until meat drops from bones—about 2 hours. Remove all bones and skin and cut meat up with scissors. Return meat to stock, add spices and simmer. Brown flour in skillet, mix with I cup of stock to smooth paste and thicken soup. Twenty minutes before serving, add cooter eggs. Add sherry and garnish with thin slices of lemon. Serves 6–8.

*Mrs. Clarence Steinhart*
*(Kitty Ford),*
*from Charleston Receipts*

# AWENDAW SEAFOOD CHOWDER

We especially enjoy this chowder in the summer, when we are able to catch the shrimp and dig the clams—a family effort. Awendaw is a small community north of Charleston.

*—Jane Gilmore Riley*

### Yield: 10 servings

½ cup vegetable oil
2 cups peeled and diced potatoes
1 large green bell pepper, finely
    chopped
1 large onion, finely chopped
1 large clove garlic, minced
½ cup chopped celery
1 can (28 ounces) tomatoes (or 10
    small fresh tomatoes)
1 can (6 ounces) tomato paste
2 cups water
2 bay leaves
2 tablespoons Worcestershire sauce
Salt and freshly ground pepper, to
    taste
3 large carrots, sliced
2 pounds shelled clams, chopped and
    drained
1 pound peeled, cleaned, and
    deveined shrimp
1 small lemon, thinly sliced
2 tablespoons chopped parsley

**1.** In a Dutch oven, heat the oil and brown the potatoes, green bell pepper, onion, garlic, and celery over medium heat.
**2.** Add the tomatoes, tomato paste, water, bay leaves, Worcestershire sauce, salt and pepper, and carrots, and simmer over low heat until the carrots are tender, about 30 minutes.
**3.** Add the clams, shrimp, lemon, and parsley and cook until the clams and shrimp are cooked through, about 15 minutes. Serve hot, in cups or bowls.

## CHARLESTON OKRA SOUP

1 large beef bone (plenty of meat)
2 medium onions, chopped
3 pounds fresh okra, chopped fine
3 quarts water
1 piece breakfast bacon
8 large, fresh tomatoes, or 2
    (No. 2½) cans tomatoes (7 cups)
Salt and pepper, bay leaf

Cook meat in water slowly for two hours. Add okra, bacon, and peeled tomatoes, bay leaf, onions, salt and pepper to taste; let cook another two hours; add more water, if needed. Hot rice and buttered cornsticks are a tasty accompaniment. Serves 8–10.

*Mrs. Daniel E. Huger
(Louise Chisholm),
from Charleston Receipts*

## BOBBY G'S CLAM CHOWDER

This is a great "warmer-upper" for late afternoon and evening oyster roasts. Bobby G.'s oyster roasts are well known in the Charleston area, and they always begin with clam chowder.

—*Jennifer Wertz Hendricks* (Mrs. Ralph Martin Hendricks, Jr.)

*Yield: 12 servings*

5 slices bacon
1½ cups diced onion (about 3
   medium onions)
1½ cups diced celery
½ cup diced carrots
½ cup (1 stick) butter
7 cups peeled and diced potatoes
   (about 12 medium potatoes)
Water
1 teaspoon Old Bay Seasoning
1 teaspoon garlic salt
1 teaspoon freshly ground pepper
2 cans (10 ounces each) whole clams
2 cans (12 ounces each) evaporated
   milk

**1.** Place the bacon in an 8-quart pot with a heavy bottom and cook over medium heat until just browned; pour off the grease. Add the onions, celery, carrots, and butter to the bacon and sauté until the vegetables are tender, about 10 minutes.

**2.** Add the potatoes and water to cover (about 2 cups). Add the seafood seasoning, garlic salt, and pepper. Bring the mixture to a boil over medium heat; reduce to simmer and cook, stirring occasionally, for 10 minutes. Add the cans of clams and their liquid and simmer for an additional 10 minutes.

**3.** Remove the pot from the heat and stir in the evaporated milk. Return to the burner and reheat over very low heat (do not boil).

"*The* food itself is often the entertainment at social gatherings such as the barbecue, the oyster roast, and the fish fry. Everyone pitches in and joins the cooking, then sits down at the communal table when all the food is prepared."

**Hoppin' John's Lowcountry Cooking,** *John Martin Taylor*

## GRAMPA'S CATFISH STEW

"Grampa" is my grandfather, Mr. John Tieclemann.

— *Christine Rodenberg*

---

*Yield: 8 servings*

---

1 pound slab bacon, diced
2 pounds onions, chopped
1 can (46 ounces) tomato juice
1 can (6 ounces) tomato paste
1 bottle (32 ounces) catsup
3 cloves garlic, minced
Salt and freshly ground pepper, to
   taste
Tabasco sauce, to taste
Worcestershire sauce, to taste
3 pounds catfish, skin and bones
   removed
6 hard-cooked eggs, chopped

**1.** In a large pot cook the bacon until it is almost crisp. Add the onions and sauté until they are translucent. Drain off the excess grease. Add the tomato juice, tomato paste, catsup, and garlic and cook, covered, over low heat for 2½ hours.

**2.** Season with the salt and pepper, Tabasco, and Worcestershire. Add the catfish and the chopped eggs and cook over low heat for 30 minutes, breaking up the fish as it cooks.

---

## COLD CUCUMBER SOUP WITH SHRIMP AND CRABMEAT

This soup is extremely refreshing and well suited to a hot summer day, especially since it requires no cooking. The garnish of shrimp and crabmeat makes it an excellent starter for an elegant meal. The recipe was given to me by John Nee.

— *Kathleen Blanchard Smith* (Mrs. Gregory L. Smith)

---

*Yield: 4 to 6 servings*

---

3 medium cucumbers, peeled,
   seeded, and coarsely
   chopped
¼ teaspoon Tabasco sauce
½ teaspoon onion juice
4 cups buttermilk
2 cups sour cream
Salt and white pepper, to taste
½ cup diced, peeled, and deveined
   cooked shrimp
½ cup lump crabmeat, picked over
   and shells discarded

**1.** Place the cucumbers, Tabasco, onion juice, and 1 cup of the buttermilk in a blender or the bowl of a food processor. Purée until the mixture is smooth.

**2.** Transfer the mixture to a large bowl and whisk in the remaining buttermilk, the sour cream, and the salt and pepper. Serve immediately or refrigerate.

**3.** To serve, ladle the soup into cups or small bowls and top each serving with some of the shrimp and crabmeat.

## GAZPACHO

I tried in vain to obtain a recipe for gazpacho from one of Charleston's premier food shops and finally decided to attempt it on my own. After many tries, this is the version I most enjoy. Notice that the recipe does not call for oil—good for the weight-conscious.

— *Ruth Ellen Conway Smythe* (Mrs. David McCord Smythe)

*Yield: 6 to 8 servings*

3 carrots, quartered
3 cucumbers, peeled and seeded
2 green bell peppers, seeded and
 quartered
12 fresh tomatoes, peeled and
 quartered
½ teaspoon chopped cilantro
½ teaspoon salt
½ teaspoon ground cumin
½ teaspoon dried dill weed
Sour cream or low-fat plain yogurt,
 for garnish
Cumin, for garnish

**1.** Place the carrots, cucumbers, green bell peppers, and tomatoes in the bowl of a food processor and process just until chunky (you may need to do it in two batches).
**2.** Transfer the mixture to a large bowl and season with the cilantro, salt, cumin, and dill weed (you may want to add more, to taste). Chill for at least 2 hours and serve with a dollop of sour cream and a sprinkling of cumin.

## COLD AVOCADO SOUP

Delicious on a hot summer day!

— *Pamela McCain Pearce*

*Yield: 4 servings*

1 ripe avocado, peeled and coarsely
 chopped
½ cup heavy or whipping cream
½ cup milk
1 cup chicken broth
1 teaspoon fresh lime juice
Salt and white pepper, to taste
Sour cream, snipped chives for
 garnish

**1.** Place the avocado, cream, milk, chicken broth, lime juice, and salt and pepper in a blender or the bowl of a food processor and process until smooth. Chill for at least 2 hours.
**2.** To serve, top each cup or bowl with a dollop of sour cream and sprinkle with chives.

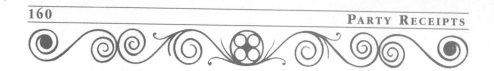

## SUMMER SOUP

A delicious, low-calorie soup for hot summer days.
— *Nancy Cohen Dudley* (*Mrs. William G. Dudley III*)

---
### Yield: 2 or 3 servings
---

1 large or 2 small cucumbers, peeled,
    seeded, and finely diced
3 bunches scallions (green onions),
    finely diced (white part only)
1 green bell pepper, finely diced
¾ cup low-fat plain yogurt
½ cup imitation sour cream
2 cubes chicken bouillon, crushed
Salt and white pepper, to taste

Place all the ingredients in a blender or
food processor and process until
smooth. Chill for at least 2 hours.

## SHRIMP TERRINE SEASIDE

My mother, Mary Ellen Long Way, combined several recipes to come up with this
one. Various greens and vegetables may be used as a garnish for the slice of
terrine.

— *Ellen Way Dudash* (*Mrs. Stephen Dudash*)

---
### Yield: 8 servings
---

¾ pound raw peeled and deveined
    shrimp
3 egg whites
3 tablespoons chopped chives
3 tablespoons sliced scallions (green
    onions)
½ teaspoon dried dill weed
½ teaspoon salt
¼ teaspoon white pepper
1½ cups heavy or whipping cream,
    cold

**1.** Preheat the oven to 350°F. Line an
8 x 4 x 2-inch loaf pan with enough
foil to completely cover the top of the
loaf. Oil the foil.
**2.** Place the shrimp in the bowl of a

food processor and process until
smooth, stopping frequently to scrape
the sides of the bowl. Add the egg
whites, chives, onion, dill weed, salt,
and pepper and process until the mixture resembles a thick paste.
**3.** With the processor running, gradually add the cream. Process for 1
minute.
**4.** Pour the shrimp mixture into the
prepared loaf pan. Place the loaf pan
in a 13 x 9 x 2-inch pan and fill the
larger pan with hot water to a depth
of 1 inch. Bake the terrine until a knife
inserted in the middle comes out
clean, about 30 minutes. Cool and
chill.
**5.** Slice the terrine and serve on individual plates or unmold onto a platter.

## SALMON MOUSSE

Accompany the mousse with a bowl of your favorite horseradish sauce.
— *Capers Alexander Grimball (Mrs. Francis E. Grimball)*

---
*Yield: 8 to 10 servings*
---

2 envelopes unflavored gelatin
1½ cups cold water
1 cup low-fat no-cholesterol
    mayonnaise
½ cup bottled French dressing
½ cup drained nonfat yogurt
1 can (14¾ ounces) pink salmon,
    drained, bones removed, and
    mashed
1 small onion, finely chopped
1 cup finely chopped celery

**1.** Oil a 1½-quart mold.
**2.** Place the gelatin and water in a small saucepan and stir over low heat until the gelatin is dissolved, 3 to 5 minutes. Set aside to cool.
**3.** Combine the mayonnaise, French dressing, and yogurt in a medium-size bowl and stir in the gelatin. Chill until slightly thickened, about 30 minutes.
**4.** Fold in the salmon, onion, and celery and pour the mixture into the prepared mold. Chill until set, 2 to 3 hours.

## AVOCADO MOUSSE

Summer luncheons are my favorite time to serve this easy and yummy first course.
— *Leigh Tyler Deas (Mrs. Jules Deas, Jr.)*

---
*Yield: 8 servings*
---

1 envelope unflavored gelatin
3 tablespoons fresh lemon juice
1 heaping cup puréed avocado
½ cup sour cream
½ cup mayonnaise
¼ teaspoon salt
⅛ teaspoon pepper
Dash of cayenne
¼ teaspoon onion salt
¼ teaspoon dried dill weed
1 cup cooked small shrimp (optional)

**1.** Lightly oil a 1½-quart ring mold.
**2.** In a large bowl soften the gelatin in ¼ cup cold water. Add 1 cup boiling water and the lemon juice to the gelatin mixture. Chill until slightly thickened.

**3.** In a medium-size bowl combine the avocado purée, sour cream, mayonnaise, and seasonings, mixing well. Add the avocado mixture to the gelatin mixture, mix well, and fold in the shrimp.
**4.** Pour into the prepared mold and chill until set, about 3 hours. Unmold on a bed of lettuce and fill the center of the ring with additional shrimp if you wish.

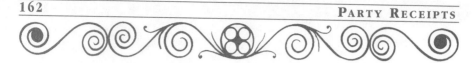

# STONO RIVER CRAB QUICHE

To make the quiche easier to handle at stand-up parties, bake it in individual tart shells.
— *Florance Robinson Anderson* (Mrs. Thomas R. Anderson)

*Yield: 8 servings*

1 cup cottage cheese
½ teaspoon salt
3 eggs
1 tablespoon white wine
2 cups fresh lump crabmeat, picked
  over and shells discarded
1 cup grated Swiss cheese
1 9-inch deep-dish pastry shell,
  unbaked

**1.** Preheat the oven to 350°F.
**2.** Place the cottage cheese, salt,

eggs, and white wine in a blender and blend at high speed until the mixture is creamy, about 2 minutes.
**3.** Transfer the egg mixture to a large bowl and stir in the crabmeat.
**4.** Sprinkle ½ cup of the grated cheese over the bottom of the pastry shell and pour in the egg mixture. Bake until the top is golden brown, about 45 minutes.
**5.** Sprinkle the remaining cheese over the top of the quiche and return the pan to the oven just long enough to melt the cheese, about 5 minutes.

# VIDALIA ONION PIE

This is a variation of a recipe given to me by my mother. There are many ways to serve the pie besides cutting it in serving-size pieces and placing it on a plate. It may be sliced in thin wedges easily manageable without a fork, or the filling may be baked in mini-quiche shells. For mini-quiches, the onions should be diced.
— *Charlotte Cochran*

*Yield: 12 first course servings*

½ cup (1 stick) butter or
  margarine
5 medium-size Vidalia or Wadmalaw
  sweet onions, sliced
¼ teaspoon salt
¼ teaspoon pepper
2 shakes Tabasco sauce
¼ teaspoon dry mustard
3 eggs, well beaten
1 cup sour cream
1 9-inch deep-dish pastry shell,
  unbaked
½ cup grated sharp Cheddar
  cheese

**1.** Preheat the oven to 450°F.
**2.** Heat the butter in a frying pan, add the onions, and sauté until the onions are translucent but not brown.
**3.** Combine the salt, pepper, Tabasco, mustard, eggs, and sour cream in a medium-size bowl and mix well. Stir in the onions. Pour the mixture into the pastry shell and top with the grated cheese.
**4.** Bake for 20 minutes, then reduce the oven temperature to 325°F and bake until the filling is set and the top is golden brown, about 20 minutes more. Let cool for at least 10 minutes before cutting into serving pieces.

# ROQUEFORT CHEESECAKE

This appetizer cheesecake, a recipe from my sister Chane, may be prepared one to four days ahead of the time you plan to serve it. It's quite rich, so cut in small wedges.

— *Hamer Dillard Salmons* (Mrs. Richard Salmons, Jr.)

---

*Yield: 12 servings*

---

½ *cup bread crumbs, lightly toasted*
¼ *cup freshly grated Parmesan cheese*
½ *pound sliced bacon*
*1 medium onion, chopped*
*3 ounces prosciutto*
*1¾ pounds cream cheese, at room temperature*
½ *pound Roquefort cheese, crumbled*
*4 eggs*
⅓ *cup heavy or whipping cream*
½ *teaspoon salt*
*2 to 3 drops hot pepper sauce*

**1.** Preheat the oven to 325°F. Butter a 9-inch springform pan.
**2.** In a small bowl combine the bread crumbs and the Parmesan cheese. Sprinkle the mixture over the bottom and sides of the pan, turning to coat. Refrigerate until set, at least 30 minutes.
**3.** Fry the bacon in a skillet until it is crisp. Drain on paper toweling. Pour off all but about 1 tablespoon of the bacon fat (leaving 1 tablespoon in the pan). Add the onion, cover, and cook over low heat until the onion is translucent, about 10 minutes.
**4.** Crumble the bacon. Chop the prosciutto. Combine the cream cheese and Roquefort in a blender or the bowl of a food processor and process until smooth. Add the eggs, cream, salt, and hot pepper sauce and process again until smooth. Add the bacon, prosciutto, and onion and process just to combine the ingredients; the mixture should retain some texture.
**5.** Pour the filling into the prepared pan. Bake for 1 hour and 20 minutes. Turn the oven off and let the cheesecake cool in the oven with the door ajar for 1 hour. Remove to a wire rack and cool to room temperature before removing from the pan and cutting in small wedges.

*W*admalaw Sweets are similar to Vidalia onions (but sweeter, according to Lowcountry cooks). They are grown on Wadmalaw, a barrier island just south of Charleston.

# SWEET ONION TARTLETTES

The onion filling for these bite-size tarts may be made up to two days before you want to serve them. Just reheat the mixture over low heat one hour before serving and fill the pastry shells.

*— Therese Trouche Smythe (Mrs. George B. Smythe)*

*Yield: 48 tartlettes*

6 tablespoons unsalted butter
4 medium red onions, very thinly
  sliced (about 4 cups packed)
¼ cup red wine
¼ cup sherry vinegar or red wine
  vinegar
¼ cup crème de cassis
Salt and freshly ground pepper, to
  taste
4 dozen tartlette shells

**1.** In a large frying pan with a lid, melt the butter. Add the sliced onion and cover tightly. Allow the onions to cook ("sweat") over low heat until they are very soft but not brown.

**2.** Add the wine, vinegar, and crème de cassis to the frying pan and cook until most of the liquid has evaporated, about 20 minutes. Season with the salt and pepper.

**3.** Just before serving fill each tartlette shell with approximately 1 tablespoon of the onion mixture. Serve warm.

# SPICED ASPARAGUS

Spring is the best time for fresh asparagus and my favorite asparagus recipe!

*— Sissy Graham Bradham (Mrs. P. Welbourne Bradham)*

*Yield: 6 servings*

1 bunch (about 1 pound) asparagus
  (thin stalks are best), trimmed
⅓ cup vinegar
¼ cup water
¼ cup sugar
½ teaspoon salt
3 whole cloves
1 stick cinnamon
¼ teaspoon celery seed

**1.** Blanch the asparagus in a large pot of boiling water until crisp-tender, 3 to 5 minutes. Immediately plunge the asparagus into a bowl of ice water to stop the cooking. Drain well and place in a shallow dish.

**2.** In a medium-size saucepan combine the vinegar, water, sugar, salt, cloves, cinnamon stick, and celery seed and cook over low heat, stirring frequently, until the sugar has dissolved.

**3.** Pour the marinade over the asparagus and let it marinate for several hours or overnight in the refrigerator.

**4.** At serving time, remove the asparagus from the marinade and place on individual plates or a platter.

## ASPARAGUS WITH LEMON-MUSTARD SAUCE

The lemon-mustard sauce goes equally well with other lightly cooked vegetables and with chicken fingers.

— *Marsha Hemphill Huggins*
*(Mrs. James Alden Huggins)*

---

*Yield: 8 to 10 servings*

---

2 bunches (about 2 pounds)
    asparagus (medium-size stalks),
    trimmed
1 cup mayonnaise
2 tablespoons fresh lemon juice
2 tablespoons prepared yellow
    mustard
2 to 3 teaspoons sugar, to taste

**1.** In a vegetable steamer set in a large saucepan, steam the asparagus over boiling water until tender when pierced with a fork, about 5 to 8 minutes. Immediately plunge the asparagus into a bowl of ice water, to stop the cooking. Remove when cool and set aside to drain.
**2.** Make the sauce: In a small bowl combine the mayonnaise, lemon juice, mustard, and sugar and mix with a whisk. Let stand for about 2 minutes, then whisk again. Taste and add more sugar or lemon juice, as needed.
**3.** Serve the asparagus at room temperature or chilled, on individual plates with the sauce spooned on top or on a platter with the sauce used as a dip.

## CHILLED LEEKS WITH LEMON SAUCE

The most important part of this recipe is to be sure to clean the leeks thoroughly, to remove all traces of sand.

— *Mary Bennett Morrison*
*(Mrs. J. Hagood Morrison)*

---

*Yield: 4 servings*

---

1 bunch leeks (at least 4)
5 tablespoons olive oil
2 tablespoons fresh lemon juice
Salt and freshly ground pepper, to
    taste

**1.** Scrub the leeks, remove the root ball, and slice in half vertically. Cut off all but ½ inch of the green. Run the trimmed leeks under cold water to remove all sand. Steam the leeks in a vegetable steamer set in a large saucepan until just tender, 8 to 10 minutes. Transfer the leeks to a bowl of ice water to stop the cooking. Drain well and refrigerate.
**2.** In a small bowl combine the olive oil, lemon juice, and salt and pepper. Refrigerate until ready to use.
**3.** At serving time, arrange the leeks on individual plates and spoon over the sauce.

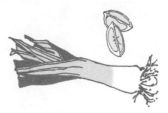

# BABY EGGPLANT ROUNDS WITH CREAMY PESTO

All you need is a little bit of sun and a little bit of earth to grow eggplant and basil in the South, so I have a thriving crop of both (the eggplants are baby) in my tiny garden in historic downtown Charleston. This recipe is one of my favorite ways to use the eggplant; the pesto topping can be kept in the refrigerator for up to a week.

*— Laura Wichmann Hipp (Mrs. George Preston Hipp)*

*Yield: 8 to 10 servings*

4 ounces cream cheese, at room
   temperature
1 to 2 tablespoons freshly grated
   Parmesan cheese
1 small clove garlic
½ cup fresh basil leaves
1 tablespoon pine nuts
1 tablespoon olive oil
2 baby eggplants (very fresh)
Salt

**1.** Make the pesto: Place the cream cheese, Parmesan cheese, garlic, basil, and pine nuts in the bowl of a food processor and process until smooth.

**2.** Slice the eggplant into rounds ¾ inch thick and sprinkle with salt.

**3.** Heat the olive oil in a frying pan over medium heat.

**4.** Pat dry the eggplant with paper toweling and place in the frying pan. Sauté for 4 minutes on each side.

**5.** Carefully spoon enough pesto onto each round to cover the top. Cover the pan and sauté until the pesto is warmed through, about 3 minutes. Place one round on each of 8 to 10 small plates and garnish with a tiny sprig of fresh basil or with a small edible flower, such as impatiens, pansy, or marigold, placed in the center of each round.

"But Porgy best loved the late afternoons, when the street was quiet again, and the sunlight, deep with color, shot level over the low roof of the apothecary shop to paint the cream stucco on the opposite dwelling a ruddy gold and turn the old rain-washed tiles on the roof to burnished copper. Then the slender, white-clad lady who lived in the house would throw open the deep French windows of the second story drawing-room, and sitting at the piano, where Porgy could see her dimly, she would play on through the dusk until old Peter drove by with his wagon to carry him home."

**Porgy,** *Du Bose Heyward*

# PAPAYA STUFFED WITH CURRIED CRAB

I have prepared this dish often for my friend Tom Sullivan, former art director for *Gourmet* magazine. Diced chicken or turkey may be substituted for the crab.

— *Kay Elizabeth Kennerty*

---
*Yield: 8 servings*
---

1 can (6 ounces) lump crabmeat,
    picked over and shells discarded
2 scallions (green onions), white part
    only, diced
¼ cup diced celery
¼ cup mayonnaise
1 teaspoon fresh lemon juice
½ teaspoon curry powder
Salt and white pepper, to taste
4 papayas, halved and cored

**1.** Preheat the broiler.
**2.** In a medium-size bowl toss togeth-er the crabmeat, scallions, and celery.
**3.** In a small bowl combine the mayonnaise, lemon juice, curry powder, and salt and pepper. Add three-quarters of the mayonnaise mixture to the crabmeat mixture, and combine well. Reserve the remaining mayonnaise mixture.
**4.** Stuff each papaya half with some of the crabmeat and top with a dab of the reserved mayonnaise mixture. Place the stuffed papayas on a baking sheet and run under the broiler until the tops are slightly brown, 2 to 3 minutes (watch carefully).

# SAUCY SALMON

Here is a copycat attempt at a dish we were served at a restaurant—we have come to *love* our version.

— *Sara Thackston Shelnutt (Mrs. David L. Shelnutt)*

---
*Yield: 4 servings*
---

½ cup sour cream
2 tablespoons prepared horseradish
1 teaspoon grated onion
1 teaspoon minced garlic
1 tablespoon drained capers
4 lettuce leaves
4 to 6 ounces smoked Norwegian
    salmon
Capers, for garnish (optional)

**1.** In a small bowl combine the sour cream, horseradish, onion, garlic, and capers. Chill for at least 1 hour.
**2.** Place the lettuce leaves on four individual plates, arrange the slices of

"*Everywhere*, in all directions, sprawled the harbor, widening out beyond the point of the city like an enormous fan, the city itself a small tongue tasting the bay's immensity."

**The Golden Weather,**
*Louis Rubin*

salmon on the lettuce, and top with the sauce. Garnish with additional capers if you wish.

# ESCARGOTS À LA SAN DIEGO

Gary Graupmann, my husband, deserves the credit for this recipe, created when we were living in San Diego.

*— Lynn Du Bois Graupmann (Mrs. Gary Graupmann)*

---

*Yield: 2 servings*

2 cups water
4 ice cubes
½ cup fresh lemon juice
1 can (7 ounces) escargots (snails),
    drained (there should be 12)
1 shallot, finely diced
1 clove garlic, minced
1½ tablespoons chopped parsley
1 tablespoon finely snipped
    chives
½ cup (1 stick) butter, melted
French bread

**1.** In a medium-size bowl combine the water, ice cubes, and lemon juice. Add the escargots and allow them to soak for 3 hours in the refrigerator.

**2.** Preheat the oven to 450°F.

**3.** In a small bowl mix together the shallot, garlic, parsley, chives, and butter.

**4.** Drain the escargots and pat dry with paper toweling. Insert the escargots into ceramic shells or arrange six in each of two shallow 5-inch baking dishes.

**5.** Top with the butter mixture, dividing it equally among all the escargots. Bake until bubbling, about 8 minutes. Serve immediately with French bread.

"Here they landed and built a little town and called it 'Albemarle Point,' afterwards 'Charles Town.' . . . At Albemarle Point they endured all the first horrors of colonization. Want, hunger, sickness, danger from Indians and so on. Their food was for a time reduced to one pint of 'damnified peas' a day, and but for the help of the friendly Indians they might have starved."

**Charleston: The Place and the People,** *Mrs. St. Julien Ravenel*

# COOKIES·CAKES
## AND
# CONFECTIONS
## FOR THE BUFFET TABLE

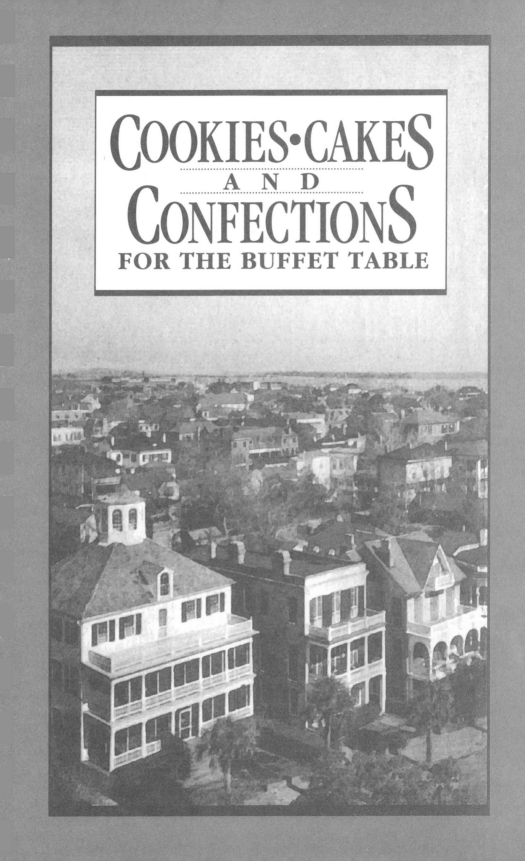

# RITA'S BENNE COOKIES

Cooks in plantation house kitchens used the rich, spicy, honey-colored benne seed to make delicious and exotic concoctions, many of which are still Lowcountry traditions.

— *Robin Carlisle Inabinett (Mrs. Edward L. Inabinett III)*

---

*Yield: 4 dozen cookies*

---

½ *cup (1 stick) butter or margarine,*
    *at room temperature*
2 *cups light brown sugar*
1 *egg, well beaten*
1 *teaspoon vanilla extract*
1 *cup self-rising flour*
1 *cup benne seed (sesame)*

**1.** Cream together the butter and sugar in a large bowl. Add the egg and vanilla and mix well. Add the flour and benne seed, mixing well after each addition.

**2.** Divide the dough into six equal parts. Roll each into a cylinder 1 inch in diameter and wrap in aluminum foil. Freeze overnight or until ready to bake.
**3.** Preheat the oven to 325°F. Line baking sheets with aluminum foil.
**4.** Slice the frozen dough thin and bake on a prepared baking sheet until light brown, 8 to 10 minutes. Let the cookies cool thoroughly before removing them from the aluminum foil.

---

# DATE STICKS

This recipe dates back to 1943 and is from my grandmother's wartime collection.
— *M. Elizabeth Bennett Sheridan (Mrs. John C. Sheridan)*

---

*Yield: 3 dozen cookies*

---

1 *cup sifted unbleached all-purpose*
    *flour*
1 *teaspoon baking powder*
½ *teaspoon salt*
2 *eggs, well beaten*
1 *cup sugar*
1 *tablespoon melted butter*
2 *cups chopped dates*
½ *cup chopped walnuts or pecans*
1 *tablespoon hot water*
*Confectioners' sugar*

**1.** Preheat the oven to 325°F. Grease a 13 x 9 x 2-inch pan.
**2.** Sift the flour once, measure, add the baking powder and salt, and sift together three times.
**3.** Place the eggs in a mixing bowl and gradually add the sugar, stirring after each addition. Add the butter and beat in the dates and nuts. Add the flour alternately with the hot water. Mix well.
**4.** Spread the batter thinly in the pan and bake for 30 to 35 minutes, until brown. Cool, cut in 2⅔ x 1-inch strips, remove from the pan, and roll in confectioners' sugar.

# ALMOND TEA COOKIES

One of the highlights of my visits to Charleston as a child was getting dressed up and going to the formal drawing room of my grandmother, Juliette Wiles Staats, for a Sunday afternoon tea party. As long as I was quiet and well behaved, I could sidle up to the tea table and sneak some of her fabulous tea cakes and cookies, including these almond fingers.

— *Cathy Huffman Forrester (Mrs. Darryl Forrester)*

---
*Yield: 4 dozen cookies*
---

1 cup (2 sticks) butter, at room
   *temperature*
*1 cup almond paste*
*¼ teaspoon salt*
*1⅔ cups unbleached all-purpose flour*
*1 cup confectioners' sugar combined*
   *with ground cinnamon, to taste*

**1.** Cream the butter thoroughly in a large bowl, then add the almond paste and incorporate well. Stir the salt into the flour and add gradually to the butter mixture, mixing well after each addition.

**2.** Chill the dough until firm, at least 3 hours or overnight.
**3.** Preheat the oven to 325°F.
**4.** Cut off thin slices of the dough, and, using your hands, roll out on a floured surface into rolls about the size and thickness of a pencil.
**5.** Bake on an ungreased baking sheet for 15 minutes. Let cool slightly before removing from the baking sheet, then remove while still warm and carefully roll in the mixture of confectioners' sugar and cinnamon. (These cookies break easily, especially if removed from the pan too soon.) Cool on a wire rack and store in an airtight tin.

# SCOTCH SHORTBREAD

This is a quick and easy shortbread, with no rolling or cutting involved.

— *Susan Mikell Mills (Mrs. David N. Mills)*

---
*Yield: 48 squares*
---

1 cup (2 sticks) butter, at room
   *temperature*
*1 cup confectioners' (4X) sugar*
*1 cup unbleached all-purpose*
   *flour*
*2 tablespoons cornstarch*

**1.** Preheat the oven to 425°F. Butter a 9 x 13 x 2-inch pan and dust it with flour.
**2.** In a medium-size bowl cream the butter and sugar. Sift together the flour and cornstarch and work into the butter and sugar mixture, blending well.
**3.** Pat the dough into the pan, making sure it reaches the edge on all sides. Stick all over with a fork.
**4.** Bake for 5 minutes. Reduce the oven temperature to 350°F and bake for 10 minutes, until barely brown (watch carefully). Remove from the oven, immediately cut in squares, and place the pan on a wire rack to cool.

# CHOCOLATE COCONUT MACAROONS

Guests won't eat just one of these — they're like peanuts!

*— Marjorie Cantwell*

---
*Yield: 3 to 4 dozen cookies*
---

*1 package (14 ounces) sweetened
    coconut*
*1 can (14 ounces) sweetened
    condensed milk*
*2 teaspoons vanilla extract*
*3 tablespoons butter*
*½ cup cocoa*

**1.** Preheat the oven to 350°F. Grease a baking sheet.
**2.** In a large bowl combine the coconut and the condensed milk. Add the vanilla extract and mix well.
**3.** Melt the butter over low heat or in a microwave oven. Add the cocoa to the melted butter and stir until it dissolves.
**4.** Add the warm butter and cocoa mixture to the coconut mixture and stir until well blended.
**5.** Drop teaspoonsful of the dough onto the prepared baking sheet and bake for 10 minutes (they will be moist). Remove the cookies from the baking sheet and cool on a wire rack.

# CHOCOLATE MACAROONS

This cookie makes a nice addition to a tray of sweets for luncheons, parties, and special family and holiday gatherings.

*— Eleanor Wilson Taylor (Mrs. J. Van Wyck Taylor)*

---
*Yield: 10 dozen small cookies*
---

*2 cups sugar*
*½ cup vegetable oil*
*4 eggs*
*2 cups unbleached all-purpose flour*
*2 teaspoons baking powder*
*1 teaspoon salt*
*4 ounces unsweetened chocolate,
    melted*
*1 teaspoon vanilla extract*
*2 cups chopped pecans or walnuts*
*Confectioners' sugar*

**1.** In a large bowl combine the sugar and oil and beat well. Add the eggs, one at a time, incorporating each one.
**2.** Sift the flour with the baking powder and salt. Add the flour to the sugar and egg mixture, stirring after each addition. Stir in the chocolate, incorporating it well; stir in the vanilla and nuts.
**3.** Chill the dough until it is very firm, about 3 hours.
**4.** Preheat the oven to 325°F. Cut several sheets of waxed paper to fit the dimensions of your baking sheet.
**5.** Form the dough into small balls and roll in confectioners' sugar. Bake on the prepared baking sheet for about 10 minutes. Cool on wire racks.

# CHEESE WHEELS

These pastry pinwheels are not very sweet and add variety to a tray of cookies.

*— Mary Simpson Lang (Mrs. Albert G. Lang)*

*Yield: 4 to 5 dozen*

*6 ounces cream cheese, at room temperature*
*1 cup (2 sticks) butter, at room temperature*
*3½ cups unbleached all-purpose flour*
*1 cup apple butter*
*⅔ cup finely chopped pecans*

**1.** In a large bowl cream together the cream cheese and butter. Gradually add the flour, mixing well after each addition, to form a dough.
**2.** Divide the dough in half and roll out each half on a floured surface to form a thin rectangular crust. Spread the surface of each crust with half of the apple butter and sprinkle on half of the chopped nuts. Starting with one of the long sides, roll as for a jelly roll, into a cylinder about 1 inch in diameter. Repeat with the other crust.
**3.** Chill the rolls overnight.
**4.** Preheat the oven to 300°F.
**5.** Using a sharp knife, cut the rolls of dough in ⅛-inch slices and bake on an ungreased baking sheet until barely brown, about 20 minutes. Cool on wire racks.

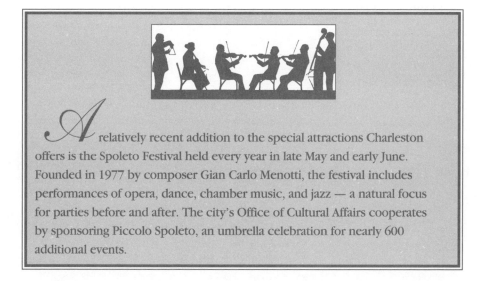

A relatively recent addition to the special attractions Charleston offers is the Spoleto Festival held every year in late May and early June. Founded in 1977 by composer Gian Carlo Menotti, the festival includes performances of opera, dance, chamber music, and jazz — a natural focus for parties before and after. The city's Office of Cultural Affairs cooperates by sponsoring Piccolo Spoleto, an umbrella celebration for nearly 600 additional events.

# ROLLED SUGAR COOKIES

This wonderful recipe was given to me by my friend Denise Fraser. It is her great-grandmother's recipe, which makes it 80 to 100 years old. The various generations of Denise's family get together at Christmastime for a session of sugar cookie baking.

— *Nella Barkley Schools (Mrs. David Schools)*

*Yield: 8 to 10 dozen cookies*

*1 cup vegetable shortening*
*1½ cups sugar*
*2 eggs*
*1 teaspoon vanilla extract*
*2 tablespoons grated lemon zest*
*2 tablespoons grated orange zest*
*3 tablespoons fresh lemon juice*
*7 tablespoons fresh orange juice*
*5 cups unbleached all-purpose flour*
*1 teaspoon baking soda*
*1 teaspoon baking powder*
*½ teaspoon salt*
*Sugar*

**1.** In a large bowl cream together the shortening and sugar. Add the eggs, vanilla, lemon rind, orange rind, lemon juice, and orange juice and mix well.
**2.** In another large bowl combine the flour, baking soda, baking powder, and salt. Gradually add the dry ingredients to the butter and sugar mixture, stirring well after each addition. The dough will be stiff.
**3.** Divide the dough into four sections, wrap each in aluminum foil, and chill until firm, several hours or overnight.
**4.** Preheat the oven to 300°F. Lightly grease a baking sheet.
**5.** Working with one section of dough at a time, roll out the dough on a floured surface and cut into shapes with cookie cutters. Sprinkle the shapes with sugar and bake on the prepared baking sheet until barely beginning to brown, 10 to 12 minutes. Cool on wire racks.

**"BOYS BIRTHDAY PARTY, FEB. 2, 1888**

*18 children — 4 nurses — 12 lookers on*

*8 qts. cream — not a spoonful left, too little.*

*2 iced pound cakes — breakfast plate size.*

*6 doz. sponge biscuit — 3 doz. poppers, 2 lbs. chocolate drops."*

**From the party notebook of**
**Mrs. Samuel Gaillard Stoney, Sr.**
**(Louisa Cheves Smythe Stoney)**

# Aunt Daisy's Secret Cookies

My Great Aunt Daisy used to serve these squares at her tea parties.
— *Margaret McIntyre McCormack* (Mrs. David B. McCormack)

### Yield: 60 squares

1 box (10 or 11 ounces) pastry mix
2 eggs
2 cups dark brown sugar
2 teaspoons unbleached all-purpose
   flour
1 cup sweetened coconut
1 cup chopped pecans
1 teaspoon vanilla extract

**Icing**

Juice of 1 small lemon
2 teaspoons melted butter
1½ cups sifted confectioners'
   sugar

**1.** Preheat the oven to 350°F.
**2.** Make the cookies: Press the pastry mix (just as it comes from the box, without additional ingredients) into the bottom of a jelly-roll pan, making sure it extends to the edges of the pan.
**3.** In a medium-size bowl beat the eggs well. Add the brown sugar, flour, coconut, pecans, and vanilla and combine well. Spread this mixture over the pastry and bake until the filling is set, 15 to 20 minutes.
**4.** Make the icing: Place the lemon juice and butter in a medium-size bowl and gradually add the confectioners' sugar, stirring well to incorporate it.
**5.** Remove the pastry from the oven and spread with the icing while the pastry is still warm. Once the icing forms a crust, cut the pastry into squares and transfer them to a flat surface to cool.

# "Whatsits"

Nanny, my great-grandmother, wrote "simply grand for parties" on her copy of this recipe; and Little Dell, my great aunt, has underlined "very grand" three times on her file card.
— *Margaret Jenkins Donaldson* (Mrs. Robert J. Donaldson III)

### Yield: 3 dozen

2 egg whites
1 cup sifted light brown sugar
2 cups chopped pecans or walnuts
1 tablespoon unbleached all-purpose
   flour

**1.** Preheat the oven to 250°F. Lightly butter a baking sheet.
**2.** In a medium-size bowl beat the egg whites until they are stiff but not dry. Gradually add the brown sugar, stirring after each addition.
**3.** Place the nuts on a sheet of waxed paper, sprinkle with the flour, and roll until the nuts are coated. Gently fold the nuts into the egg white and sugar mixture.
**4.** Drop the mixture by teaspoonsful onto the prepared baking sheet. Bake until light brown, about 30 minutes.

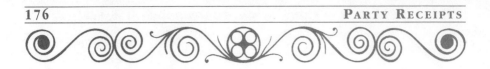

## SANTA'S SESAMES

These are a favorite cookie for our family's Christmas open house. Easily made ahead of time, they are rich and delicious.

*— Susan Smith Maguire (Mrs. Francis Maguire)*

*Yield: 4 dozen cookies*

1 cup (2 sticks) butter, at room
   temperature
1½ cups sugar
3 cups unbleached all-purpose flour
1 cup sesame (benne) seeds
2 cups shredded coconut
½ cup finely chopped almonds

**1.** In a large bowl cream the butter and sugar. Add the flour, sesame seeds, coconut, and almonds, mixing well after each addition.

**2.** Divide the dough into three parts and roll each into a cylinder 1½ inches in diameter. Wrap the rolls in waxed paper and chill until firm, about 3 hours. (The rolls can also be frozen for future use.)

**3.** Preheat the oven to 300°F. Grease a baking sheet.

**4.** Slice the rolls of dough in ¼-inch slices and bake on the prepared baking sheet for 30 minutes. Cool on a wire rack.

## CHRISTMAS FRUITCAKE COOKIES

Notice that these cookies must be started a day ahead, since the mixed fruits need to soak for 24 hours.

*— Lynn Du Bois Graupmann (Mrs. Gary J. Graupmann)*

*Yield: 4 dozen cookies*

2¼ cups mixed candied fruit
1 cup raisins
½ cup brandy or dark rum
2 eggs
½ cup dark brown sugar
⅓ cup (⅔ stick) butter or margarine,
   melted
½ teaspoon baking soda
1 teaspoon ground cinnamon
¾ teaspoon ground cloves
Dash of ground nutmeg
¾ teaspoon vanilla extract
1½ cups unbleached all-purpose
   flour, sifted
1 cup chopped walnuts

**1.** In a medium-size bowl soak the candied fruit and raisins in the brandy for 24 hours, stirring the mixture several times during that period.

**2.** When ready to proceed with the recipe, preheat the oven to 375°F.

**3.** Beat the eggs and sugar in a large bowl until they are well combined. Add the melted butter, baking soda, cinnamon, cloves, nutmeg, and vanilla. Mix well. Gradually add the flour, combining well after each addition.

**4.** Stir in the brandied fruits and their liquid and the chopped nuts. Mix well.

**5.** Drop the dough by rounded teaspoonful onto ungreased baking sheets. Bake until the cookies are light brown, about 15 minutes. Remove from the oven and cool on wire racks.

# GRANDMA'S NUTHORNS

Grandma's Nuthorns have been a traditional holiday treat in our family for more than three generations. They are great with coffee or tea or as a light dessert. Raspberry preserves may be substituted for the nut filling, to make "raspberry crescents."

— *Dawn Elizabeth Rehak*

---

*Yield: 5 dozen pastries*

---

### Dough

7 cups unbleached all-purpose flour
½ teaspoon salt
2 cups vegetable shortening
1 can (12 ounces) evaporated milk
1 cake (.6 ounce) yeast
4 eggs
¼ teaspoon vanilla extract

### Filling

1 pound walnuts, ground
½ teaspoon vanilla extract
3 tablespoons butter, at room
    temperature
4 to 8 tablespoons sugar, to taste

**1.** Make the dough: In a large bowl combine the flour, salt, and shortening and mix well.
**2.** Place half of the can of evaporated milk and the yeast in a small saucepan and cook over low heat just until the yeast dissolves; do not boil.
**3.** Place the remaining evaporated milk, the eggs, and vanilla in a medium-size bowl. Beat well. Add the yeast mixture. Combine the liquid mixture with the flour mixture, incorporate well, cover the dough with a clean, dry towel and refrigerate for no more than 6 hours.
**4.** Make the filling (just prior to baking): Combine all the ingredients in a medium-size saucepan and cook over low heat, stirring, until the butter has melted, about 3 minutes.

**5.** Preheat the oven to 350°F.
**6.** Assemble the pastries: Sprinkle a clean surface with sugar. Divide the dough into two parts and roll each into a thin square. Cut each square into 2- to 3-inch small squares.
**7.** Place 2 teaspoons of the filling mixture on each square of dough and fold into a crescent shape. Bake on baking sheets until slightly browned, 12 to 15 minutes. Cool on wire racks.

### CHRISTMAS EVE DROP-IN

*Ham Biscuits*

*My Mother's Crab Dip*

*Shrimp Wadmalaw*

*Asparagus Roll-Ups*

*Santa's Sesames*

*Christmas Fruitcake Cookies*

*Scotch Shortbread*

*Bourbon Balls*

*Party Pralines*

*Sour Cream Pecans*

*Holiday Fruit Punch*

*Eggnog*

# CHOCOLATE SQUARES

These squares are a favorite sweet from my childhood — an easy recipe to make with your children as a family project. The result is a pale brownie.

— *Virginia Gayle Grimball (Mrs. Henry E. Grimball)*

### Yield: 12 squares

¾ cup sugar
½ cup (1 stick) butter, at room
    temperature
2 eggs
½ cup unbleached all-purpose flour,
    sifted
1 ounce unsweetened chocolate,
    melted
1 teaspoon vanilla extract
1 cup chopped walnuts or pecans
    (optional)

**1.** Preheat the oven to 350°F. Lightly butter an 8-inch square pan.
**2.** In a medium-size bowl cream the sugar and butter. Add the eggs and mix well. Gradually add the flour, incorporating well. Add the melted chocolate, vanilla, and nuts. Stir just to combine.
**3.** Pour the batter into the prepared pan and bake for 25 minutes. Allow to cool in the pan, then cut into squares.

# COFFEE BARS

For an elegant finish, frost these bars with an icing made by combining ½ cup confectioners' sugar with 1 tablespoon hot coffee. The recipe was given to me by Ruth Tisdale Geer.

— *Helen Lyles Geer*

### Yield: 16 bars

¼ cup (½ stick) butter or margarine,
    at room temperature
1 cup light brown sugar
1 egg
½ cup hot coffee
1½ cups unbleached all-purpose
    flour, sifted
½ teaspoon baking powder
½ teaspoon baking soda
½ teaspoon salt
½ teaspoon ground cinnamon
½ cup raisins
½ cup chopped walnuts or
    pecans

**1.** Preheat the oven to 350°F. Lightly butter an 8-inch square pan.
**2.** In a medium-size bowl cream together the butter and brown sugar. Add the egg and coffee and mix well.
**3.** In another bowl combine the flour, baking powder, soda, salt, and cinnamon and mix well. Gradually add the dry ingredients to the creamed mixture, stirring well after each addition. Stir in the raisins and nuts.
**4.** Spread the batter in the prepared pan and bake until golden brown, about 20 minutes. Allow to cool in the pan, spread with icing, if you wish, and cut into bars.

# POUND CAKE

I find that this cake is better if it is baked the day before I plan to serve it.

— *Betty Fowler Davis* (Mrs. Gordon D. Davis)

---
*Yield: 12 to 15 servings*
---

3 cups sugar
1 cup (2 sticks) butter, at room
   temperature
½ cup vegetable shortening
5 eggs
3 cups unbleached all-purpose flour
½ teaspoon baking powder
Pinch of salt
1¼ cups milk
1 teaspoon almond extract
1 teaspoon vanilla extract
1 teaspoon lemon extract

**1.** Preheat the oven to 325°F. Lightly butter and flour a tube or bundt pan.
**2.** In a large bowl cream together the sugar, butter, and vegetable shortening. Add the eggs, one at a time, stirring well after each addition.
**3.** Sift together the flour, baking powder, and salt three times. Add the flour to the creamed mixture in 4 parts, alternating with the milk and starting and ending with flour. Stir in the almond, vanilla, and lemon extract.
**4.** Bake in the prepared pan until the cake tests done, 1 hour and 30 minutes. Cool the cake in the pan for 10 minutes, then invert it over a cake rack to continue cooling.

# DALE'S CREAM CHEESE POUND CAKE

Dale Welch is a longtime business associate. After she brought her delicious pound cake to numerous departmental staff meetings, I begged for the recipe.

— *Pamela McCain Pearce*

---
*Yield: 12 to 15 servings*
---

1½ cups (3 sticks) butter, at room
   temperature
8 ounces cream cheese, at room
   temperature
2⅔ cups sugar
6 eggs
1 tablespoon vanilla extract
1 tablespoon butter flavoring
3 cups cake flour
¼ teaspoon salt

**1.** Preheat the oven to 300°F. Lightly butter and flour a bundt pan.

**2.** In a large bowl cream together the butter, cream cheese, and sugar. Add the eggs, one at a time, mixing well after each addition. Stir in the vanilla and butter flavoring.
**3.** Combine the flour and salt and gradually add to the batter, mixing well after each addition.
**4.** Pour the batter into the prepared pan and bake until the cake tests done, 1 hour and 15 minutes. Cool the cake in the pan for 10 minutes, then invert it over a wire rack and unmold. Continue to cool for 1 hour.

# APPLESAUCE FRUIT CAKE

I used this receipt to make the groom's cake for my daughter's wedding. If you wish to do the same, slice and cut the cake into 1¼-inch squares and pack the squares in tiny boxes. Arrange the boxes on a silver tray placed near the door. Departing guests can then take home a bit of cake to tuck under their pillows — to dream on.

— *Barbara Gaines Hood* (Mrs. William C. Hood)

---
*Yield: 15 to 20 servings;*
*30 to 40 squares*

---

3 cups unbleached all-purpose flour
2 teaspoons baking soda
1 teaspoon baking powder
½ teaspoon ground cloves
½ teaspoon ground nutmeg
½ teaspoon ground cinnamon
½ teaspoon salt
1 pound candied cherries
½ pound candied green pineapple
½ pound candied white pineapple
¾ cup chopped dates
1 cup raisins
1½ cups chopped pecans
1½ cups chopped walnuts
½ cup (1 stick) butter, at room
    temperature
1 cup sugar
2 eggs
½ cup bourbon
1½ cups chunky applesauce

**1.** Preheat the oven to 275°F. Butter and flour a 10-inch tube pan.
**2.** Sift together the flour, baking soda, baking powder, cloves, nutmeg, cinnamon, and salt. Set aside.
**3.** Cut up the candied fruits. Place in a colander and pour over boiling water, to wash away the preservatives. Drain well.
**4.** In a medium-size bowl mix together the candied fruits, dates, raisins, pecans, and walnuts.
**5.** In a large bowl cream together the butter and sugar. Add the eggs, one at a time, beating well after each addition. Alternately add the flour mixture and the bourbon to the creamed mixture, mixing well after each addition. Stir in the fruits and nuts and the applesauce (the batter will be stiff; you may want to use your hands to be sure the ingredients are blended thoroughly).
**6.** Place the batter in the prepared pan and bake until the cake tests done, about 2 hours and 30 minutes. Cool the cake in the pan, then remove to a wire rack to continue cooling. Wrap in plastic wrap or aluminum foil and store in the refrigerator.
**Note:** If the cake is to be cut in squares, use two 9 x 5-inch loaf pans and bake for 2 hours.

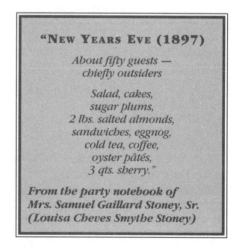

**"NEW YEARS EVE (1897)**

*About fifty guests —*
*chiefly outsiders*

*Salad, cakes,*
*sugar plums,*
*2 lbs. salted almonds,*
*sandwiches, eggnog,*
*cold tea, coffee,*
*oyster pâtés,*
*3 qts. sherry."*

*From the party notebook of*
*Mrs. Samuel Gaillard Stoney, Sr.*
*(Louisa Cheves Smythe Stoney)*

# DREAM CHEESECAKES

These are heavenly!

*—Jean Dozier Blackmon*

---

*Yield: 6 dozen cheesecakes*

---

**Filling**

1½ pounds cream cheese, at room
  temperature
1½ teaspoons vanilla extract
1 cup sugar
5 eggs

**Topping**

1 pint sour cream
¼ cup sugar
1 teaspoon vanilla extract

**1.** Preheat the oven to 350°F. Line 1½-inch muffin tins with paper liners.
**2.** Make the filling: Place the cream cheese and vanilla in a large bowl and cream with an electric mixer. Add the sugar and eggs and mix well.
**3.** Spoon approximately 1 tablespoon of the filling into the prepared muffin cups and bake until the tops crack (they will not be brown), about 20 minutes.
**4.** Make the topping: Combine the ingredients in a medium-size bowl and mix well.
**5.** Spoon a small amount of the topping onto each cheesecake. Bake for 5 minutes. Let cool and refrigerate until ready to serve.

---

Mrs. St. Julien Ravenel's description of the "salons" held in the rented rooms of a Mrs. Holland, the widow of an Englishman and herself of Greek descent: "The refreshments were the simplest possible. Lemonade or claret-sanger, and sweet wafers, made crisp and fresh at the moment by her own maid; — nothing more. Yet so great was the charm of the reunions that gentlemen and ladies would leave the handsomest parties to go to them."

**Charleston: The Place and the People, *Mrs. St. Julien Ravenel***

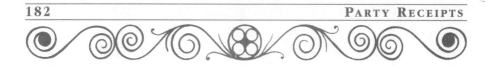

# MINIATURE CHOCOLATE ECLAIRS

Mini-éclairs are perfect for the tea table or as a dessert for a cocktail buffet.
— *Anne Smith Hutson (Mrs. Richard Woodward Hutson, Jr.)*

---

*Yield: 24 éclairs*

---

**Pastry**

*1 cup water*
*½ cup (1 stick) butter*
*1 cup unbleached all-purpose*
*    flour*
*4 eggs, beaten separately*

**Filling**

*1 cup milk*
*½ cup sugar*
*3 tablespoons unbleached all-purpose*
*    flour*
*Pinch of salt*
*2 egg yolks*
*2 teaspoons vanilla extract*
*1 cup heavy cream, whipped*

**Icing**

*2 teaspoons butter*
*2 ounces unsweetened chocolate*
*2 cups confectioners' sugar*
*4 tablespoons hot water*
*Milk*

**1.** Preheat the oven to 400°F.
**2.** Make the pastry: Place the water and butter in a medium-size saucepan and bring to a full rolling boil. Reduce the heat to low, add the flour, and stir vigorously until the mixture begins to form a ball. Remove from the heat and stir in 1 beaten egg at a time.
**3.** Drop the dough by spoonfuls or shape into small logs and place on an ungreased baking sheet. Bake for 30 minutes.
**4.** Make the filling: Heat the milk in a small heavy saucepan over low heat until it is hot but not boiling.
**5.** In a medium-size bowl combine the sugar, flour, and salt. Stir in the hot milk. Beat with a whisk until well blended.
**6.** Pour the mixture back into the saucepan and stir vigorously for 4 to 5 minutes, until it is thick and smooth. Add the egg yolks and cook for about 2 minutes, stirring constantly. Cool by stirring. Add the vanilla and whipped cream.
**7.** Make the icing: Heat the butter and chocolate in a medium-size saucepan until melted. Remove from the heat and blend in the confectioners' sugar. Add the hot water and enough milk to achieve a consistency that can be drizzled over the pastry (as opposed to spread). Stir until smooth.
**8.** Assemble the éclairs: Using a sharp knife, gently cut off the top of the pastry. Remove the moist insides and fill with the filling. Replace the top and drizzle icing over the surface. Refrigerate, lightly covered, until ready to serve.

---

**DEPARTURE**

*". . . But I will dream of houses on the bay;*

*Tall houses casting velvet shadows where*

*The shrimp man cries his catch, and vendors bear*

*Bright baskets on their heads, and children play. . . ."*

*Elizabeth Verner Hamilton, from* **Tall Houses,** *Tradd Street* **Press**

# PEACH TARTS

Stonewall peaches are grown in the hill country of Texas, my home state. Any particularly juicy peach will work well in this recipe.

— *Kara Anderson Berly* (Mrs. J. Anderson Berly III)

*Yield: 24 tarts*

### Pastry

3 ounces cream cheese, at room
   temperature
½ cup (1 stick) butter, at room
   temperature
3 tablespoons sugar
1 teaspoon fresh lemon juice
1½ cups unbleached all-purpose flour

### Filling

4 tablespoons plus 3 tablespoons
   sugar
4 tablespoons cornstarch
2 cups puréed fresh peaches
¾ cup chopped pecans
1 tablespoon butter

**1.** Make the pastry: In a medium-size bowl cream together the cream cheese, butter, sugar, and lemon juice until the mixture is fluffy. Gradually add the flour, stirring after each addition, to make a soft dough. Refrigerate for 30 minutes.

**2.** Preheat the oven to 375°F.

**3.** Pinch off pieces of dough to make 24 1-inch balls and press the balls into miniature muffin tins (the dough should be about ¼ inch thick). Bake for 10 minutes, lightly press down the center of each pastry cup, and continue baking until light brown, about 10 minutes. Cool.

**4.** Make the filling: In a medium-size saucepan combine the 4 tablespoons of sugar and the cornstarch. Add the 3 tablespoons of sugar to the puréed peaches and gradually add the peaches to the sugar and cornstarch.

**5.** Bring the mixture to a boil over medium heat, stirring constantly. Add the pecans and cook until the mixture has thickened, about 5 minutes. Remove from the heat and stir in the butter. Cool slightly and spoon into the tarts.

"*T*hough they have as great variety of good Peaches, as there are in any Country, perhaps, in the whole World, yet the principal use made of them is to feed Hogs; for which purpose large orchards of them are planted."

**A Description of South Carolina,** *London, 1761*

# ALMOND POPPY BREAD

A wonderful quick and easy treat!

*— Louise Liebenrood Owens (Mrs. Stuart C. Owens)*

*Yield: 2 loaves*

3 cups unbleached all-purpose flour
1 teaspoon salt
1½ teaspoons baking powder
2¼ cups sugar
1½ tablespoons poppy seeds
3 eggs
1½ cups milk
1⅛ cups cooking oil
1½ teaspoons vanilla extract
1½ teaspoons almond extract

### Glaze

¾ cup confectioners' sugar
¼ cup lemon juice
2 teaspoons melted butter
½ teaspoon almond extract
½ teaspoon vanilla extract

**1.** Preheat the oven to 350°F. Butter and flour two 9 x 5-inch loaf pans or three smaller pans.
**2.** In a large bowl stir together the flour, salt, baking powder, sugar, and poppy seeds. In a medium-size bowl combine the eggs, milk, oil, vanilla, and almond extract.
**3.** Add the egg mixture to the flour and sugar mixture and stir just to combine (do not overbeat). Pour the batter into the prepared pans and bake until the bread tests done, about 1 hour and 15 minutes (less if small pans are used).
**4.** Allow the bread to cool in the pans for 10 minutes, then turn out onto a wire rack to continue cooling.
**5.** Make the glaze: Combine the confectioners' sugar, lemon juice, melted butter, almond extract, and vanilla extract in a small bowl and whisk well.
**6.** When the bread is cool, place waxed paper under the wire rack and pour the glaze over the tops and sides of the loaves.

## MOLDY MICE (SAND TARTS)

1 stick butter
1 cup flour
1½ teaspoons vanilla
1 tablespoon sugar
½ cup chopped pecans
4X sugar

Mix butter and sugar. Add vanilla. Flour nuts and put together. Roll in small bars about the size of your thumb. Bake at 425° about 15 minutes. When done roll in powdered sugar while very hot. Yield: 3 dozen.

*Mrs. W. H. Barnwell (Mary Royall), from* Charleston Receipts

# CHOCOLATE CHIP BANANA NUT BREAD

The chocolate chips turn standard banana bread into a real treat — especially popular with the young at heart.

*— Anne M. Lamble*

*Yield: 10 to 12 servings*

½ cup (1 stick) margarine
1 cup sugar
2 eggs
2 cups unbleached all-purpose flour
1 teaspoon baking soda
2 cups mashed bananas
1 teaspoon vanilla extract
½ cup chopped walnuts or pecans
¾ cup chocolate chips

**1.** Preheat the oven to 350°F. Lightly butter and flour a 9 x 5-inch loaf pan.
**2.** In a large bowl cream together the margarine and sugar. Beat in the eggs. Add the flour and baking soda. Add the bananas and stir until well blended. Add the vanilla, nuts, and chocolate chips.
**3.** Pour the batter into the prepared pan and bake until the bread tests done, about 1 hour.

# BOILED CUSTARD

Boiled custard has been a tradition in our family as long as I can remember. According to my grandmother, her mother always served the custard in a punchbowl on Christmas Eve, instead of eggnog. My great uncles would secretly add their own "cheer" to the bowl. I like to serve boiled custard in a small stemmed glass accompanied by cookies or as a sauce for pound cake and fresh raspberries.

*— MariAnn Felton Seybold (Mrs. James R. Seybold, Jr.)*

*Yield: 8 servings*

¾ cup sugar
1 tablespoon unbleached all-purpose
   flour
1 quart whole milk
4 eggs
½ teaspoon vanilla extract
Pinch of salt

**1.** In a small bowl combine the sugar and flour.
**2.** Place the milk in the top of a double boiler and stir in the sugar and flour. Over medium heat, cook the mixture until the sugar dissolves, stirring constantly.
**3.** Separate 3 of the eggs, reserving the whites for another use. In a small bowl beat the 3 egg yolks and 1 whole egg and stir them into the milk mixture. Stir constantly until the mixture coats a spoon, about 30 minutes.
**4.** Remove the pan from the heat, stir in the vanilla and salt, and let cool. Pour into a bowl and chill overnight in the refrigerator.

# SYLLABUB

This recipe came from my Great-Great-Grandmother Miles, which makes it over 100 years old. There is disagreement in our family about the best time to eat syllabub; I like it just after it has been prepared, but other family members prefer to let it season. Though the mixture will separate after several hours in the refrigerator, it can be stirred back together in the glass with no harm done to the flavor.

— *Stephanie Snowden Atkinson* (Mrs. Bert Connor Atkinson)

*Yield: 6 servings*

4 egg whites
1 cup heavy cream
½ cup (scant) sugar
½ to 1 ounce sweet wine (homemade
    is preferable)
½ to 1 ounce whiskey
Freshly grated nutmeg

**1.** In a medium-size bowl using an electric mixer, beat the egg whites until they are stiff but not dry. Set aside.

**2.** In another medium-size bowl, beat the cream, gradually adding the sugar, until it is stiff. Gently fold the cream into the egg whites. Fold in the wine and whiskey to taste (the amount really depends on the sweetness of the wine and how much alcohol content you wish to have).

**3.** Spoon the mixture into six sherbet dishes and garnish with the nutmeg. Chill.

**Note:** The recipe can be doubled successfully.

"This afternoon, from 3 to 5, the Lyric Verse Society will hold a meeting at the home of Mrs. Bradwell Sancton on Tradd Street. Syllabub will be served, with curried sandwiches, and the minor poems of Elbert Hubbard."

**Syllabub,** *Patricia Colbert*

# GRAND MARNIER DIP

This dip resembles a sabayon sauce and may be placed in a bowl surrounded by bite-size pieces of fruit or passed as a topping for individual servings of cut-up fruit.
— *Susan Still Clement*
*(Mrs. Robert L. Clement III)*

*Yield: 2 cups*

*3 egg yolks*
*½ cup sugar*
*¼ teaspoon salt*
*¼ cup Grand Marnier liqueur*
*2 cups heavy or whipping cream*

**1.** In a small saucepan combine the egg yolks, sugar, and salt. Cook over medium heat, stirring constantly, until the sugar dissolves, 2 to 3 minutes. Remove from the heat and stir in the Grand Marnier. Let cool.
**2.** Beat the cream until stiff peaks form. Fold the cream into the Grand Marnier mixture just until well combined. Cover and chill for 1 to 2 hours. Serve with assorted fresh fruits.

## PEACH OR APRICOT LEATHER

This conserve is a favorite in Charleston. It is usually made with dried peaches, but I prefer apricots.

*1 pound dried peaches or apricots*
*1 cup sugar*

Wash the peaches or apricots and soak in water overnight. Cover with water (allow room, for they will swell) and boil as they are, until tender. Drain. Then run them through meat chopper, add the sugar, mix well and return to the stove to melt the sugar. Spread the mixture fairly thin on tin cookie sheets. Next you will substitute, as best you can, the conveniences—I have a table with a galvanized iron top and screen frame to cover it. Place sheets on table in hot sunshine and move with the sun. Tin attracts it. When not too dry, sprinkle with granulated sugar. Cut in strips, roll into little rolls. Then roll in sugar and enjoy.

*Miss Ellen Parker*
*from* **Charleston Receipts**

# SOUR CREAM FRUIT DIP

This is my friend Lynn's fast and easy dip for all kinds of fruit — your choice.
— *Martha Ann Kelly Hill* (Mrs. E. Burrow Hill III)

*Yield: 8 to 10 servings*

*1 cup sour cream*
*1 tablespoon light brown sugar*
*½ teaspoon ground cinnamon*
*4 cups bite-size pieces chilled fruit*
*(strawberries, pineapple, melon, etc.)*

**1.** In a medium-size bowl combine the sour cream, brown sugar, and cinnamon and mix well. Refrigerate for at least 1 hour.
**2.** Place the bowl of dip on a platter and surround with the fruits. Pass toothpicks.

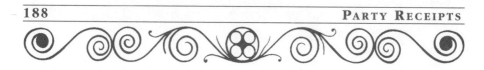

# CHOCOLATE-CAPPED FRUITS

These are a great complement to traditional hors d'oeuvres; they not only taste good but are decorative as well. Kiwi fruit, bananas, and apples may be used instead of, or in addition to, the strawberries (stems left on) and pineapple.

— *Donna Smith FitzGerald* (Mrs. James Perdue FitzGerald)

---

*Yield: 12 to 15 servings*

8 ounces semisweet chocolate
2 tablespoons vegetable shortening
½ teaspoon orange extract
1 pint strawberries
1 pineapple, peeled, cored, and cut in
   bite-size pieces

**1.** Melt the chocolate and shortening in the top of a double boiler over simmering water or in a microwave oven. Stir in the orange extract.
**2.** Dip the fruits in the warm chocolate mixture and place on waxed paper to set (make sure the pieces are not touching one another). Refrigerate until ready to serve.

# WHITE FUDGE

The combination of red cherries and white fudge makes this candy a perfect addition to holiday platters.

— *Amy Carswell Willis* (Mrs. Thomas L. Willis)

---

*Yield: 2 to 3 dozen pieces*

2¼ cups sugar
½ cup sour cream
¼ cup milk
2 tablespoons butter
1 tablespoon corn syrup
¼ teaspoon salt
2 teaspoons vanilla extract
1 cup chopped walnuts
⅓ cup quartered candied cherries

**1.** Line an 8-inch square pan with foil.
**2.** In a medium-size saucepan combine the sugar, sour cream, milk, butter, corn syrup, and salt. Bring to a boil over medium heat and continue cooking until the temperature reaches

238°F on a candy thermometer. Remove the pan from the heat and let stand until the mixture is lukewarm, about 1 hour.
**3.** Add the vanilla and beat until the mixture loses its gloss. Stir in the nuts and cherries. Pour the mixture into the prepared pan and let it set until firm. Cut the fudge into squares.

# PARTY PRALINES

Pralines make an excellent dessert for a Mexican buffet or whenever you need a taste of something sweet but not filling.

— *Kate Bauer Palanica (Mrs. William J. Palanica)*

### Yield: About 40 pralines

2 cups light brown sugar
1 cup sugar
¾ cup light cream
1 tablespoon light corn syrup
1 tablespoon butter
1 teaspoon vanilla extract
3 cups chopped pecans

**1.** In a large saucepan combine the brown sugar, granulated sugar, cream, and corn syrup. Bring to a boil and continue cooking until the mixture reaches the soft-ball stage, 238°F on a candy thermometer.
**2.** Remove the pan from the heat and add the butter, vanilla, and pecans. Beat the mixture, to cool (to accelerate the process, set the pot in cool water while you are beating).
**3.** Drop the mixture in heaping teaspoonful onto waxed paper. If the mixture hardens too fast, reheat it and add extra cream to soften it.

# BOURBON BALLS

For a different taste, you may substitute crème de menthe for the bourbon in this recipe.

— *Glenn Edmunds Puckhaber (Mrs. Edward Allen Puckhaber)*

### Yield: 2 dozen

1 cup finely chopped pecans
⅓ cup bourbon
¼ cup (½ stick) butter, at room
    temperature
1 pound confectioners' sugar (10X)
2 ounces bittersweet chocolate,
    melted

**1.** In a small bowl, soak the pecans in the bourbon for at least 30 minutes.
**2.** In a large bowl, cream together the butter and confectioners' sugar. Add the pecans and bourbon and stir to combine well.
**3.** Roll the mixture into small balls and dip the balls in the melted chocolate. Cool on waxed paper.

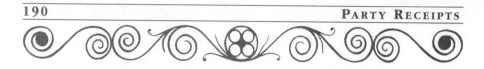

## MANDARIN CHOCOLATE CANDY

These confections are a cross between a cookie and a candy — and delicious!
— *Dorsey Glenn Condon (Mrs. Clarence M. Condon III)*

*Yield: 4 dozen*

1 cup sweetened condensed milk
4 ounces unsweetened chocolate
¼ teaspoon salt
2½ cups flaked sweetened coconut
½ cup chopped pecans
1½ teaspoons orange extract

**1.** Preheat the oven to 350°F. Lightly grease two baking sheets.
**2.** In a heavy saucepan, combine the milk, chocolate, and salt and cook over low heat, stirring frequently, until the chocolate melts and the mixture thickens.
**3.** Remove the pan from the heat and quickly stir in the coconut, pecans, and orange extract. Form the mixture into small balls (about a teaspoonful of the mixture) and place on the prepared baking sheets.
**4.** Bake until the candies are firm, 6 to 7 minutes. Immediately transfer the candies to waxed paper to cool. Store in an airtight container.

## RUTH'S SOUR CREAM CANDY

My sisters and I used to make this candy for my grandfather, Russell Wolfe, on Valentine's Day. We would put our homemade valentines and a box of the candy by his front door, ring the doorbell, and then run and hide in the camellia bushes. He was always delighted and "surprised" to find his favorite valentines on the doorstep.

— *Connor H. Gantt (Mrs. John M. Gantt, Jr.)*

*Yield: About 2 dozen*

1 cup sour cream
2 cups light brown sugar
1 cup chopped walnuts or pecans
1 teaspoon vanilla extract

**1.** Spray a large rectangle of waxed paper with vegetable oil spray.
**2.** Combine the sour cream and brown sugar in a medium-size heavy saucepan, bring the mixture to a boil over medium heat, and boil until it reaches the soft ball stage (238°F) on a candy thermometer.
**3.** Remove the pan from the heat and beat the mixture until it is creamy (this can take a long time). Stir in the nuts and vanilla and drop by teaspoonsful onto the prepared waxed paper.

# CANDIED PECANS

This is a favorite recipe of my mother, Sara Clark Vardell.

*— Laura Nowell Vardell*

---
*Yield: 2 cups*
---

1 egg white
1 cup dark brown sugar
1 teaspoon vanilla extract
2 cups pecan halves (about 1 pound)

**1.** Preheat the oven to 225°F. Grease a baking sheet.

**2.** Beat the egg white until stiff in a medium-size bowl. Fold in the brown sugar and vanilla and then gently fold in the pecans.

**3.** Drop the pecans in small mounds (1 to 2 halves in each) onto the prepared baking sheet. Bake for 45 minutes. Cool on a wire rack and store in an airtight container.

# SOUR CREAM PECANS

No baking is required in this version of sugared pecans, but you will need a candy thermometer.

*— Margaret Edwards Lee (Mrs. Douglas B. Lee)*

---
*Yield: 4 cups*
---

1 cup sour cream
2 cups sugar
1 teaspoon vanilla extract
2 tablespoons butter
¼ teaspoon baking soda
4 cups pecan halves (about 2 pounds)

**1.** Lightly butter a jelly-roll pan.
**2.** Combine the sour cream and sugar in a medium saucepan and cook over medium low heat, stirring, until the mixture almost reaches the hard ball stage (250°F on a candy thermometer). Remove from the heat.
**3.** Add the vanilla, butter, and baking soda and beat with a spoon for 1 or 2 minutes. Add the pecans, stirring to coat.
**4.** Turn the mixture out onto the prepared pan. Let it cool, then separate the pecans into individual pieces. Store in an airtight container.

> "They pass a horse-drawn carriage, tourists gawking at the tall houses, the young driver standing with reins in his hands; two boys on skateboards confusing traffic, knees padded, arms out, daring the cars; a lady with a splotchy dog leashed to her wrist and pulling her along faster than she wants to go."
>
> **Dreams of Sleep,**
> *Josephine Humphreys*

# INDEX

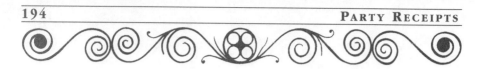

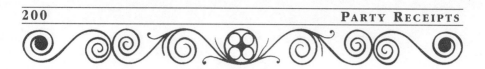

For information about ordering **CHARLESTON RECEIPTS** and **CHARLESTON RECEIPTS REPEATS**, complete the form below and mail or FAX it to:

**The Junior League of Charleston, Inc.**
**51 Folly Road**
**Charleston, S.C. 29407**
**Telephone (803) 763-5284     FAX (803) 763-1626**

Name

Address

City                                    State          Zip

Phone (          )

---

For information about ordering **CHARLESTON RECEIPTS** and **CHARLESTON RECEIPTS REPEATS**, complete the form below and mail or FAX it to:

**The Junior League of Charleston, Inc.**
**51 Folly Road**
**Charleston, S.C. 29407**
**Telephone (803) 763-5284     FAX (803) 763-1626**

Name

Address

City                                    State          Zip

Phone (          )